CATALOGUE 2.0

THE FUTURE OF THE LIBRARY CATALOGUE

CATALOGUE 2.0

THE FUTURE OF THE LIBRARY CATALOGUE

EDITED BY SALLY CHAMBERS

Neal-Schuman

An imprint of the American Library Association

Chicago • 2013

First published in the United Kingdom by Facet Publishing, 2013.
This simultaneous U.S. Edition published by Neal-Schuman,
an imprint of the American Library Association, 2013.

16 15 14 13 12   5 4 3 2 1

ISBN: 978-1-55570-943-3 (paper)

For Elaine

Contents

Acknowledgements

I would like to thank the wonderfully supportive editorial team at Facet Publishing, in particular Louise Le Bas, who commissioned this book and supported me in its initial stages; Sarah Busby, who helped me in the intermediate stages of putting the book together, especially during the challenging year when I was commuting between the Netherlands and Germany; and finally Jenni Hall, whose friendly, yet motivational, support helped me to see this book through to its conclusion.

I would like to thank the book's contributors; Anne, Emmanuelle, Driek, Karen, Lorcan, Lukas, Marshall, Rosemie, Silvia and Till, for agreeing to work with me on the book in the first place and then bringing their expertise, commitment and patience. Without you, there would be no book!

I have made every effort to contact the holders of copyright material reproduced in this text. I would like to thank them for their permission to reproduce the material ijn the book. However, if there are queries, please contact the publisher.

I would like to thank my colleagues at The European Library, DARIAH-EU and the Göttingen Centre for Digital Humanities, who patiently listened to me when I 'went on' about 'the book'; my cataloguer friends, Christoph (thanks for the authority record) and John, who are both passionate cataloguing librarians to the core; and not forgetting those catalogue and library 'enthusiasts' on Twitter, including @hochstenbach, @L_OS_Cymru, @ostephens, @rtennant, @saschel and @yo_bj.

A special thank you goes to my loved ones, both friends and family; my Mum and Dad, my brother David and his partner Phil, Martin, Michel, Morag, Pauline, Carmen, Chun and my life-coach Sally Lever, who supported me throughout the process.

Finally, I would like to dedicate this book to Elaine, whose kindness, love and strength lives on.

Sally Chambers,
Göttingen, Germany

Foreword

Marshall Breeding

Catalogue 2.0 provides an interesting and important exploration of the realm of the emerging technologies, products and projects that impact the way that libraries provide their customers with access to their collections and services. Library catalogues have gone through a transformative evolution from modules of library management systems, which eventually came to be outmoded and cumbersome, through a set of discovery interfaces that modernized them and expanded their scope, up to the current crop of index-based discovery services that ambitiously aim to deliver access to the full breadth of library collections spanning print, electronic and digital materials. The authors who have contributed to this book address a wide variety of topics, including both practical projects and concepts in play, that will help shape the design and capabilities of library catalogues as they continue to evolve and develop.

The book was ably managed and edited by Sally Chambers. She has recruited a range of contributing authors coming from a broad international base and representing several different areas of interest and expertise, who bring to the project a wide variety of conceptual perspectives. She frames the topic in her Introduction, pulling together some of the issues to be covered in the following chapters.

Readers will gain important insights about the implications of seminal topics. No book on access or organization of content would be complete without a discussion of the Semantic Web and Emmanuelle Bermès provides an excellent treatment of the topic. Karen Calhoun, former Vice President of OCLC responsible for WorldCat and Metadata Services, gives an authoritative discussion on the fundamental impact that the web has had on scholarship. She calls for research libraries to rethink bibliographic control, co-operative cataloguing systems and library catalogues in order to remain relevant in the future. Rosemie Callewaert helps us think through how catalogue interfaces can improve presentation and organization of results by following the principles of the FRBR. Lorcan Dempsey, OCLC's Vice President for Research, gives a thoughtful analysis of library catalogues from the perspective of information abundance and the scarcity of attention, and how the impact that libraries can have is amplified when globally consolidated. Till Kinstler explores different approaches to search and retrieval technology as applied to library catalogues.

Several chapters provide practical information regarding projects and products. The chapter I contributed describes some of the major discovery services and products marketed internationally as well as some important European projects. Lukas Koster and Driek Heesakkers give an important treatment of bringing the catalogue to mobile devices.

Consistent with the fundamental premise that catalogues exist to satisfy the needs of users and not librarians, Anne Christensen contributes a very interesting chapter on user reactions to next-generation catalogues.

I find myself thoroughly impressed with the quality of writing and the depth of content assembled in this edited volume on current and forward-looking issues surrounding library catalogues and discovery services. Some of the top thought leaders and practitioners in the field share information and insights that others involved with planning the next steps of their catalogue will not want to miss. Those involved with library administration and management who are responsible for planning and strategy, cataloguers and metadata specialists with interests in tuning the catalogue to best represent their work, and programmers and other technologists will all find material relevant to their interests and professional responsibilities. Even apart from those in these roles, anyone with a personal interest in the future of library catalogues will appreciate this volume.

Of all the areas of technology that I cover in my work, the ones that consistently rise to the top in strategic importance are those involving the ways that libraries deliver their content and services to their users. This book makes strong contributions in this area; it should encourage additional discourse and spark further work that will lead to the advancement of the state of the art of the library catalogue.

Introduction

Sally Chambers

Does the library catalogue have a future? This is often the first question that people ask me when I tell them that I am editing a book on the future of the library catalogue. And, indeed, it is one of the key themes that we will explore in this book.

Until recently, the library catalogue has provided the key to unlocking the treasures of a library's collections. Without exploring the library catalogue, a user will not know which books are to be found in the library or, where they can be found.

In the last 25 years, the nature of the library catalogue has changed immensely. Even within my own working life as a librarian, I have seen library catalogues in many forms: the huge, heavy tomes of the printed versions of both the British Museum and Library of Congress catalogues; the wooden drawers filled with neatly ordered card catalogues; the first electronic library catalogues on small black screens with fluorescent green letters; the first-generation web OPACs; the federated search portals; the discovery systems; the mobile library catalogues; and, increasingly, the opening of Linked Data applications setting library bibliographic data free for use by other applications, outside the library, on the web.

Not only has the library catalogue changed, but cataloguing, the essential skill of bibliographic description and therefore of catalogue creation, is undergoing a steady evolution. One of the traditional tools of the cataloguing trade, the *Anglo-American Cataloguing Rules*, 2nd edition (AACR2), a detailed set of rules telling librarians how books and other library materials need to be described for inclusion in the library catalogue, is expected, albeit over a period of several years, to be replaced by *Resource Description and Access* (RDA). RDA, the cataloguing standard for the 21st century, was published in June 2010 and following a thorough testing process in the United States,[1] was due to be implemented by the Library of Congress from 'RDA Implementation Day One', 31 March 2013.[2]

The development of RDA has not been the only recent historical event within the bibliographic universe. MARC, MAchine Readable Cataloguing, the standardized way of encoding bibliographic data, is in the process of being replaced by a newer web-enabled standard. In 2002, Roy Tennant sentenced MARC to death in his famous article in *Library Journal*, 'MARC must Die'.[3] Similar authors, such as Lukas Koster, one of the contributors to this volume, asked the question 'Who needs MARC?' on his blog,[4] eliciting some passionate comments. Yet it was only in 2011, almost 10 years after Roy Tennant's original proclamation, things really started to change.

In May 2011, I facilitated what turned out to be a timely workshop at the European Library Automation Group (ELAG) 2011 conference entitled 'MARC must Die?'[5] The workshop aimed to get a deeper understanding of why library technologists want to kill MARC and at the same time explore the value that cataloguers see in MARC records. The overall goal was to develop a shared vision of how the workshop attendees would like library bibliographic metadata to evolve. The results of the workshop were delivered via a tongue-in-cheek presentation[6] that called for a globally accepted data model, which should be developed on the basis of use cases and supported by technical specifications, one of which was that the use of URIs (Uniform Resource Identifiers) would be essential. It was recommended that appropriate tools would need to be developed to enable *agile cataloguing*, which would create data not records.

The timely nature of the workshop became apparent when one of the workshop participants, Barbara Tillett from the Library of Congress, reacted to the workshop announcement on my blog, notifying the workshop attendees that on almost the same day as the workshop the Library of Congress would be announcing its 'Bibliographic Framework Transition Initiative'.[7] The aim of the initiative is to undertake

... a review of the bibliographic framework to better accommodate future needs. A major focus of the initiative will be to determine a transition path for the MARC 21 exchange format in order to reap the benefits of newer technology while preserving a robust data exchange that has supported resource sharing and cataloging cost savings in recent decades.

In short, the Library of Congress was proposing to develop the 'globally accepted data model' that the workshop had concluded was necessary. A general plan for the initiative was published in October 2011.[8]

In May 2012, the Library of Congress announced that it had signed a contract with an organization that will 'translate the MARC 21 format to a Linked Data (LD) model while retaining as much as possible the robust and beneficial aspects of the historical format.'[9] In September 2012, at the International Group of Ex Libris Users (IGeLU) 2012 conference, Sally McCallum, from the Library of Congress, presented the next steps in the model development, including an early experimentation phase in autumn 2012, followed by model, mapping and tools development to encourage wider experimentation.[10] In November 2012, just as this book was going to press, the Library of Congress published the draft BIBFRAME data model, *Bibliographic Framework as a Web of Data: Linked Data Model and Supporting Services*[11] for community discussion.

The year 2013 will be an important one for libraries. In the United States, implementation of RDA, the new 'cataloguing code', is scheduled for implementation from 31 March 2013. The replacement of MARC 21, for encoding bibliographic data, is likely to be launched and maybe even implemented in 2013.

The idea behind 'Catalogue 2.0' is to provide an overview of the current state of the art of the library catalogue and then to look to the future to see what the library catalogue might become.

The book starts with a look at the catalogue from the user perspective. In her chapter, 'Next-generation catalogues: what do users think?', Anne Christensen, a user services librarian from Germany, helps to understand how we can develop a more user-centric way of developing library catalogues for our users. Using her own experience in developing Beluga,[12] a next-generation catalogue for the universities in Hamburg, as a basis, Anne provides us with a background on the different methodologies that can be employed to understand what our users want. From anthropological studies on the information-seeking behaviour of students to involving users in an iterative, agile, user-centred development process, Anne shows how we can make the library catalogue into a service that users like and want to use again.

From a more technical perspective, Till Kinstler, an information scientist and library software developer from Germany, explores how search engine technologies – which influence what users expect from library catalogues – can be used in the 'back-end' of library information systems, to improve the user experience. In 'Making search work for the library user', Till explains the technological differences between traditional 'Boolean-based' library catalogues and 'information retrieval-based' search engines. Using the practical example of the German National Licences project, he shows how search engine functionalities, such as search suggestions, e.g. 'did you mean?' and faceted browsing can be integrated into the library catalogue.

Marshall Breeding, a world-renowned library technology expert and catalogue watcher, provides us with an overview of the current state of the art of the technology products that libraries can choose from in order to implement a next-generation library catalogue. In his chapter 'Next-generation discovery: an overview of the European scene', Marshall provides an overview of both commercial and open-source products, as well as library-developed solutions, including practical examples of which libraries have implemented which systems. This chapter also includes a case study of an implementation of the open-source library system VuFind, by Silvia Gstrein, a digital library specialist from Innsbruck University Library, for the European eBooks on Demand service.

The next section of the book moves on to looking at new ways of presenting the data that is deeply buried in library catalogues. The first chapter in this area comes from Lukas Koster and Driek Heesakkers, who both work at the University of Amsterdam library. In their chapter on 'The mobile library catalogue', Lukas and Driek introduce us to a range of considerations that we need to take into account when working with mobile technology. Taking a user-centred approach, they turn to the application of mobile technology for academic library users, by exploring in detail the mobile catalogue that they developed for the University of Amsterdam library. This case study is then set within a wider context of mobile catalogues that have been implemented in a range of libraries. Building on their experience in Amsterdam, they offer a checklist of what you need to consider when thinking about offering mobile services in your library.

Moving on from providing library catalogue services to the palm of the user's hand to exploring what can be done to make bibliographic metadata work harder, in 'FRBRizing your catalogue' Rosemie Callewaert, an information architect from Belgium, explores how FRBR, the Functional Requirements for Bibliographic Records – a user-centred method of modelling the bibliographic universe – can be applied practically within the library catalogue. Despite having been published almost 15 years ago, FRBR has yet to be widely implemented in library catalogues. However, Rosemie shows how the theoretical model of FRBR has been applied within the Open Vlacc, the Union Catalogue of Dutch-speaking public libraries in Belgium, to improve the user experience.

Today, it's not about the catalogue, it's about the data. In her chapter, Emmanuelle Bermès, a librarian and Semantic Web expert from France, introduces the idea that it may be time for libraries to start moving beyond the deeply buried data silos that are today's library catalogues towards freeing bibliographic data from the confinements of the catalogue and making it open, available and reusable as part of the global 'Web of Data'. In 'Enabling your catalogue for the Semantic Web' Emmanuelle provides an introduction to the Semantic Web and its practical implementation, Linked Data, before moving on to explore the key issues that libraries need to consider when embarking on a Linked Data project. Emmanuelle also explains the technical basics of Linked Data. What are RDF and those URIs that we hear so much about? Is data modelling really as daunting as it sounds? Is a SPARQL endpoint important for my triple store? However, as Emmanuelle discusses, the real added value of library Linked Data is in its (re)use beyond the library domain.

Even if we are looking towards a Linked Data future, have the digital revolution and the web had a more fundamental impact on the scholarship that it is the mission of research libraries to support? Placing the library catalogue in the broader context of bibliographic control, co-operative cataloguing systems and open access repositories, Karen Calhoun, former Vice-President of OCLC responsible for WorldCat and Metadata Services and author of the 2006 report *The Changing Nature of the Catalog*, looks in her chapter at how the rise of digital scholarship has a profound impact on the way that libraries deliver services for their users. By exploring the impact that the 'digital' has had on library collections and in turn on how they are described, do we need to rethink how the library catalogue fits into a global web-based world? Is, Karen asks, 'Catalogue 2.0' a catalogue at all?

Which leads nicely on to the final chapter, by Lorcan Dempsey, Vice President and Chief Strategist from OCLC. In 'Thirteen ways of looking at libraries, discovery and the catalogue: scale, workflow, attention', Lorcan sets the library catalogue in the broader context of the web-based, networked world. He looks at how information use and creation has changed from the physical to the digital, from the local to the global network. By explaining that the catalogue emerged when information resources were scarce, but attention was abundant, Lorcan describes how there has been a switch in the way information resources are used. Once the library service, and the catalogue within it, were the centre of attention. Users would build their workflows around the library; now, Lorcan argues, this is no longer the case. As users are accustomed to the web and multiple ways of digital delivery, will the library catalogue, describing only part of the 'global collection', remain as an identifiable library service?

Editing this book has been an interesting exploration – both the act of editing itself, and learning that it needs physical and mental time and space, as well as a professional exploration into the world of the library catalogue. I have been able to work with some fantastic international colleagues and have developed lasting friendships. I have been able to dive into the topics that surround the library catalogue.

As a librarian, I am concerned that if libraries fully embrace the web, then we will somehow lose expertise and professionalism, especially in the areas of the library catalogue and bibliographic control. However, I am aware that if librarians, as a profession, do not fully embrace the web, there will be no profession left to hold on to. Therefore, we need to take a deep breath and co-operate fully with professionals from outside the library world.

Digital scholarship, digital humanities and e-Science offer an emerging role for libraries. As the academic disciplines are changing and, indeed, are being enhanced by the opportunities that the web are offering, so are libraries, librarianship and catalogues. The role of libraries in digital scholarship is a relatively new terrain for us and our role has yet to be fully mapped out. However, it is important that we see the potential.

So, does the library catalogue have a future? I hope that this book at least goes some way towards answering this question.

References

1   www.loc.gov/aba/rda/rda_test_archives.html.
2   www.loc.gov/catdir/cpso/news_rda_implementation_date.html.
3   www.libraryjournal.com/article/CA250046.html.
4   http://commonplace.net/2009/05/who-needs-marc.

5   http://elag2011.techlib.cz/en/855-07-marc-must-die.

6   www.slideshare.net/schambers3/marc-must-die.

7   www.loc.gov/bibframe.

8   www.loc.gov/bibframe/news/framework-103111.html.

9   www.loc.gov/bibframe/news/bibframe-052212.html.

10   http://igelu.org/wp-content/uploads/2012/09/IGeLU-sally-McCallum.pptx.

11   www.loc.gov/bibframe/pdf/marcld-report-11-21-2012.pdf.

12   http://beluga.sub.uni-hamburg.de.

Editor and contributors

Sally Chambers started working in libraries in the mid-1990s, initially working in academic libraries in the UK. In 2000 she turned her focus to digital libraries. Since then she has co-ordinated a forerunner of Enquire, a digital enquiry service for UK public libraries, and the development of an online library for distance learning students at the University of London. In January 2005 she joined The European Library based at the National Library of the Netherlands, where her work focused on interoperability, metadata and technical project co-ordination for a range of European projects. In May 2011 Sally decided to explore the digital humanities, alongside her role at The European Library. To do this, she joined the European co-ordination team for DARIAH-EU, the Digital Research Infrastructure for the Arts and Humanities, based at the Göttingen Centre for Digital Humanities in Germany. In January 2012 she moved to DARIAH-EU full-time. Sally is convinced that libraries have a key role to play in the digital humanities and is dedicated to understanding this role and encouraging libraries to rise to the challenge. She is active in the European digital library community via the European Library Automation Group (ELAG). She tweets as @schambers3.

Emmanuelle Bermès is Head of Multimedia Services at the Centre Pompidou in Paris, where she leads the Centre Pompidou digital museum project. After graduating from the École nationale des Chartes and École nationale supérieure des sciences de l'information et des bibliothèques in France, Emmanuelle started working as a librarian in the French National Library (Bibliothèque nationale de France, BnF) in 2003. From 2003 to 2008 she contributed to the creation of a new version of the digital library, Gallica, and participated in the design of the digital preservation system. From 2008 to 2011, still at BnF, she was involved in metadata standardization and management, and started working on the application of Semantic Web technologies to library data in general and library catalogues in particular. Meanwhile she was also involved in several European and international groups as an expert; within Europeana she contributed to designing the Europeana Data Model and in 2010–11 she was a co-chair of the Library Linked Data W3C incubator group. She is the convener of the Semantic Web special interest group (SWSIG) created by IFLA in 2011.

Marshall Breeding is an independent consultant, speaker, and author. He is the creator and editor of *Library Technology Guides* and the lib-web-cats online directory of libraries on the web. His monthly column Systems Librarian appears in *Computers in Libraries*; he is the Editor of *Smart Libraries Newsletter*, published by the American Library Association, and has authored the annual Automation Marketplace feature published by *Library Journal* since 2002. He has authored nine issues of ALA's *Library Technology Reports* and has written many other articles and book chapters. Marshall has edited or authored seven books, including *Next-Gen Library Catalogs* (2010) and *Cloud Computing for Libraries*, published in 2012 by Neal-Schuman, now part of ALA TechSource. He regularly teaches workshops and gives presentations at library conferences on a wide range of topics. Marshall Breeding held a variety of positions for the Vanderbilt University Libraries in Nashville, Tennessee, from 1985 to May 2012, including Director for Innovative Technologies and Research and Executive Director of the Vanderbilt Television News Archive. Breeding was the 2010 recipient of the LITA LITA/Library Hi Tech Award for Outstanding Communication for Continuing Education in Library and Information Science.

Karen Calhoun joined the University Library System at the University of Pittsburgh in July 2011, where she serves as an assistant university librarian, leading strategic initiatives in collaborative planning, service innovation and implementation, organizational development and assessment. From 2007 to 2011 Karen was Vice President, OCLC WorldCat and Metadata Services, where she was charged with helping to chart a course for future services, engaging with OCLC member libraries, and extending WorldCat's global relevance. From 1996 to 2007 she served in leadership positions at Cornell University Library, most recently as Senior Associate University Librarian for Information Technology and Technical Services. Active professionally as a writer, researcher and speaker, Karen is perhaps best known for her role as principal investigator and author of *The Changing Nature of the Catalog and its Integration with Other Discovery Tools*, a Library of Congress-commissioned study that proposed new directions for the library catalogue in the digital era. She holds a bachelor's degree from Bucknell University, an MS in Library and Information Science from Drexel University and an MBA from Franklin University.

Rosemie Callewaert is a freelance information architect and usability expert. Previously, she worked as a metadata architect for Bibnet, a project organization funded by the Flemish Government, building digital library platforms for public libraries in Belgium. In the past 15 years Rosemie has worked on various projects, both initiating and co-ordinating user workflows for library and museum collection interfaces. Her specific interest is designing the user experience for information and content-based interfaces for the internet with all kinds of datasets and using the philosophy of the Semantic Web. Based on her experience in different large conversion projects, she is also an expert in translating metadata schemas between web-based formats and metadata languages from the library community.

Anne Christensen is Head of User Services at the University Library of Leuphana University, Lüneburg, Germany. Prior to this position, Anne was in charge of Beluga, a next-generation discovery tool developed at the State and University Library in Hamburg. This project was renowned for the participation of users in the development of both user interface and functionality. Anne frequently speaks at national and international conferences, including the European Library Automation Group (ELAG) and the Ticer International Summer School. She has also played a key role in introducing unconferences to the German library scene. In her personal blog she reflects the impact of new technologies and changes in user behaviour on both libraries and the profession (http://xenzen.wordpress.com, in German). Anne holds a Master's degree in Library and Information Science from Humboldt University in Berlin.

Lorcan Dempsey is Vice President and Chief Strategist at OCLC, where he oversees the research division and participates in planning. He is a librarian who has worked for library and educational organizations in Ireland, England and the USA. Lorcan has policy, research and service development experience, mostly in the area of networked information and digital libraries. He writes and speaks extensively, and can be followed on the web at Lorcan Dempsey's weblog (http://orweblog.oclc.org) and on Twitter (http://twitter.com/lorcanD). Before moving to OCLC Lorcan worked with JISC in the UK, overseeing national information programs and services, and before that was Director of UKOLN a national research and policy unit at the University of Bath. Lorcan is Irish, and before moving to the UK he worked in public libraries in Dublin, Ireland.

Silvia Gstrein is Head of the Department of Digital Services at the University and Regional Library of Tyrol, University of Innsbruck, Austria. Since 2002, she has led several national and international IT related projects in the area of e-learning and digitization matters, contributed to European projects such as Digitisation on Demand (DOD), EuropeanaConnect, EuropeanaTravel and ARROW and is co-ordinator of the eBooks on Demand network (http://books2ebooks.eu), a digitization and document delivery service of public domain books with more than 30 participating libraries from 12 European countries.

Driek Heesakkers is Project Manager at the University of Amsterdam library. Besides the library's Mobile Web project in 2010, he has managed projects on diverse subjects such as virtual research environments, research data, enhanced publications and an award-winning RFID-based self-service solution for closed stacks. He studied Economic and Social History at the University of Amsterdam.

Till Kinstler studied both information and computer science at the Universität des Saarlandes, Saarbrücken, Germany. After implementing virtual learning environments based on constructivist learning theories, he now develops search applications for libraries at the Common Library Network Head Office (GBV Verbundzentrale) in Göttingen, Germany. His main focus is using open source software to improve the findability of library materials on the web. He is a contributor to the VuFind open source discovery interface project. As a member of the programme committee for the annual conferences of the

European Library Automation Group (ELAG) he aims to improve international knowledge exchange about library information technology.

Lukas Koster is Library Systems Co-ordinator at the University of Amsterdam library, responsible for digital library information systems, ILS/LMS, federated search, link resolver, discovery and delivery tools. He studied sociology at the University of Amsterdam. After additional training in ICT, systems design and development, he worked as systems designer and developer in institutions of higher education and scientific information. Since 2003 he has been involved in library search and discovery systems, first at the National Library of the Netherlands and currently at the University of Amsterdam, where he participated in the library's Mobile Web project in 2010. Lukas believes that linked open data is a necessary next step for libraries. He promotes this through blogging at Commonplace.net (http://commonplace. net), making presentations at national and international conferences and contributing to local and global initiatives and publications.

1

Next-generation catalogues: what do users think?

Anne Christensen

Introduction

In the wake of the digital revolution, libraries have started rethinking their catalogues and reshaping them along the lines that have been set by popular search engines and online retailers. Yet it has also become a hallmark of next-generation catalogues to reflect the results of studies concerning user behaviour and user needs and to rely on the participation of users in the development and testing of the new tools. A wide array of methods for user-driven design and development are being employed, which ideally leverage discovery platforms that reflect the specifics of library metadata and materials as well as the need for attractive design and useful new functionalities.

After looking back at the history of user studies on online catalogues, we will briefly investigate methods to involve users actively in the design and development processes for new catalogues before describing and examining the outcomes of studies of users' perceptions.

Catalogues: where are we coming from?

The catalogue is the core product of any library. The accessibility of the catalogue via Telnet or later the web was considered a huge achievement because – to quote from one of Ranganathan's famous *Five Laws of Library Science* (Ranganathan, 1931), it 'saved the time of the reader' in terms of saving them the trip to the library. But the first generation of online catalogues has to be considered as a by-product of the automation of circulation processes or metadata exchange between libraries. The early online catalogues served internal purposes in the first place, rather than being meant as a service for users.

It is therefore not surprising that there is little to no evidence about the consideration of user needs and perspectives in the literature about the development of the early Online Public Access Catalogues (OPACs). They were, however, the subject of quite extensive research after they had been introduced. Early user studies identified significant problems with subject searching (Cochrane and Markey, 1983). There is plenty of literature from the 1980s about preventing users from failing with searches other than 'known-item' searches. In response to the results from these studies, a lot of research has been conducted about supporting users with subject searching, for instance by helping them to match their terms with those used in the catalogue or by offering linguistically enhanced retrieval functionality such as stemming or spelling correction (Walker, 1987).

Frameworks for next-generation user studies: anthropological and ethnographic approaches

Sadly, the features proposed after the early user studies of online catalogues have not been extensively implemented in the standard first-generation catalogues. It is therefore not surprising that with the rise of the world wide web and its powerful search engines, library users have quickly switched to websites other than library catalogues to conduct their research. Within ten years, academic libraries lost what used to be a monopoly position for the provision of scientific information. The changes in the behaviour of users, from all types of library, have been documented in a large study by the Online Computer Library Center in 2005 (OCLC, 2005). Around the same time, two highly significant studies were published that provided valuable insights into the information-seeking behaviour of students. Both these studies employed anthropological and ethnographic approaches that had not been used before in a library context, and, interestingly, resulted in the development of new, home-grown catalogues at the respective institutions. At the University of Rochester, anthropologist Nancy Fried Foster and her team published a comprehensive report not only on searching habits of undergraduates, but on their academic work in general (Foster and Gibbons, 2007). In parallel, the library started to develop its own next-generation discovery solution with a strong emphasis on user-centred design.[1]

Denmark's State and University Library in Aarhus examined the information-seeking behaviour of their users by encouraging them to write journals and then analysing these 'cultural probes'. This resulted in the definition of three different behavioural patterns (drive-in users, worker bees and library enthusiasts), which serve as personas for whom appropriate services can be developed (Akselbo et al., 2006). Since the improvement of the current catalogue aroused the most interest in their users, the library decided to embark on their own catalogue project, the development of 'Summa'.[2]

Similar research has been conducted elsewhere (Hennig, 2006; Rowlands et al., 2008). The findings regarding the further development of catalogues recommend seemingly straightforward user requirements: make catalogues more convenient (Calhoun et al., 2009). But how does convenience translate into features? A concern that is expressed both often and urgently is the availability of delivery options; limiting searches to available items, both print and electronic, seems to be more important to users than the actual discovery of relevant material. On the other hand, the user studies that concentrate on catalogues specifically indicate a great necessity for support in the discovery process, as well as help with the evaluation of search results. But this support would need to be very unobtrusive, since users generally feel confident about their abilities regarding the research process.

Another outcome of the user behaviour studies, which is important for catalogue design, is the time factor; users will visit the catalogue site only very briefly and a vast majority of users only conduct simple searches and look at no more than a few items from the top of the results list. A possible solution to this could be the work on new relevance ranking algorithms.

Great expectations: the next-generation catalogue

Research from the 1980s proves that librarians have been aware of their users' problems with OPACs for a long time, and they have developed what from today's perspective looks like an impressively wide range of ideas for improvement (Hildreth, 1982). Michael E. Koenig proposed the idea of enriching the catalogue with what he called 'user-supplied metadata' as early as 1990 (Koenig, 1990). Koenig was concerned about the large increase in scientific information and claimed that user-supplied metadata would help librarians and users with the evaluation of authoritativeness, etc. The idea must have been completely forgotten, because the use of folksonomies in library information systems seemed very new when, around 2005, the University of Pennsylvania introduced *PennTags*.[3]

However, innovative ideas for catalogues date back even further. In 1964, Don R. Swanson published an article called 'Dialogues with a catalogue' (Swanson, 1964). The features listed by Swanson read like requirements for a next-generation catalogue; enrichment of bibliographic metadata with tables of contents, browsing functionality, combination of discovery and delivery services, search for similar titles and exploiting circulation data for recommendation services.

Why haven't libraries been able to implement features they knew would help users better? It is not the purpose of this chapter to answer this question. However, a look at the history of library automation indicates that vendors for library management system (LMS) software (and thus also OPACs) have been busy developing a market for themselves.[4] Only after the introduction of open-source indexing solutions like Solr[5] have libraries started developing their own search tools and, knowingly or not, have come back to ideas for catalogue functionality which are sometimes more than 45 years old.

The other reason for libraries to engage in rebuilding the catalogue has been mentioned before. With the advent of the web, users started doing their research anywhere but in the library, because catalogues (as well as other bibliographic research tools) were simply too hard to use in comparison with other platforms. This motivated libraries not only to finally start rebuilding catalogues, but also to involve users in the process. There is scarcely any implementation of a new discovery solution that has not been usability-tested or released as a beta version for discussion within the user community prior to launch.

Methods of user-centred design

The methods employed for the development, implementation and testing of next-generation catalogues are mainly usability studies and focus groups. Both these methods require only a reasonable amount of effort, at least compared to the large anthropological and ethnographic studies. Henrik Lindström and Martin Malmsten describe what a user-centred design process could look like (Lindström and Malmsten, 2008). Features are developed, preferably in short cycles, which always involve user collaboration and feedback. In the Beluga project at the State and University Library in Hamburg,[6] new or planned features were presented to focus groups where users could discuss and comment on the features. The features were then implemented and subsequently usability tests were conducted in order to assess whether users understood and used the offered functionality as intended (Christensen, 2009).

Other implementation projects follow the same or similar routes. Results of focus groups and usability tests are mainly published informally; Yale University Library put its reports on usability tests of their VuFind installation (as well as other tools) on a specific website,[7] created by a group around Director of Usability and Assessment Kathleen Bauer. Users' reactions to Bibliocommons, a next-generation catalogue implemented at the Canadian Queen's University, have been researched by Martha Toub and Steve Whitehead and presented at the Access conference in Hamilton 2008 (Whitehead and Toub, 2008). Graham Stone published about the experiences with the VuFind installation at the University of Huddersfield, UK (Stone, 2010).

Alongside such studies, there are two other significant publications on new catalogues that examine the users' perspective on a larger scale. The OCLC report *Online Catalogs: what users and librarians want* was published in 2009 (Calhoun et al., 2009). It is, among other methods, based on a survey with more than 11,000 participants. In 2011, a German consortium conducted a web-based study and recruited nearly 24,000 respondents (Nienerza, Sunckel and Maier, 2011). With numbers of respondents this large, these studies complement the data from usability tests and focus groups (which typically have no more than 6–12 participants).

A distinctive feature of the OCLC report is the investigation of librarians' attitudes towards next-generation catalogues. The findings of this report, and the experience of libraries that have introduced their next-generation catalogues, would make for a chapter of its own. Librarians seem to be most concerned about data quality in next-generation catalogues. These new architectures require bibliographic metadata from (mostly) proprietary LMS systems to be mapped into other formats. Librarians are worried about resulting inaccuracies and the lack of possibility of exploiting authority files, thesauri and classification systems. These concerns are important, but are not really in the focus of what users expect from new catalogues. Still, with librarians as a main constituency for catalogues, these concerns must be taken into account by development and implementation teams.

User study findings
Catalogue enrichment

The enrichment of bibliographic metadata with additional information has been a requirement for several years, both by librarians and by users. An undoubted outcome of these user studies is the need for tables of contents as well as other evaluative content, such as summaries, abstracts or excerpts.

Findings concerning other enrichments, especially user-generated metadata, are much more inconsistent. There seems to be some interest in contributing ratings, reviews and tags to the catalogue, but users are also harbouring numerous concerns. In the focus groups for Beluga, both students and faculty members made a strong case for the neutrality of the catalogue, accepting only descriptive and non-judgemental information like tables of contents and rejecting the inclusion of reviews and ratings from non-academic users. Also, the motivation of users to contribute to the catalogue – either with ratings, reviews or tags – is low. In the unlikely event of them adding any significant content, they would feel uncomfortable sharing this with strangers. These results are backed up by the German study (Nienerza, Sunckel and Maier, 2011) where only 24% of the respondents stated interest in adding their own content to the catalogue.

A study from the UK's Research Information Network published in 2010 defined *trust* and *quality* as the main barriers for researchers contributing content to information systems (Procter and Williams, 2010). Students seem to be reluctant to contribute because it does not seem beneficial to them to invest time in sharing information. While *openness* and *sharing* are two core concepts of the 2.0-generation of web services, there seems to be little acceptance of this in the context of library services. It is therefore unlikely that a critical mass of user-generated metadata will be created any time soon. A possible direction for the further development of next-generation catalogues is the aggregation of this content. In order to eventually exchange social metadata between different catalogues, a standardized format would need to be developed as well as corresponding policies for terms of use.

The search process

As we know from the studies about information-seeking behaviour, users want the catalogue to be a convenient and efficient tool. Ease of use is the most important paradigm for next-generation catalogues. They typically offer a number of features to meet these needs: autocompletion, spell checking and *did you mean?* functionality, faceted browsing or limiting searches to electronic and currently available items.

The feature that has been examined most extensively is faceted browsing. The Endeca-based catalogue at North Carolina State University (NSCU) was the one of the first catalogues to employ this functionality (Antelman, Lynema and Pace, 2006). There is quite a lot of research, both qualitative and quantitative studies, on the use of faceted browsing (Fagan, 2010). When asked, users sometimes seem to prefer text searching to more structured searching through facets. At the same time, results of the studies cited by Jody Condit Fagan consistently show a high level of satisfaction with faceted browsing options in general, as well as good outcomes of the conducted searches. Both labelling and order of the facets play an important role regarding the usability, but in general, users seem to understand intuitively their purpose and how to make best use of them. There is even a debate about forgoing the advanced search interface in favour of faceted navigation (Morville and Callender, 2010).

Quite surprisingly, users in the usability tests for Beluga complained about the simplicity of the user interface, specifically the lack of an advanced search interface. This seemed very odd to the development team, given how seldom the advanced search is used in the current catalogue. It seems to be very surprising for users to see such a simple interface in a library catalogue. However, when people started using the simple search, they quickly forgot about Boolean searching and advanced searching options. A recent study that compares the searching behaviour of users in classic and next-generation catalogues shows that users are 15 times more likely to refine their searches when facets are available (Ballard and Blaine, 2011).

Facets obviously seem to help users with the translation of their information needs into searchable queries. Another way to accomplish this is by using authority files and controlled vocabularies. Libraries worldwide have spent decades compiling this data, but large parts of it cannot be exploited for next-generation catalogues because it is locked away in proprietary LMS systems. To be able to use this data in next-generation catalogue environments, it is crucial that the data is made available in appropriate formats and through open interfaces. Users could be offered recommendations for search terms or expand searches on the basis of this data. This is important because evidently not only students but also scholars have huge difficulties establishing appropriate search terms (Siegfried, 2011).

Evaluating search results

Meeting the demand for convenient and efficient searching also includes working on the presentation of search results. With many of the next-generation catalogues it is easy to find at least something on any given subject. But are users able to make sense of a typical results list? As mentioned before, facets help users to refine result sets subsequent to searching. However, there is plenty of evidence that users expect the library catalogue to work like Google in the way the results are ranked. They want to see the most relevant results at the top of their lists, and don't realize that this is not the case in most classic catalogues (Schneider, 2006).

Even though more advanced library catalogues and discovery interfaces typically offer a ranking based on term statistics, this method has certain limitations and will not always produce sufficiently convincing results (see Chapter 2 for more information). The architecture of next-generation catalogues, however, allow for new and entirely different algorithms to be implemented. Dirk Lewandowski suggests a set of factors that go far beyond the standard text matching – for instance, the inclusion of popularity information (Lewandowski, 2009). The idea of mining circulation data to establish popularity factors might indeed be viable, especially if this data is aggregated from a large number of libraries, as preliminary results from the JISC-funded Library Impact Data Project indicate (Stone, Ramsden and Pattern, 2011).

Other than circulation data, libraries have even more information available that can be useful to establish relevance. The relevance of a title could be boosted in accordance with the number of items held by the library. Bibliographic metadata may also contain useful information to assist relevance ranking. For instance, ranking could be provided for a certain target audience, based on whether an item is classified as an introduction to a subject.

Testing the results of relevance-ranking algorithms is undoubtedly difficult, and even more so with several different factors in action. Additionally, there is enough evidence that just one algorithm might not be sufficient. For example, Ken Varnum developed Project Lefty the prototype of a system that takes a user's expertise level into account to establish an appropriate ranking algorithm (Varnum, 2010). Working on ranking algorithms is most certainly a very challenging task, but its complexity may not keep information professionals and librarians from trying to make the search experience more satisfying for their users.

Discovery

Next-generation catalogues are sometimes also referred to as discovery tools. Consequently, most solutions claim to be particularly helpful when it comes to subject searching. Aside from faceted browsing, there are other features in next-generation catalogues to look at as far as discovery is concerned. All studies indicate that keyword searching is the predominant way used to access a catalogue initially, but the qualitative research, especially, shows that users like the idea of being given starting points for their research. Virtual shelf browsing is one solution to that, a feature which has been brought to perfection by the Harvard Library Innovation Lab under the auspices of David Weinberger. The application ShelfLife[8] not only lets users explore the library collections but colour-codes the works according to their 'community relevance'. This is a measure which takes into account not only the circulation data, but also the usage in courses.

Collecting reading lists for courses in order to determine the local relevance is something that was discussed extensively in the context of the Beluga project. One aim of the project was to integrate the catalogue seamlessly with the learning management systems used by the universities in Hamburg. However, both students and academic staff were reluctant to share their lists. Faculty members felt that their lists were often very personal and would need revision and continued updating before being made public. Students said that they would not want others to profit from lists that had been a lot of work to compile in the first place.

It is apparent that libraries have to explain the value of openness better. We know that one quality users appreciate most in libraries is their trustworthiness (OCLC, 2005). As a result of – and not in spite of – this trustworthiness, libraries must engage in leveraging the principles of openness. The functionalities that at least students wish for can only be implemented if the necessary data, reading lists for courses or papers, are made publicly available.

Meanwhile, the users' keenness for discovery can be met otherwise. There is an obvious potential for both faculty and subject specialists in working together on providing selected, preferably annotated bibliographies for certain topics. The requirement for the transformation of the next-generation catalogue into a knowledge hub with reader advisory functions could be met (Tarulli, 2010).

Delivery

The reason why library catalogues are perceived as inadequate in comparison to Google seems to have much to do with delivery. Google provides users not only with search results, but also with full text. This paradigm shapes our users' expectations and explains why the improvement of delivery rates scores highly in all studies.

Easy-to-understand information on the availability of catalogue items is a key factor in meeting the demands for convenience. Information on the location of a physical item and its circulation status or the link to an electronic full text should be provided in the results list already. It should also be possible to limit searches to available items.

But the demand for convenient delivery options can also be interpreted in a wider sense. This demand suggests next-generation catalogues should hold more content than their predecessors. And they do indeed often contain journal information on an article level and go beyond local holdings, for instance by including other bibliographic databases or data from full-text repositories. This poses a challenge for the development of interfaces, because libraries will want to make sure that their holdings are successfully identified by their users and users will want manageable amounts of relevant information. Nevertheless, the Google paradigm is very much in place regarding delivery, and if libraries want to retain or even regain users, it seems advisable to strive for comprehensiveness as well as a steady increase of electronically available resources.

Most studies broach the subject of the export of bibliographic data to reference management tools or social networks. These features are generally met with only very little enthusiasm. This may have to do with the fact that only a very small proportion of students use these platforms. There might be more potential in creating connections between catalogues and learning management systems, but this has not been sufficiently researched as yet.

Towards user experience: likeable features

There is not much enthusiasm for connections between catalogues and social networks. Thus the integration of buttons to export data from catalogues to social networks would be 'putting lipsticks on pigs', as Roy Tennant succinctly put it back in 2005 (Tennant, 2005). Ensuring a modern look and feel to the catalogue is however still important and both librarians and vendors for library-related software have started taking up the idea of user experience (Sadeh, 2008).

Creating a catalogue interface that offers a positive user experience goes further than user-centred design. The aim is to offer a service that users like and want to use again. This still means that they have to be able to fulfil their tasks effectively. But with the high level of frustration with current catalogues, it might be advisable to put some thought into the development of particularly easy-to-use and likeable interfaces or features. The implementation team for Summon at the University of Huddersfield was rewarded with an 84% satisfaction rate, with users claiming the ease of use and simplicity as best features.

In the Beluga project, users were presented with different ideas for the visualization of the database's content and results lists. They have proven to be very fond of visualizations in general, particularly a shelf-browsing functionality and graphical representations of topics and contexts. The ability to make unexpected discoveries of content is a form of information behaviour that has often been described as 'serendipity'. Users may not actively ask for 'serendipity', but there is enough evidence that they will enjoy this functionality greatly if offered in addition to efficient goal-directed searching (Björneborn, 2008). Another example of a feature that is useful and likeable at the same time is the presentation of holdings information on a map, as employed in the Swedish union catalogue LIBRIS.[9] There is no record of users' reactions to this functionality, but with the high emphasis that users are putting on delivery information, it can be expected that it would be received very favourably, particularly in urban regions with lots of library locations.

Conclusion

The term 'catalogue 2.0' shows that functionality and design elements which are typically associated with the 'Web 2.0' seem to be relevant to library catalogues. However, it is not the 2.0-features that users want to see in the next generation of library catalogues.

Developing catalogues in the direction of social networks or folksonomies does not seem feasible because of the reluctant attitude of library users regarding the production of user-generated content. The 'social' features of catalogues are not at all what create the most enthusiasm in today's library users. Instead, users call for features which help them to search the catalogues more efficiently and conveniently. As pointed out before, at least some such features have been sketched in very early stages of the electronic catalogue, for instance relevance ranking, catalogue enrichment or browsing functionality.

But libraries are still very much social places, and tools like ShelfLife or collaborative reference management systems communities may help users to develop a deeper understanding that many of the features they wish for in searching and evaluating scientific information can only be met when more people share their expertise and experience.

The studies highlighted in this chapter have helped with the development of understanding for users' needs. Librarians who have helped to conduct these studies have characterized their work with users as satisfying and inspiring. The library catalogue is still very much the core product of any library, and librarians themselves have high stakes in this tool and fear that the involvement of users in the catalogue development might endanger the quality of the product. Qualitative and authoritative data, however, remains one of the most prominent wishes of users and libraries can provide this. The next-generation catalogue is one important interface to this data and it needs to reflect the changing patterns of user behaviour as well as the users' own ideas to fulfil its tasks.

References and further reading

Akselbo, J. L., Arnfred, L., Barfort, S., Bay, G., Bagger Christiansen, T., Hofman Hansen, J., Jensen, H.T., Markussen, G. B., Morthorst, A. M. and Nielsen, M. P. (2006) *The Hybrid Library: from the user's perspective*, Aarhus, www.statsbiblioteket.dk/summa/fieldstudies.pdf/at_download/file.

Antelman, K., Lynema, E. and Pace, A. K. (2006) Toward a Twenty-first Century Library Catalog, *Information Technology and Libraries*, **25** (3), 128–39, http://cat.inist.fr/?aModele=afficheN&cpsidt=18125337.

Ballard, T. and Blaine, A. (2011) User Search-limiting Behavior in Online Catalogs: comparing classic catalog use to search behavior in next-generation catalogs, *New Library World*, **112** (5/6), 261–73, http://dx.doi.org/10.1108/03074801111136293.

Björneborn, L. (2008) Serendipity Dimensions and Users' Information Behaviour in the Physical Library Interface, *Information Research*, **13** (4), 1–15, http://search.ebscohost.com/login.aspx?direct=true&db=lxh&AN=36027244&site=ehost-live.

Calhoun, K., Cantrell, J., Gallagher, P. and Hawk, J. (2009) *Online Catalogs: what users and librarians want*, Dublin, OH, OCLC, www.oclc.org/reports/onlinecatalogs/fullreport.pdf.

Christensen, A. (2009) Partizipative Entwicklung von Diensten in der Bibliothek 2.0: Methoden und Ergebnisse aus Katalog 2.0-Projekten, *Bibliotheksdienst*, **43** (5),

527–37, http://beluga-blog.sub.uni-hamburg.de/blog/wp-content/uploads/2009/
05/user_studies1.pdf.

Cochrane, P. A. and Markey, K. (1983) Catalog Use Studies Since the Introduction of
Online Interactive Catalogs: impact on design for subject access, *Library &
Information Science Research*, **5** (4), 337–63.

Fagan, J. C. (2010) Usability Studies of Faceted Browsing: a literature review,
Information Technology and Libraries, **29** (2), 58–66,
http://connection.ebscohost.com/c/articles/50741400/usability-studies-faceted-
browsing-literature-review.

Foster, N. F. and Gibbons, S. (eds) (2007) *Studying Students: the undergraduate research
project*, Chicago, Association of College and Research Libraries,
www.ala.org/acrl/sites/ala.org.acrl/files/content/publications/
booksanddigitalresources/digital/Foster-Gibbons_cmpd.pdf.

Hennig, N. (2006) *Embedding Library Services in the Trusted Networks of MIT Students*,
www.hennigweb.com/presentations/ncaaist-embeddedlibrary-hennig.pdf.

Hildreth, C. R. (1982) *Online Public Access Catalogs: the user interface*, Dublin, OH,
OCLC, http://gso.gbv.de/DB=2.1/PPNSET?PPN=025274058.

Koenig, M. E. D. (1990) Linking Library Users: a culture change in librarianship,
American Libraries, **21** (9), 844–9.

Lewandowski, D. (2009) Ranking library materials, *Library Hi Tech*, **27** (4), 584–93,
http://dx.doi.org/10.1108/07378830911007682.

Lindström, H. and Malmsten, M. (2008) User-Centred Design and Agile
Development: rebuilding the Swedish National Union Catalogue, *The Code4Lib
Journal*, **5** (5), http://journal.code4lib.org/articles/561.

Morville, P. and Callender, J. (2010) Design Patterns: faceted navigation. In Morville,
P. and Callender, J. (eds), *Search Patterns*, Sebastopol, CA, O'Reilly, 95–101,
www.alistapart.com/articles/design-patterns-faceted-navigation.

Nienerza, H., Sunckel, B. and Maier, B. (2011) Unser Katalog soll besser werden!
ABI-Technik, **31** (3), 130–49.

Oberhauser, O. (2010) Relevance Ranking in den Online-Katalogen der 'nächsten
Generation', *Mitteilungen der Vereinigung Österreichischer Bibliothekarinnen &
Bibliothekare*, 2010, **63** (1/2), 25–37, http://hdl.handle.net/10760/14655.

OCLC (2005) *Perceptions of Libraries and Information Resources: a report to the OCLC
membership*, 12–19, OCLC Reports, www.oclc.org/reports/pdfs/Percept_all.pdf.

Procter, R. and Williams, R. (2010) *If You Build It, Will They Come? How researchers
perceive and use web 2.0*: a Research Information Network report,
www.rin.ac.uk/system/files/attachments/web_2.0_screen.pdf.

Ranganathan, S. R. (1931) *The Five Laws of Library Science*, Madras, Madras Library

Association, http://catalog.hathitrust.org/Record/001661182.

Rowlands, I., Nicholas, D., Williams, P., Huntington, P., Fieldhouse, M., Gunter, B., Withey, R., et al. (2008) The Google Generation: the information behaviour of the researcher of the future, *Aslib Proceedings*, **60** (4), 290–310, http://dx.doi.org/10.1108/00012530810887953.

Sadeh, T. (2008) User Experience in the Library: a case study, *New Library World*, **109** (1/2), 1–36, http://dx.doi.org/10.1108/03074800810845976.

Schneider, K. G. (2006) How OPACs Suck, Part 1: relevance rank (or the lack of it), *ALA TechSource Blog*, www.alatechsource.org/blog/2006/03/how-opacs-suck-part-1-relevance-rank-or-the-lack-of-it.html.

Siegfried, D. (2011) World Wide Wissenschaft – Wie professionell Forschende im Internet arbeiten, *Informationsdienst Wissenschaft*, http://idw-online.de/pages/de/news409574.

Stone, G. (2010) Searching Life, the Universe and Everything? The implementation of Summon at the University of Huddersfield, *Liber Quarterly*, **20** (1), 25–52, http://eprints.hud.ac.uk/7155.

Stone, G., Ramsden, B. and Pattern, D. (2011) Looking for the Link between Library Usage and Student Attainment, *Ariadne*, **67**, www.ariadne.ac.uk/issue67/stone-et-al.

Swanson, D. R. (1964) Dialogues with a Catalog. *Library Quarterly*, **34** (1), 113.

Tarulli, L. (2010) *Social Catalogues and Readers' Advisory Services: building trust, promoting community and enhancing RA service outside the physical library*, www.slideshare.net/laureltarulli/social-catalogues-and-readers-advisory-services-building-trust-promoting-community-and-enhancing-ra-services-outside-the-physical-library.

Tennant, R. (2005) Digital Libraries: 'lipstick on a pig', *Library Journal*, www.libraryjournal.com/article/CA516027.html.

Varnum, K. (2010) Project Lefty: more bang for the search query, *Computers in Libraries*, **30** (3), www.infotoday.com/cilmag/apr10/Varnum.shtml.

Walker, S. (1987) OKAPI: evaluating and enhancing an experimental online catalog, *Library Trends*, **35** (4), 631–45.

Whitehead, M. and Toub, S. (2008) User-generated Content and Social Discovery in the Academic Library Catalogue: findings from user research, *Access 2008*, Hamilton, www.slideshare.net/stoub/usergenerated-content-and-social-discovery-in-the-academic-library-catalogue-findings-from-user-research-presentation.

References

1 www.extensiblecatalog.org.
2 www.statsbiblioteket.dk/summa.
3 http://tags.library.upenn.edu.
4 www.librarytechnology.org/automationhistory.pl.
5 http://lucene.apache.org/solr.
6 www.uni-hamburg.de/eLearning/eInfo/eLearning_Foerderprojekte_e.html#
   BELUGA.
7 https://collaborate.library.yale.edu/usability/reports.
8 http://librarylab.law.harvard.edu/blog/shelflife-alpha.
9 http://libris.kb.se.

2

Making search work for the library user

Till Kinstler

Introduction

With the advent of the world wide web, using search engines to find information has become a daily activity for many people. Before the web, searching in electronic databases was a complex process, usually carried out by information professionals. As search engines have become more popular, users' expectations of search interfaces have increased. Users now demand self-service from intuitively usable search engines that deliver the right results, quickly. Just as users expect this from search engines, they also expect it from library catalogues.

The foundations of both search engines and library catalogues lie in the science of information retrieval. Whereas search engines harness a range of modern information retrieval techniques to provide relevant results for their users, library catalogues are lagging somewhat behind. This chapter will start by describing how Boolean search, using operators such as 'AND', 'OR' and 'NOT' to combine search terms, which is the key information retrieval paradigm used in library catalogues, differs from the Vector Space Model that is used in many search engines. The chapter will then go on to explore how such search engine technologies can be applied to library catalogues and, indeed, if combined with Boolean-based search techniques can lead to a powerful and usable search experience for the library users. Finally, other features of modern search engines, such as search suggestions and facets, are also explored. If all of these technologies can be combined and implemented within a library context, it can help the library catalogue get a step closer to meeting the expectations of today's web-savvy users.

A short history of electronic library catalogues

Library catalogues are information retrieval systems.

Information retrieval (IR) deals with the representation, storage, organization of, and access to information items such as documents, Web pages, online catalogs, structured and semi-structured records, multimedia objects. The representation and organization of the information items should be such as to provide the users with easy access to information of their interest.

(Beaza-Yates and Ribeiro-Neto, 2010, 1)

Library card catalogues were designed to help users find information items in libraries. This is still the primary task of library catalogues today.

First-generation electronic catalogues

Libraries began transferring card catalogues to computer-based catalogues in the 1970s. These first-generation electronic catalogues were simply electronic versions of the well known card catalogues. They offered alphabetic browsing in a selected number of pre-coordinate[1] indexes (e.g. author, title, subject), just as card catalogues did. A second generation of electronic library catalogues emerged in the 1980s, adding features common in commercial database systems of that time. These systems offered a wider choice of post-coordinate indexes[2] for keyword and term searching. Formulation of advanced searches across different indexes was possible using formal query languages. These languages typically offered Boolean operators, parentheses for grouping of query parts and features like truncation and wildcard searching. In the second half of the 1990s web-based user interfaces were added to these second-generation electronic catalogues to enable users to search the library catalogue on the internet. However, the search functionality basically remained the same as in the earlier terminal-based second-generation systems. Further development of these systems then focused more on web interface improvements than on search technology enhancements. In this way, the Online Public Access Catalogues (OPACs) in today's integrated library management systems (LMS) are still based on the second-generation paradigms of Boolean search.

Next-generation library catalogues

Discussions about the features of a next generation of library catalogue that would acknowledge the shortcomings of the second-generation OPACs had already taken off in the 1980s. The main problems observed with second-generation catalogues were summarized, for example, by Hildreth in 1987 in an article entitled 'Beyond Boolean' (Hildreth, 1987):

- they offer no options for exploratory searching and discovery
- there is no automatic assistance to correct spelling mistakes or help the user find alternative formulations of the search statement
- there is no lead from successful free-text search terms (e.g. title words) to the corresponding subject headings or class numbers assigned to a broader range of related materials
- they provide insufficient information in the retrieved bibliographic records (such as tables of contents, abstracts, and book reviews)
- there is no ranking in large retrieval sets in decreasing order of probable relevance or 'closeness' to the user's search criteria.

Some experimental and research implementations of electronic catalogues in the 1980s and 1990s, such as the CITE system of the US National Library of Medicine[3] and the Cheshire 2 project[4] (a joint US/UK initiative at the University of California, Berkeley and the University of Liverpool), used search technology beyond the Boolean retrieval model. However, the next-generation features of these OPACs did not make it into commercially available software products for libraries. Belkin and Croft concluded that

> ... there is a disquieting disparity between the results of research on IR [Information Retrieval] techniques, which demonstrate fairly conclusively, on both theoretical and empirical grounds, the inadequacy of the exact match paradigm for effective information retrieval and the status of operational IR systems, which use almost exclusively just one exact match technique – Boolean logic.
>
> (Belkin and Croft, 1987, 129)

This is still true. OPACs today still implement the exact match, Boolean retrieval model, while research in information retrieval was already focusing in the 1980s on best match technologies like the vector space and probabilistic retrieval models.[5]

The rise of search engine technology

In recent years, search engine technology beyond the Boolean retrieval model became widely available, for example in commercial products like Fast

Enterprise Search[6] or Endeca Information Access Platform (IAP)[7] and open source projects like Solr/Lucene[8] Xapian,[9] YaCy[10] or Elastic Search.[11] Development of these products was driven by the rising demand for search engine technology caused by the evolution of the world wide web and enterprise intranets in the last 15 years.

Based on these search engine products, OPACs offering next-generation features discussed from the 1980s are now finally being implemented in libraries.

What is wrong with Boolean searching?
Boolean operators

The Boolean search is one of the earliest information retrieval models and is still widely implemented. Its fundamental principle is exact matching of queries and indexed documents. Queries are formulated using query terms and the basic Boolean operators (see Figure 2.1):

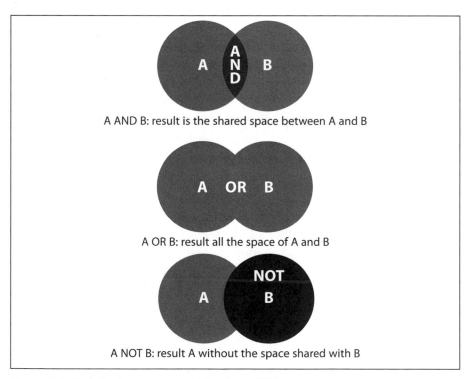

A AND B: result is the shared space between A and B

A OR B: result all the space of A and B

A NOT B: result A without the space shared with B

Figure 2.1 *Basic Boolean operators AND, OR and NOT*

- AND means all terms in the query have to match in returned documents (all terms must match).
- OR means one or more of the query terms have to match in returned documents (any term must match).
- NOT means a term cannot be in a matching document.

Some systems offer additional operators such as XOR (exclusive OR: either one OR the other of the terms must match, but not both) or NEAR (matching terms have to be close to each other – close is often defined as within five words' distance). Usually either AND or OR is used as the default operator if a user enters only query terms. In addition, Boolean systems usually support the use of parentheses to build nested queries such as (A OR B) AND C. Replacing parts of words or single characters, using truncation or wildcard operators, are other typical features.

Boolean systems enable the precise formulation of queries. A document in such a system either precisely matches a query or it does not.

The shortcomings of Boolean

The longstanding shortcomings of the Boolean retrieval model stem from both information retrieval theory and user research. Gerard Salton summarized this critique in a 1984 article as: 'The conventional Boolean retrieval methodology is not well adapted to the information retrieval task' (Salton, 1984). He lists several reasons, such as:

- User studies show that formulation of good Boolean queries is very difficult for untrained users.
- Users have no control over the size of a result set: some queries do not deliver any hits, while others return result sets too huge to browse.
- There is no ranking of results in any order of presumed usefulness for the searcher: all results are assumed to be equally good by the system as long as they match the query.
- All query terms are considered equally important by the system.
- For OR-queries a document containing only one query term is considered to be as important as documents containing all query terms; even if only one single term in a document does not match an AND-query, the document is not returned.

Porter and Galpin (1988) added to the critique: 'The number of documents retrieved is usually too large or too small, and a certain amount of juggling with terms is necessary to get a retrieved set of manageable size. Users frequently cannot compose Boolean expressions, and require an expert to do it for them. The retrieved set of documents is usually not ranked in any way, and so it is necessary to inspect the entire list in the search for relevance.' Cooper (1988) also stresses the counter-intuitive meaning of AND and OR in Boolean queries: '[...] in ordinary conversation a noun phrase of the form "A AND B" usually refers to more entities than would "A" alone, whereas in the information retrieval usage it refers to fewer documents than would be retrieved by "A" alone.'

All these shortcomings of Boolean information retrieval still exist in many of today's library OPACs, because they are based on the Boolean retrieval model.

Today, there is an additional reason why users struggle with library catalogues; library users expect OPACs to work in a similar way to search interfaces they use every day on the web. However, web search engines like Google or Bing or search interfaces to shopping sites like Amazon or eBay are not based on the Boolean exact matching paradigm. They typically allow fault-tolerant search, provide search suggestions, apply relevance ranking to result sets and offer refinement and browsing of result sets. They follow the best match paradigm instead of the exact match paradigm.

The vector space model: relevance ranking in information retrieval

Best match searching

In the Boolean retrieval model, queries either match documents exactly or they do not. The vector space model, however, implements best match searching. Willet (1988) characterizes this as: 'A best match search matches the set of query stems against the sets of stems corresponding to each of the documents in the database, calculates a measure of similarity between the query and each document, and then sorts the documents into order of decreasing similarity with the query.' In this way, 'best match' systems enable the output of a list of documents sorted by their similarity to the query. The best matching documents are on top of the list.

Calculating relevance

In information retrieval this concept is called relevance or relevancy ranking. Relevance is a measure of similarity between documents and queries. There are several ways to calculate relevance in search engines, the vector space model being a widely implemented one.

In the vector space model[12] each individual term in the documents to be searched is assigned a weight. This weight is a numeric value for the importance or significance of a term in a document. Documents and queries are represented as lists of these weights forming vectors. The term weights are the numeric components of the vectors. Therefore, documents can be mathematically treated as vectors within a vector space.

Figure 2.2 shows a simple vector space of three terms (T1, T2, T3), three documents (Doc1, Doc2, Doc3) and one query. The term weights of the three terms in each document are the components (t1, t2, t3) of the document vectors. In a vector space, it is possible to calculate the distance between the documents and the query terms. As the vectors for documents with similar term weights point in similar directions, the distance between the vector of the terms within each document and the query terms is a measure of the similarity of the documents. There are several ways to calculate the distance

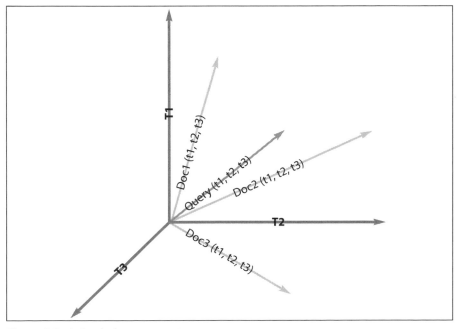

Figure 2.2 *A simple document vector space*

in vector spaces. Such calculations are called similarity measures. Cosine similarity[13] is a commonly used similarity measure. The result is a single value for the similarity of the documents and the query terms. This value can then be used as a score for sorting search results according to their similarity to a query in vector space search engines.

Term weights

Term weights play an essential role in the vector space model. This is because they are the numerical components of the vectors and therefore determine their direction. In turn, the direction of the vectors determines the similarity calculation.

The simplest way to express the weight of a term in a document is as a binary number. Either the term occurs in a document (1) or it does not (0). Using this method, however, means that all the terms in a document are considered to be equally representative of the content of the document. A general assumption in the vector space model is that terms appearing frequently in a document are important and significant for the content of that document. Therefore, the term frequency (tf) within a document is one of the values that are used to measure the weight of a term in search engines using the vector space model.

The 'tf-idf' model

Using term frequency alone, however, boosts common words that occur frequently in language – articles (e.g. the, a), pronouns (e.g. I, she, him, it) and conjunctions (e.g. and, or, but), etc. These terms are not useful as descriptors for the content of a document, because they are so common. The vector space model therefore uses inverse document frequency (idf) to identify such common terms and reduce their weight. The idf for a term is calculated as the number of documents in a collection divided by the number of documents that contain that term.[14] So, therefore, terms occurring in only a few documents have a high idf value, while terms occurring in all documents have an idf value of 1. The product of tf and idf is used to calculate the final weight of a term in a document. This is often called the tf-idf weight. In this way, terms occurring frequently within in a document, but not occurring in many documents, have a high tf-idf weight. While terms occurring infrequently in a single document or frequently all over the document collection have a lower tf-idf weight.[15]

Calculating similarity

Relevance ranking, is therefore, the calculation of the similarity between the documents and the query terms based on the term weights in a vector space model. In this way, relevance ranking is simply a statistical analysis of the occurrence of terms in the query against the occurrence of the terms in the documents.

Software implementations of the vector space model usually offer ways to influence the similarity calculation. For example, the Solr[16] search engine technology from the Apache Lucene project,[17] which is used in many new library catalogues and discovery interfaces, allows the weights of individual terms in documents and queries to be boosted. It also offers ways to add additional or custom formulas to the similarity calculation. The ranking calculation can therefore be finely tuned for different use cases.

Search engine software based on the vector space model usually offers additional exact matching options. For example, the use of operators + and − to mark query terms as being mandatory in, or excluded from, the results are common. Some search engines also offer Boolean searching, with all common Boolean operators, in addition to the best match functionalities. Result sets are then calculated based on the exact Boolean query, but ranked using the vector space model. In this way, real-world search engines users can use the best of both paradigms.

Relevance ranking of library resources

Concern has been expressed about the use of the term-statistics based vector space model for search in library collections.[18] Such concern is based on the assumption that vector space search works better, or only, on full-text collections. It is assumed that the short metadata records typically found in library catalogues would not be suitable for relevance calculation. From a mathematical point of view, this is not true. Common implementations of the vector space model take into account the length of the documents concerned by normalizing the vectors over the document length. The document length is therefore not important for the ranking calculation. In this way, the vector space model works perfectly well with short texts like catalogue records.

Ranking catalogue records

The problem with catalogue records is more that the snippets of text (such as titles, person names, subject headings and sometimes abstracts) only express a few, highly condensed, and sometimes not even significant aspects of a resource. For example, a title might be chosen to attract readers, not to describe the content of the book. A record might be calculated as being relevant, based on term statistics but the resource it describes might still be irrelevant because the content of the record does not exactly match the content of the book. This, however, is not a retrieval model problem. A book selected from an alphabetically sorted card catalogue might turn out to be irrelevant as well. The issue just becomes more obvious in relevance ranked lists, because users expect most helpful results on top of the list.

Relevance ranking in vector space search engines can even improve exact matching. For example, in classic Boolean OPACs, finding journals like *Nature* or *Science* is a hard task. In long result lists for common terms like 'nature' or 'science' sorted by year of publication or title, these journals tend to be quite low down in the result list. However, if the ranking in a vector space engine is done well, these journals can appear at the top of the result lists of a search for 'nature' or 'science'. In this way, dealing with large result lists can be much easier for users, because the best matches are at the top of the list.

How are best matches determined? Best matches that are calculated based on term statistics do not necessarily meet an individual user's information need in a specific context. For that reason, popular web search engines use lots of different ranking factors beyond term statistics to sort a result list. For example, Google says it uses 'more than 200' different factors (called signals) to calculate result ranking.[19]

Additional ranking factors

For library material, too, additional ranking factors beyond term statistics can be used to calculate a result list. There has been intense discussion of such factors in the literature. However, only a few catalogue implementations seem to use any of them. Hildreth (1995) mentions 'Many ranking criteria: most likely to be relevant first, most recent, most cited, most circulated, etc.' Lewandowski (2009) discusses similar factors in more depth, including popularity, freshness and locality. Dellit and Boston (2007) refer to websites whose business relies on successful search applications (e.g. Google for the web, Amazon for the products they sell) that apply users' patterns of behaviour for ranking calculation. They suggest using popularity, as an important expression of users' behaviour, as a ranking factor.

Popularity

For web resources, popularity is often calculated based on the link structure, as Google's PageRank algorithm is (Page et al., 1999). If many links point to a website, it is considered popular and important for a topic. To measure the popularity of library resources different methods are being discussed. Frequently mentioned indicators include the number of holdings (of a resource in a library or across several libraries), circulation rates, clicks on records in catalogues or explicit ratings of resources by users. 'Most cited', as mentioned by Hildreth (1995), belongs to this category. Figure 2.3 shows how the University of Huddersfield library uses circulation data to show 'People who borrowed this item, also borrowed . . .' recommendations in its catalogue.[20] Other recommendation services, that can be added to library catalogues, like BibTip[21] or Ex Libris' bX,[22] calculate recommendations for similar items based on use frequency of electronic resources and click rates in library catalogues.

Figure 2.3 *'People who borrowed this item, also borrowed . . .' feature in the University of Huddersfield library catalogue*

Freshness

Freshness is another ranking factor often discussed. Ranking by freshness is often available, in a basic form, in traditional OPACs as an option to sort search results by year of publication. However, if freshness is the only factor used for the ranking calculation, this will make, for example, the journal *Nature* hard to find. Vector space search engines can use freshness as an extra ranking factor in addition to term statistics. On the other hand, the importance of the freshness of resources depends heavily on a user's information needs. For that reason, in library catalogues based on vector space search engines, freshness does not seem to be commonly used as an additional ranking factor.

Availability

Availability of a resource is another additional ranking criteria. If the best resource is not available for use, it is rather useless. Availability of library resources has many aspects. Books and journals might be borrowed or only on the shelf in a different branch library or only available through inter-library loan with a long delivery time. Online resources are often considered to have better availability than printed material. In an office, in front of a computer, online access is convenient. However, if users are in the library without a network device, they might prefer printed resources. What availability means therefore depends on the individual user's context. For example, OCLC's WorldCat local[23] ranks resources available at the local library higher than those only available through inter-library loan. Suchkiste,[24] a joint discovery interface for electronic resources licensed by German libraries, gives the highest ranking to the resources that a user has immediate online access to because his or her library holds a licence for the resource.

The user context

This short discussion of some possible ranking factors for library material shows that their usefulness very much depends on the individual information needs of users. A fresh resource on the web might be useful for one user, but an ancient hand-drawn map might be the best for a second. Information needs are, by definition, always within a user's individual context. Talja, et al. (1999) write in their study on the use of context in information seeking research, that 'In practice, context . . . usually refers to any factors or variables that are seen to affect individuals' information-seeking behaviour: socio economic conditions, work roles, tasks, problem situations, communities and organizations with their structures and cultures, etc.' Web search engines collect and use data on users' contextual situations to rank search results. For example, Google uses (among many other factors) preferred language settings in the web browser, the (assumed) location and the search and browsing history of users to rank resources matching the personal context higher. In this way, users searching for 'weather' in London get differently sorted results from users entering the same query in Sydney, Australia.

The JISC (Joint Information Systems Committee)-funded MOSAIC project[25] investigated the personalization of library catalogue search results based on users' contexts. The user's context in the project's prototype implementation[26] can be defined by different parameters, such as institution, academic level, course title, or academic year. The system ranks search results differently for different user contexts. An undergraduate student at University A gets a differently ranked result list from a professor at University B. The assignment of resources to context parameters in the prototype is based on circulation data and course reading lists. The project promotes the idea of building up contextual data by sharing circulation and other usage data among universities to reach a broader assignment of library materials to context parameters.

Some concerns have been raised about using usage data for personalizing search results. There are the obvious data protection and privacy issues to be solved when collecting and using user data for ranking. Beyond that, there is some discussion about ethical questions around personalization of search results, for example pointed out in a blog post by Roy Tennant.[27]

More features of modern search engines

Besides the fundamental change from Boolean to vector space retrieval models, modern search engines have a number of other additional features that can be used to improve user experience in library catalogues.

Search suggestions

Spelling suggestions are well known from web search engines. If a query does not return any or only few results, the search engine suggests similar search terms to the ones originally entered. This is a way to help users navigate out of zero-hit dead ends. There are different ways to determine the terms to suggest. Some search engines work with dictionaries, some use words in the search index, others provide suggestions based on previous successful searches.

A related feature is the suggestion of search terms or search results while users are typing in their queries. This feature is sometimes called autocomplete, autosuggest or live search. 'Autocomplete involves the program predicting a word or phrase that the user wants to type in without the user actually typing it in completely.'[28] It is well known from the address bars of web browsers. As the user types, the browser suggests previously entered URLs in a drop-down list. Users can select from this list, saving them from typing in complete URLs. In systems where users repeatedly enter the same terms (such as browser address bars or login forms), suggestions are usually based on users' previous input. In library catalogues and other search engines, where users typically enter different queries over time, suggestions are usually based on the searchable content and successful or frequent searches from other users. Some systems suggest search terms based on index entries. This can be a useful application for library authority data. For example, OCLC provides an autosuggest service based on the Virtual International Authority File (VIAF).[29] The service looks up matching names in VIAF and suggests best matching entries. Users can then select the suggested names as search terms. This autosuggest service has been implemented on the VIAF website itself.[30] Another approach is to suggest search results, instead of search terms, as users type. The Suchkiste project[31] implemented search result suggestions in the search interface[32] for the German Research Foundation's (DFG) Nationallizenzen digital collection.[33] The system suggests titles of best matching search results in a drop-down list, based on what the user types. Google has gone one step further and introduced a feature called 'instant search'[34] that updates the result list while users are typing their query.

Facets

Card catalogues were designed for browsing records by a selected number of access points, usually person names, titles and subjects. Library data still follows the concept of catalogue cards. Defining access points is still a fundamental principle in cataloguing. Unfortunately, the browsing functionality of card catalogues was lost in second-generation OPACs. Instead, keyword search is the typical user interface in these systems. Modern search engines give the opportunity to provide advanced browsing functionality in user interfaces through a feature usually called faceting, faceted search or drill-down. Faceting breaks up the search results into multiple categories or clusters, typically showing the number of results for each facet. Users can browse result sets based on these categories. They can even combine aspects from different categories while browsing. Faceted browsing is a feature often found on shopping websites to help users narrow down search results by different aspects of products (price, technical data, manufacturer, etc.). Fagan (2010) reviews the usefulness of facets in user interfaces, concluding: 'Reviewing user studies about faceted browsing revealed empirical evidence that faceted browsing improves user performance. Yet this evidence does not necessarily point directly to user success in faceted library catalogs, which have much more complex databases than those used in these experimental studies.'

In library catalogue user interfaces facets are often shown in a column on the left or right hand side of search results. There are two main differences between traditional card catalogue browsing and faceted search. Faceted search works in combination with keyword searching in the same user interface. Users may browse, structure and refine the results of a keyword search by several categories using facets. Users are also able to create their own custom navigation by combining various facets instead of using a few static, pre-coordinated indexes, as in card catalogues.

Technically, facets are statistics on recurring aspects of categories of a data set. A data set can be a search result, the complete search index or a part of it. The categories often correspond to metadata fields. Highly structured data, like library data, is well suited for faceting. Data fields such as person names, subject headings, series and journal titles, publication years, publishers and publication format are possible facet categories. As in cataloguing, there are two types of possible facet categories: descriptive categories and subject categories.

It is not possible to provide a general answer as to which data fields are most useful as facet categories in a catalogue. One way to find a useful choice of categories is to examine typical use cases and navigation patterns of users in the library catalogue. The typical display of facets, as lists of the options within in a particular category, sorted by number of occurrence, is not always the most suitable. For example, instead of offering a list of single publication years or fixed ranges of publication years as facets, a visualization of values over the whole result set with an option to select flexible date ranges is possible: see Figure 2.4 on the next page.

Another limit for facet categories is imposed by the library data itself. Faceting only makes sense for fields that occur in all, or at least the vast majority of, records. Otherwise if users select a facet category, all records not having that data field are excluded. That is especially a problem with subject headings and classifications. These knowledge organization systems[35] are perfectly suited for faceting, because they allow clustering of search results by topics. However, a study by Karen Smith-Yoshimura, et al. (2010) shows that subject-added entries occur only in about 46% of 146 million records in OCLC WorldCat. Dewey Decimal Classification (DDC),[36] the most common classification scheme, only occurs in 14% of the records. Therefore, more than half the records are not findable through a topic facet based on the subject-

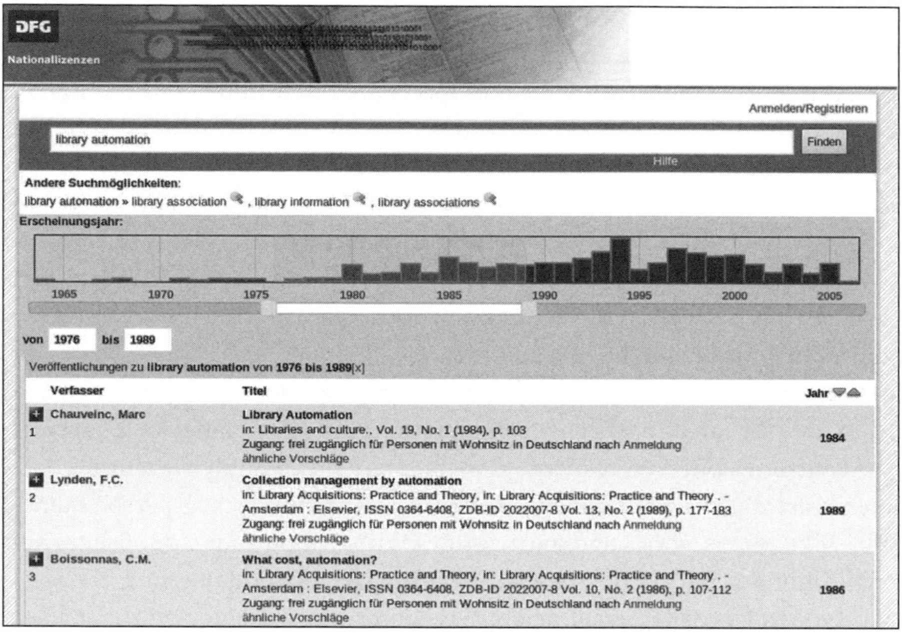

Figure 2.4 *Visualization of the year of publication facet in the 'Suchkiste' interface*

added entry field and fewer than every sixth record would be findable in a DDC facet. The situation may be different in a well maintained, small local library catalogue compared to large data aggregations from lots of sources like WorldCat. However, this example shows that statistics on field occurrence in data records are important when deciding on facet categories.

Conclusion

Search is the core of a library catalogue. Up-to-date search technology can help fulfil some of the long-discussed promises of next-generation library catalogues that make libraries more usable. The change from the exact match paradigm to best match search with ranked result lists is overdue. The shortcomings of Boolean search have been well known for many years. As many users are now familiar with search interfaces on the web, they simply expect library catalogues to work similarly. With the rising number of library resources being findable in large-scale, aggregated search indexes,[37] relevance ranking is a must, because result lists of thousands of resources are not manageable. However, there is no simple standard recipe for providing relevance ranking in library catalogues. Beyond the simple term-statistics based approaches, there are lots of other possible ranking factors to consider.

Libraries should look at these and find out, for example in user studies, which ranking formula is suitable for their resources and users. Search technology for implementing such systems is readily available.

Search engine technology is becoming widely adopted in library catalogues. Catalogues 2.0 benefit from its features and the new large-scale aggregated indexes are not useful without it. It can help in making library collections accessible on the web and better usable for web-savvy users. Search and discovery is only one aspect of bringing libraries to the web, though: after discovery comes delivery. Easy access to valuable resources is a key success factor for libraries on the web. If done right, improved search interfaces help with that, but the next efforts need to go into improved delivery.

References

Baeza-Yates, R. and Ribeiro-Neto, B. (2010) *Modern Information Retrieval: the concepts and technology behind search*, 2nd edn, Pearson Education.

Belkin, N. J. and Croft, W. B. (1987) Retrieval Techniques. In Williams, M. E. (ed.), *Annual Review of Information Science and Technology*, Elsevier, 109–45.

Cooper, W. S. (1988) Getting beyond Boole, *Information Processing and Management*, **24** (3), 243–8.

Dellit, A. and Boston, T. (2007) *Relevance Ranking of Results from MARC-based Catalogues: from guidelines to implementation exploiting structured metadata*, http://1101.nla.gov.au/InfoOnline2007Paper.html.

Fagan, J. C. (2010) Usability Studies of Faceted Browsing: a literature review, *Information Technology and Libraries*, **29** (2), 58–66.

Hildreth, C. R. (1987) Beyond Boolean: designing the next generation of online catalogs, *Library Trends*, **35** (4), 647–67.

Hildreth, C. R. (1995) *Online Catalog Design Models: Are We Moving in the Right Direction?*, a report submitted to the Council on Library Resources, http://myweb.cwpost.liu.edu/childret/clr-opac.html.

Lewandowski, D. (2009) Using Search Engine Technology to Improve Library Catalogs. In Woodsworth, A. (ed.), *Advances in Librarianship*, Vol. 32, Emerald Group Publishing, 35–54.

Page, L., Brin, S., Motwani, R. and Winograd, T. (1999) *The PageRank Citation Ranking: bringing order to the web*, Technical Report, Stanford InfoLab, http://ilpubs.stanford.edu:8090/422.

Porter, M. and Galpin, V. (1988) Relevance Feedback in a Public Access Catalogue for a Research Library: Muscat at the Scott Polar Research Institute, *Program: electronic library and information systems*, **22** (1), 1–20.

Salton, G. (1984) The Use of Extended Boolean Logic in Information Retrieval. In *Proceedings of the 1984 ACM SIGMOD International Conference on Management of Data*, ACM Press, 277.

Smith-Yoshimura, K., Argus, C., Dickey, T. J., Naun, C. C., Rowlison de Ortiz, L. and Taylor, H. (2010) *Implications of MARC Tag Usage on Library Metadata Practices*, OCLC Online Computer Library Center, Inc., www.oclc.org/research/publications/library/2010/2010-06.pdf.

Talja, S., Keso, H. and Pietiläinen, T. (1999) The Production of 'Context' in Information Seeking Research: a metatheoretical view, *Information Processing and Management – Special issue on Information Seeking In Context (ISIC)*, **35** (6), 35.

Willett, P. (1988) *Document Retrieval Systems, Vol. 3, Foundations of Information Science*, Taylor Graham.

Notes

1   'Pre-coordination is the combining of elements into one heading in anticipation of a search on that compound heading.' Library of Congress, Cataloging Policy and Support Office (2007) *Library of Congress Subject Headings: pre- vs. post-coordination and related issues*, www.loc.gov/catdir/cpso/pre_vs_post.pdf.

2   'Post-coordination is the combining of headings or keywords by a searcher at the time he/she looks for materials in a catalog.' Library of Congress, Cataloging Policy and Support Office (2007) *Library of Congress Subject Headings: pre- vs. post-coordination and related issues*, www.loc.gov/catdir/cpso/pre_vs_post.pdf.

3   See Doszkoos, T. (1983) From Research to Application: the CITE natural language information retrieval system, *Lecture Notes in Computer Science*, **146**, Research and Development in Information Retrieval Proceedings, Berlin, May 18–20, 1982, 251–61, http://link.springer.com/chapter/10.1007/BFb0036350.

4   *Cheshire II project, a Next-Generation Online Catalog and Full-Text Information Retrieval System*, http://cheshire.berkeley.edu.

5   Probabilistic retrieval models calculate the probability that a query matches a document. For a discussion of different approaches to probabilistic retrieval, see for example Fuhr, N. (1992) Probabilistic Models in Information Retrieval, *Computer Journal*, **35** (3), 243–55.

6   Now a product of Microsoft Corporation called FAST Search Server 2010 for

SharePoint, http://sharepoint.microsoft.com/en-us/product/capabilities/search/Pages/Fast-Search.aspx.

7   http://docs.oracle.com/cd/E29584_01/GettingStartedGuide.pdf.

8   http://lucene.apache.org/solr.

9   http://xapian.org.

10 http://yacy.net/en.

11 www.elasticsearch.org.

12 See http://en.wikipedia.org/wiki/Vector_space_model.

13 See http://en.wikipedia.org/wiki/Cosine_similarity.

14 In real vector space model implementations, a logarithm of that quotient is usually used as value for idf.

15 For a pragmatic and plain explanation of tf-idf weighting by Eric Lease Morgan, see http://infomotions.com/blog/2009/04/tfidf-in-libraries-part-i-for-librarians.

16 http://lucene.apache.org/solr.

17 Apache Lucene open source search software, http://lucene.apache.org.

18 See for example Beall, J. (2008) The Weaknesses of Full-Text Searching, *Journal of Academic Librarianship*, **34** (5), September, 438–44.

19 Google technology overview, Search, www.google.com/corporate/tech.html.

20 Pattern, D. (2005), *Using 'circ_tran' to Show Borrowing Suggestions in HIP*, www.daveyp.com/blog/archives/49.

21 www.bibtip.com.

22 www.exlibrisgroup.com/category/bXOverview.

23 www.oclc.org/worldcat-local.en.htm.

24 http://finden.nationallizenzen.de.

25 MOSAIC project, www.jisc.ac.uk/whatwedo/programmes/inf11/mosaic.aspx.

26 MOSAIC 'Point-of-view' Library Search prototype, http://mosaic.hedtek.com.

27 Tennant, R. (2010) *When the Answer You get is Not the Answer You Need*, www.thedigitalshift.com/2010/03/roy-tennant-digital-libraries/when-the-answer-you-get-is-not-the-answer-you-need.

28 See http://en.wikipedia.org/wiki/Autocomplete.

29 Virtual International Authority File (VIAF) AutoSuggest service, www.oclc.org/developer/documentation/virtual-international-authority-file-viaf/request-types#autosuggest and Thomas Hickey's presentation at the European Library Automation Group (ELAG) 2010 conference, http://indico.cern.ch/contributionDisplay.py?contribId=18&confId=75915.

30 http://viaf.org.

31 Suchkiste project, www.slideshare.net/tillk/suchkiste-a-discovery-interface-for-dfg-nationallizenzen-1341949.

32   Suchkiste search interface, http://finden.nationallizenzen.de.

33   www.nationallizenzen.de.

34   www.google.com/instant.

35   Knowledge Organization Systems,
www.iva.dk/bh/Lifeboat_KO/CONCEPTS/knowledge_organization_
systems.htm.

36   See http://en.wikipedia.org/wiki/Dewey_Decimal_Classification.

37   See Chapter 3 for more information.

3

Next-generation discovery: an overview of the European scene

Marshall Breeding

Introduction

Dissatisfaction with the online catalogues delivered as part of the library management system sparked the emergence of a new genre of products and services that focus entirely on providing an improved experience in the way that libraries provide access to their collections and services. One of the major trends of this phase of library automation involves a separation between the library management system that provides automation support for the internal operations, such as cataloguing, circulation, serials management and new material acquisitions, from the presentation layer facing the users of the library. In this age of decoupled systems, a variety of commercial products and services, as well as projects taken on by library organizations, now find use in many libraries throughout the world.

In this chapter we will provide a brief overview of the features and general characteristics of this new genre of library software, focusing on the products that have been deployed or developed in the United Kingdom and other parts of Europe. Some of these projects include adoption of commercial products from international vendors such as Serials Solutions, EBSCO, Ex Libris and OCLC and others involve locally developed software or implementation of open source products.

Features and services

These new catalogue products, or discovery services as they are more commonly known, embrace a more robust approach to interfaces, to content and to service delivery. In these times, where most library users use the web for a wide array of daily activities, it is essential for libraries to provide interfaces that follow the conventions and meet expectations set by other successful destinations on the web. Libraries need to make dramatic improvements in the way that they provide access to their collections and deliver their services, as the current library systems in use reflect an earlier phase of the rapidly evolving history of the web.

These new-generation library discovery services aim to follow the interface conventions that have become well established in the mainstream of the web. E-commerce and social networking sites employ features that allow individuals to easily navigate through enormous quantities of information and take advantage of any services offered. While the mission and values of these other destinations differ substantially, many of the same techniques can find quite effective use by libraries as they craft their presence on the web.

Some of these basic interface techniques include:

Visually appealing interfaces with finely tuned usability

In contrast to the legacy library online catalogue, modern web interfaces employ designs that can be readily understood and navigated by typical users without any special instruction or training. They guide users through pathways that take them through the site and to the information or service of interest without making them struggle; they allow the user to think about what they want to do without the interface getting in the way.

Relevant results

When users need to search for information, modern interfaces return results ordered so that the most interesting or important items appear first. Search engines and e-commerce sites have set very high expectations with users to expect the items most closely associated with their query at the top of a list. Successful relevancy goes beyond mechanically ordered keyword matching, bringing in many other factors that help identify the items of highest importance or interest. It's often necessary to fold in use data extracted from the behaviour of previous searchers, linking frequency and social content such as end-user ratings or rankings. In a library environment, usage data from the library's circulation system, logs from link resolvers and volume of holdings in local and national libraries might be some of the factors that help libraries provide meaningful ranking of search result candidates.

Faceted navigation

Even when the system does a good job of ranking results by relevancy, the number of items retrieved often exceeds a manageable limit. Modern search environments usually employ a convention of facets, or clickable links of terms or categories, to help users narrow the results returned into a smaller number of items. Based on the content of the initial result list, the system will pull out categories and terms that when clicked will qualify the result set accordingly. In a library setting, categories of format (book, media, articles, manuscripts), dates, authors, subject headings, genre or location are examples of facets that can easily guide a user through a broad result set to specific items of interest.

Social features

Successful websites find ways to initiate interactive engagement with their users. Many individuals today expect not just one-way delivery and consumption of information, but to have the ability to provide feedback, rate the quality of items, write detailed reviews and share interesting items with their online social circle. These social interactions provide website operators with important information on the success of their services and how to identify the best and worst content within their respective systems.

Comprehensive scope

One of the major difficulties with the way that libraries have traditionally laid out their offerings was the need to work with many different separate systems to find all the material available. Separate interfaces for the online catalogue of the library management system, links to lists of e-journals or aggregated article databases, options for institutional repositories, digital collections and interlibrary lending services forced library users to follow a lengthy and complex process to find information to satisfy their research goals. One of the main goals of next-generation library interfaces focuses on providing a much simpler pathway to finding all the content and services offered. Each of the products and projects employ different techniques to attain this goal, but one of the common approaches involves building a consolidated index that includes all of the materials that constitute the library's collection. The scope of these aggregated indexes varies from those that focus mostly on the materials held in the library's local collection (print and digital) to a much more ambitious endeavour that also includes representation of all of the individual articles included in subscriptions to e-journals and article databases. The quantity of articles is vast, especially for larger academic libraries, and may number many hundreds of millions. Yet to provide convenient access to the entire library collection the aggregated index has emerged as one of the major strategies.

It should be noted that some libraries see continued value in a separate interface for their traditional collection. Such an interface can be offered either through the legacy online catalogue module associated with the library management system or through an instance of a discovery interface scoped to local content.

End-user services

These new-generation interfaces must also go beyond basic discovery of what items exist in a library's collections and deliver appropriate services for any given type of content. Within the interface itself, common expectations include personalized features that allow a library customer to login to a personal account for the purpose of establishing preferences such as subject interests or desired points of contact, creating sets of bookmarks, saving items for later reference, exporting items to a citation manager or related features.

The discovery interface also needs to perform services associated with the web-based online catalogue, including: real-time status of items displayed; ability to display items currently issued to the user; self-service tasks such as placing holds, viewing any pending fines and to make payments for fines and fees. A simple, though inelegant technique, can involve the discovery interface invoking the web-based online catalogue of the library management system, simply handing off the user to the legacy interface. A more sophisticated approach involves bringing all these user services features from the library management system into the discovery interface, taking advantage of behind-the-scenes interactions, such as APIs (Application Programming Interface) or web services, to offer these services transparently without the jarring hand-off to the legacy catalogue.

Other services of the discovery interface relate to content from other sources, such as viewing full text from subscription-based electronic content packages. To support these services, the discovery interface needs to integrate appropriate linking mechanisms, such as through OpenURL link resolvers and pass authentication credentials through proxy servers to enable simple click-and-view capabilities when the full text of an item is available in the library's collection. In general terms, the discovery interface needs to facilitate delivery of content and to enable all relevant services in addition to the basic task of letting the user know what content exists in the library collection.

Products and projects

In this section we will summarize some of the major discovery products available, focusing especially on how they have been implemented in Europe. We include commercial products, open source projects and other projects developed by European libraries.

AquaBrowser Library

One of the first products developed as a replacement for the online library catalogue came out of the Netherlands, developed by a company called Medialab Solutions, a multimedia research facility founded in 1990 by Professor M. M. 'Thijs' Chanowski as a spin-off of BSO Origin Philips. Medialab developed a search engine technology and interface called AquaBrowser that could be applied to many different kinds of information needs. The technology took hold in libraries, with Medialab customizing and refining AquaBrowser Library to suit their needs. The product was widely adopted by public libraries in the Netherlands, with as much as 80% shifting to it from their original online catalogues. Through a distribution arrangement with The Library Corporation, AquaBrowser Library found great popularity in libraries in the United States, including many public libraries and some major academic libraries such as Harvard University and the University of Chicago.

AquaBrowser makes use of a proprietary search engine developed by Medialab Solutions, called Igor, to index materials extracted from the library management system and other local repositories. It makes use of stemming and other search technologies to provide advanced search capabilities and offers faceted navigation. A unique feature of AquaBrowser is the 'cloud of associations' presented visually on a side bar that allows users to see related concepts represented in the search results and launch a new search. AquaBrowser includes an optional federated search component to provide access to external resources such as article databases. Another optional component, called My Discoveries, introduces a social dimension to the product, including tags pulled in from LibraryThing.

Medialab Solutions was acquired by R. R. Bowker in June 2007, part of Cambridge Information Group portfolio of companies, which also includes ProQuest and Serials Solutions. In 2010, the corporate structure shifted, with Serials Solutions now taking responsibility for AquaBrowser, along with the Summon discovery service it developed.

The changing corporate associations with AquaBrowser have affected some of the dynamics of its distribution in libraries. The acquisition of Medialab by R. R. Bowker meant the end of The Library Corporation's exclusive arrangement to distribute AquaBrowser in its markets, which prompted that company to develop its own end-user discovery product called LS2; Infor Library and Information Solutions, also a former distributor of AquaBrowser, has since developed its own product, called Iguana, which it hopes to place in many of the libraries using AquaBrowser. Serials Solutions continues to develop and market AquaBrowser with its own plans for future expansion.

Implementation examples
- National Library of Scotland[1]
- Carmarthenshire Libraries[2]
- Utrecht Public Library[3]
- National Library of Wales[4]
- Queen Margaret University[5]

Primo and Primo Central

Ex Libris, an international company based in Israel, specializes in automation products for national, research and academic libraries. The company launched Primo, a discovery product designed specifically for the needs of these types of library. Primo was initially launched in June 2006. The basic design of Primo includes a local index for local content including materials harvested from the library management system. Normalization, indexing and presentation rules can be customized by the library to control the way that search results are retrieved, ordered and presented. Its search facilities, based on the Lucene search engine, produce relevancy-ranked results with tuneable boosting factors that give the library control over the relative precedence of any given type of material in search results.

Primo has been designed to work independently of any library management system. It has been adopted by a large number of libraries using its own Aleph and Voyager library management systems and has also been implemented by libraries that use library management system products from competing companies. Libraries with large and complex collections can take advantage of Primo's capabilities to perform highly customized mapping and relevancy weightings to optimize access for local requirements. While most larger libraries have opted to operate local installations of Primo, Ex Libris also offers a hosted software-as-a-service version.

One area of functionality of these products involves the degree of integration with the local library management system. In addition to being able to display materials from the library management system, including real-time status and availability information, it is also helpful to enable self-service features routinely offered by web-based library catalogues through a patron's account. Functionalities such as viewing materials currently borrowed, performing renewals, placing reservations or making payments for fines and fees can also be provided via the discovery interface. Early versions of Primo would link into pages delivered by the online catalogue for these features. One of the advancements of Primo Version 3 includes the ability to perform such tasks without the need to hand users off to the legacy catalogue interface.

In order to meet the expectations for a discovery interface to offer access beyond the local collections to e-journal subscriptions at the article level, Primo has from the beginning offered an integration with the MetaLib federated search utility to retrieve results from selected products through a secondary search. This approach, while providing some exposure to e-journal content, comes with all the disadvantages of federated search such as slower performance, limitations on the number of remote targets that can be included in a search and shallow numbers of results from each target. In order to overcome these limitations and have articles available in the initial search with the same level of performance and with full indexing and relevancy rankings, Ex Libris developed Primo Central. In the same way that Primo provides a comprehensive index for content under the direct control of the library, Primo Central aggregates an expansive collection of scholarly articles drawn from the producers of databases and publishers of e-journals.

Primo Central, hosted by Ex Libris, integrates with Primo to produce unified relevancy-ranked search results including both local materials and subscribed articles. Ex Libris has worked to build the Primo Central index by developing arrangements with the major publishers and database providers that offer content to academic and research libraries. While Primo Central is not yet comprehensive, it has reached a critical mass where it represents a very large portion of these materials. Ex Libris continues to expand the Primo Central index through its efforts to develop co-operative partnerships with additional content producers. The Primo Central index has been populated with content that represents the potential universe of content products to which academic and research libraries subscribe. Through a detailed profiling of a library's actual subscriptions, search results can be scoped to exclude results to which library users will not have access. Results from its index of local content are seamlessly integrated with those from Primo Central to present to library users results with listings that include all materials available to them.

Implementation examples

- British Library[6]
- Royal Library and Copenhagen University Library Information Service[7]
- University of Oxford[8]
- University of Amsterdam Library[9]

Encore/Encore Synergy

Developed by Innovative Interfaces, Encore has been widely deployed as the next-generation catalogue for a large number of libraries using the Millennium library management system. Although designed to operate with any major library management system, to date only a small number of libraries outside the Millennium fold have adopted it. Encore embodies a service-oriented architecture and other modern technology components. In addition to the standard set of features common in the discovery services genre, such as relevancy-based results and faceted navigation, Encore's distinctive features include a word cloud for refining results by tag.

Innovative has developed a relevancy ranking technology, called RightResult, optimized for library content. General keyword search engines may not necessarily present results ordered in ways that make sense for library materials. Encore's use of RightResult helps ensure that the items most likely to match the user's query appear near the top of result lists.

Like other discovery interfaces, Encore has been designed to provide access to content beyond that managed within the library management system: libraries can bring in other content sources such as resource records from Electronic Resource Management, local digital collections or any repository that supports OAI-PMH.

Innovative, through an extended product called Encore Synergy, takes a different approach from its competitors in the way that it extends its discovery product to provide access to scholarly article content. Rather than creating a large aggregate index of articles, as do products such as Summon, Primo Central and EBSCO Discovery Service, Encore Synergy uses web services to retrieve article content dynamically from selected content sources. The basic concept of Encore Synergy involves inserting a sampling of articles into the initial result list, which then guides users to more comprehensive article search results for those interested in that type of material. Since Encore Synergy depends not on harvesting but real-time access to article resources, it avoids some of the difficulties such as gaps in current materials that may not yet be harvested and indexed, or omissions of content from publishers that have chosen not to provide their materials for harvesting. Innovative asserts that Encore Synergy is not based on a conventional federated search model but a more sophisticated implementation of web services that overcomes the issues involved in performance and depth of search results.

Implementation examples
- Bangor University[10]
- University of Bradford[11]
- City University London[12]
- University of Exeter[13]
- Wellcome Library[14]

Sorcer – Civica Library and Learning

Civica Library and Learning offers the Spydus library management system that has been implemented in many parts of the world, especially in Australia, New Zealand, Taiwan and other countries in Asia and the United Kingdom. Civica characterizes Sorcer as a consumer portal for Spydus, replacing the online catalogue with an interface that aims to be a social network for readers. It provides a modern interface and features such as lists of recommended materials, and the ability to view and contribute reviews and ratings. Sorcer offers recommendation features such as 'people who borrowed this also borrowed,' similar titles, titles by the same author, titles in the same series. The Sorcer interface uses AJAX technology to retrieve additional information as it is needed. Hovering the mouse over a link, for example, launches a small pop-up box with additional information on that item. Sorcer uses collapsible heading boxes that retrieve and display information when opened, such as holdings and availability, additional details, or a MARC display of the record. When entering a search, Sorcer will offer drop-down suggestions once a few characters have been typed. Tabbed search display offers options for categories such as 'What's New', movies, books and general interest. Facets on the right side of the page are shown initially only in category headings, but when opened display individual terms along with the number of associated items. An RSS icon provides a persistent feed for the current search. Sorcer does not offer a relevancy ordering of results, but only title, author, publication date, series and ratings.

Sorcer has been implemented by the city libraries in Bayside and Glenelg, both in Victoria, Australia, but has not yet been implemented by libraries in the United Kingdom. However, new sites are anticipated, given that Civica ranks as one of the more successful automation vendors in recent years.

Implementation examples
- Glenelg Library Service[15]
- Bayside Library Service[16]

Summon – Serials Solutions

Serials Solutions, a business unit of ProQuest, offers a discovery service called Summon that aims to provide comprehensive access to all materials in a library's collection. Summon, launched in January 2009, initiated a class of products, often referred to as web-scale discovery services, that address the universe of library content, including the vast collections of individual articles represented in subscriptions to e-journals and other content packages.

Consistent with the company's longstanding emphasis on providing libraries with tools to manage and provide access to electronic content, Summon can be seen as first addressing the incredibly challenging problem of developing a service capable of indexing and providing access in the most comprehensive way possible to all the articles to which a library might subscribe and then integrating access to local content. Technologies and methodologies for discovery within local collections have already been well established and have been incorporated into Summon as well.

The strength of Summon lies in its ambition to index the largest possible proportion of the electronic holdings of any given library's collection. Serials Solutions, as part of the ProQuest, gains access to any of the content represented across the company's broad range of content products. It has also made agreements with an expanding array of other aggregators and publishers to harvest and index their content for inclusion in the Summon index.

The fundamental design of Summon involves ingesting citation or full-text data for the purpose of indexing to support its discovery services, but when users select an item, for viewing, print or download, they link into the original provider. Summon does not republish the content, its purpose lies in providing libraries a discovery service to connect its users more efficiently with the content to which they subscribe. This model, which in many cases bypasses the search interfaces offered by aggregators and publishers, maintains, if not strengthens, the value of the content that libraries subscribe to.

Serials Solutions characterizes Summon as a discovery service that is neutral in relation to the source of the content and that does not have a built-in bias toward favouring materials associated with ProQuest. Summon also works with all of the major library management systems for integration of locally housed materials and can also ingest content from institutional repositories and digital collections.

Implementation examples
- University of Huddersfield[17]
- University of Dundee[18]
- University of London Research Library Services[19]
- London School of Economics[20]

Axiell Arena

Axiell, a major provider of automation products to libraries, archives and museums in Scandinavia and the United Kingdom, created Arena, an end-user portal that extends beyond discovery of library collections to deliver a managed environment for all of the information and services delivered through a library's website. Where most new-generation discovery interfaces replace, or supplement, the online catalogue and other search interfaces, Axiell Arena stands in for the library's entire web presence.

Axiell Arena has been designed to operate with any major library management system, though it is initially positioned to operate with the company's own products, including BOOK-IT, Origo, DDElibra, Libra.SE, Libra.FI and OpenGalaxy, the library management system developed by DS and used by over 60 library services in the United Kingdom and Ireland, including the expanding London Libraries Consortium. Axiell's involvement in the UK stems from its initial collaboration with DS in February 2008 to create a new end-user portal, DS becoming part of the Axiell Library group in April 2008, and transformation into Axiell Limited in 2009.

Arena follows established methodologies for interacting with a library management system, extracting content, displaying real-time availability status, enabling services such as viewing items on loan, performing renewals and other features with new-generation library catalogues. Arena differs in its more ambitious scope to extend beyond resource discovery and attempts to address all of the functions of a library website.

Implementation examples
- Doncaster Council Libraries[21]
- Kingston Libraries[22]
- Lewisham Libraries[23]

Infor Iguana

Another European-based supplier of library management systems, Infor Library and Information Solutions has created a new product called Iguana, which it positions as a 'marketing and collaborative user interface' for libraries. Iguana has been designed to serve as the library's complete web presence, providing not only discovery services, but a complete set of tools to build a library's website, using current web technologies, an orientation towards engendering collaboration with library users focusing on strengthening relationships. On one level, Iguana includes the expected functionality of modern discovery environments, comparable with the other new-generation library catalogue interfaces. Its approach to the way that it offers the information and services surrounding the discovery interface helps the library to market and promote its collections and services. As a comprehensive library portal product, Iguana provides the ability for a library to configure, customize and manage its entire website through a set of tools that do not require extensive technical knowledge. One of the early adopters of Iguana has been the Breda Public Library in the Netherlands.[24]

EBSCO Discovery Service

EBSCO, a major content aggregator, entered the discovery services arena in January 2010 with the release of its EBSCO Discovery Service. The company's EBSCOhost family of content products ranks as one of the most widely used platforms for access to articles for libraries. EBSCOhost includes many specialized search features, tailored indexing and controlled vocabularies designed for optimal search and retrieval as well as integrated presentation of full-text articles within many of its offerings. The EBSCO Discovery Service extends the EBSCOhost platform to provide access to content products not part of its own offerings and to the library's local collections.

EBSCO Discovery Service, like other products within this class, aims to build a comprehensive index of all the articles represented by any given library's subscriptions. Access to all of the materials represented within its own EBSCOhost products gives it quite a head start. The company has extended the scope through agreements made with many other content providers. OCLC, for example, provides a representation of its massive WorldCat, in exchange for selected EBSCOhost data that can be loaded into WorldCat.

In addition to all the remote content from EBSCOhost and third-party content providers, EBSCO Discovery Service also uses the standard techniques for harvesting content from the local library management system, with real-time availability and status display and other local repositories.

EBSCO also offers a product, announced in January 2011, which allows libraries to use the EBSCOhost interface as their local online catalogue. For libraries that rely on EBSCOhost as their primary platform for access to articles, this product will allow them to simplify their environment. Their local catalogue would appear simply as one of the selections offered to their users in the EBSCOhost interface. This online catalogue product does not include the third-party content represented in EBSCO Discovery Service.

Implementation examples
- University of Liverpool[25]
- Bournemouth University[26]

OCLC WorldCat Local

OCLC, the library membership organization, offers the WorldCat bibliographic service, originally created for the purpose of collaborative cataloguing. Based in Dublin, Ohio, in the United States, OCLC has grown into a global organization. OCLC's involvement in Europe has expanded through its acquisition of PICA, the former European-based library and information systems supplier. The WorldCat bibliographic database has grown to a massive size, with over 220 million titles represented in early 2011 from libraries in 170 different countries. WorldCat has continually evolved in functionality, providing services such as resource sharing and interlibrary loan.

Beginning in about 2007, OCLC launched WorldCat Local as an interface that could supplement or complement a library's own online catalogue. This product starts with the massive WorldCat database and incorporates filtering and scoping capabilities to replicate the functionality of an online catalogue, including linkages to the underlying library management system to show current availability and status information. When used as a discovery interface for a library, WorldCat Local would be configured to favour the library's own holdings, showing them first in result listings, followed by holdings in nearby libraries. This approach allows users to learn about resources beyond those available in the local library, presenting additional materials that might be available from interlibrary loan services or other resource sharing arrangements. With the expectation that discovery tools also provide access to articles, OCLC has expanded WorldCat with an increasing body of articles that can be made available to users associated with libraries participating in WorldCat Local.

Beginning in 2009, OCLC launched a further expansion of the functionality based on the WorldCat platform to include circulation, acquisitions and licence management of electronic resources in a new product called Web-scale Management Services. This product would essentially eliminate the necessity to operate a library management system. A small number of libraries began using Web-Scale Management Services as early adopters in late 2010. In Europe, BIBSYS, which provides library and information systems to Norway's university libraries, college libraries, a number of research libraries and the National Library, announced that it will use OCLC's Web-Scale Management Services for its new library system.

WorldCat Local has been adopted by over a thousand libraries, primarily in the United States. Many of these include OCLC member libraries that have taken advantage of the WorldCat Local Quick Start programme that allows them to make use of the product without additional cost, though without the detailed synchronization between the local library management system and WorldCat performed for those that use the full version.

Implementation example
- York St. John University[27]

OCLC's TouchPoint

In addition to WorldCat Local, OCLC also offers an 'end-user discovery service' called TouchPoint. TouchPoint is designed to offer an integrated multilingual interface for both physical and digital content that can be integrated with any library management system.

Implementation example
- Swissbib[28]

SirsiDynix Enterprise

SirsiDynix, a global library management system vendor based in Provo, Utah, in the United States, offers Enterprise as its strategic discovery interface product. Launched in July 2008, Enterprise, employing a service-oriented architecture, relies on the GlobalBrain search and retrieval technology from BrainWare. GlobalBrain was created as an enterprise-class search platform for unstructured data from organizations in many different industry sectors, offered both as a standalone product or embedded in other applications. SirsiDynix has tailored the GlobalBrain to library data as the search technology underlying its end-user products, including both the Enterprise discovery platform and its Portfolio digital asset management system.

Beyond its role as a discovery interface for access to library collections, Enterprise can also serve as a content management platform for information created by the library about its services or specialized topic areas. Content can be organized into groupings designed for different types of audiences. Carnegie Mellon University, for example, uses Enterprise not only as its primary discovery interface but also to manage its library website.

Although Enterprise has been designed to operate with any major library management system, to date it has been implemented primarily by its own sites running either Symphony or Horizon.

Enterprise offers the standard features of a new-generation library interface, including relevancy-based search and retrieval, faceted navigation and the ability to index content beyond that of the local library management system.

The technology platform for SirsiDynix Enterprise also forms the basis of the company's digital library platform Portfolio, released in November 2010. Portfolio can be used to manage and present customized interfaces for digital collections.

Implementation examples
- Blackpool Libraries[29]
- Libraries of the British Museum[30]
- Greenwich Library Service[31]

Open source discovery products

In addition to the discovery products produced and licensed by commercial companies, open source products have been created by libraries. As open source software, these products can be tested, customized, extended and implemented by libraries without licensing costs and without restrictions imposed by a vendor. While there are no direct fees for the use of the software, libraries using open source discovery products will incur costs related to any technical work that needs to be performed to implement and customize the software or to create new features not already available. Many libraries using open source software for their discovery interface may choose to engage external consultants or support firms. Libraries considering using open source discovery interfaces will need to compare the expense of local development and support with the fees paid for a commercial product along with the value of the increased control and flexibility gained. While specialized support firms have emerged which focus on open source library management systems, none have yet emerged which offer comprehensive discovery services based on any of the open source products.

For libraries considering using open source software there are an increasing number of information sources on the web to help them get started:

- SCONUL Higher Education Library Technology (HELibTech) wiki has a special page dedicated to Open Source[32]
- Open Source Software solutions for libraries mailing list[33]
- Open Source System for Libraries[34]
- The software developed as part of the JISC LMS programme that funded projects for enhancing library management systems[35]

- In addition, although not only focused on open source software, the discussions that are part of the Code4Lib community[36] may also be helpful.

The open source Apache Lucene and SOLR search engine frameworks lie at the heart of many of these open source library discovery products. Not only do products such as VuFind and Blacklight (two of the major open source discovery products available) make use of these components, but proprietary products do so as well, including Summon and Primo. The open source licence associated with Apache software allows them to be integrated into higher-level commercial products that are not themselves distributed under open source terms. Lucene has proven itself as a highly scalable search engine technology for library discovery systems, capable of indexing hundreds of millions of documents. SOLR extends Lucene with the ability to generate facets automatically, greatly reducing the effort in developing a complete discovery application.

VuFind

VuFind was originally developed at Villanova University in the United States, in an effort led by Andrew Nagy. It relies on Apache Lucene and Solr for its underlying search engine, with its interface programmed in PHP. VuFind offers a complete set of features, comparable to those seen in the commercial discovery products. Though Nagy has since left Villanova to serve as Market Manager of Discovery Services for Serials Solutions, Villanova continues its development with other personnel and in particular, Demian Katz. Demonstrating the ability to blend use of commercial and open source products, Villanova has licensed Summon from Serials Solutions and offers the deep article-level Summon index through the VuFind interface. VuFind had been implemented by many academic and public libraries in the United States, including Marmot Library Network in Colorado, the Consortium of Academic and Research Libraries in Illinois, Auburn University and by other libraries internationally such as the National Library of Australia. VuFind has an active international developer community, exemplified by the VuFind 2.0 conference in Villanova in 2010,[37] where the VuFind 2.0 Roadmap was developed.[38]

Implementation examples

- The Bielefeld University Library in Germany has created a resource, called BASE, the Bielefeld Academic Search Engine, which uses VuFind to provide access to a large collection of open access content,[39] currently indexing over 25 million documents
- Birkbeck, University of London[40]
- The German Common Library Network (Gemeinsamer Bibliotheksverbund, GBV) uses VuFind to provide access to a large collection of scientific and technical resources, including both open access and restricted content[41]
- Swansea University[42]
- National Library of Ireland[43]
- eBooks-on-Demand (EOD), the trans-European digital document delivery service, uses VuFind for its search interface.[44]

The following case study gives further details of EOD's implementation of VuFind.

VuFind Case Study: eBooks-on-Demand
Silvia Gstrein

The eBooks-on-Demand (EOD) network provides a trans-European digital document delivery service for end-users from all over the world. Currently the EOD network comprises more than 30 libraries from 12 European countries offering their holdings for the digitization on demand service.[45] An 'EOD' button linking to the order form is placed at the respective metadata record of each book provided for the service.

Currently the EOD button is placed in some 45 library catalogues, a total made up of the large number of libraries already part of the network, including those maintaining more than one library catalogue. From a users' point of view, it is very inconvenient and time-consuming to browse individual catalogues of participating libraries in isolation. In addition, sometimes the various catalogue front ends work in an idiosyncratic way and the EOD button is not always implemented identically. Above all, the catalogues in the network use a wide variety of languages for their front-end interfaces. These languages are not always ones that users are familiar with.

These issues contributed to our idea of creating a common starting point for browsing as many of the books offered for digitization on demand via EOD as possible. Potentially, in the medium term, this tool should also allow for searching those books already digitized by our participating libraries.

By the end of 2009, following an investigation of a variety of software packages, including VuFind,[46] Blacklight,[47] LibraryFind,[48] Scriblio[49] and SOPAC,[50] we decided on the software to use for setting up such a common discovery interface. Finally the choice was made in favour of VuFind – a widely used open source software, easily adaptable to our needs and already supporting multiple languages in the front end – a really important feature in a trans-European project. Moreover, the strong community of developers was of great help in setting up and customizing the interface – another factor which contributed to our decision on the software. A list of other organizations currently using or testing VuFind can be found on the VuFind website.[51]

Finally, by the end of 2010, the current implementation of VuFind was made publicly available.[52] This already included some 1.4 million records imported from about 10 libraries – a vast bulk of pre-1900 books for sale via the digitization on demand service. In co-operation with the libraries involved, we agreed on the following record metadata formats and importation methods into the 'EOD search interface':

- currently accepted metadata formats: MARC21 or MARCXML
- possible import interfaces: harvests via OAI-PMH (Open Archives Initiative Protocol for Metadata Harvesting – preferred) or batch upload via FTP.

So far, we have received encouraging feedback as well as a growing degree of awareness from both users and libraries. With the help of XML site maps, the books can easily be found via the Google search engine. This is also reflected in the increasing numbers of hits, including increasing number of users' clicks on the EOD buttons of single records. And yet, there are various details which need improvement in the near future:

- An automated update mechanism at pre-defined intervals for retrieving changes and new records from the participating library catalogues.
- Support for the import of MAB records, a format widely used in German-speaking libraries. Therefore a transformation based on already existing concordance tables[53] needs to be written which can be used for mapping the conversion of MAB to MARC.
- Finally, a solution is still to be found for integrating records of digitized card catalogues (also called IPACs). In some cases where the digitized card

catalogue has been processed through OCR, it might be possible to import results from an automated metadata comparison with online library catalogue records.

Blacklight

Blacklight follows a similar approach to VuFind, using Lucene and Solr, though it uses Ruby on Rails as its development framework instead of PHP. Development originated at the University of Virginia as a platform for access to the Nineteenth-century Scholarship Online,[54] which was further developed into a discovery interface for the library's SirsiDynix Symphony library management system and a variety of other repositories and collections.

Currently there are no known implementations of Blacklight in Europe. However, some investigation work has been undertaken as part of the JISC LMS programme for Enhancing Library Management Systems.[55] At the University of Hull, an investigation into the possibility of using the Blacklight discovery interface to extend the library search environment to cover both the library catalogue and the local institutional repository was undertaken. Further information about the project is available on the JISC LMS wiki[56] and on the Blacklight at Hull blog.[57]

Funded under the same programme, the CReDAUL project (Combing Resource Discovery for the Universities of Sussex and Brighton) has been testing Blacklight alongside VuFind to evaluate which system offers the best option for creating a combined web catalogue for the libraries of Brighton and Sussex universities. Further information is available on the project blog.[58]

In the United States, the libraries using Blacklight include:

- Johns Hopkins University[59]
- Stanford University.[60]

In addition to the discovery products mentioned above that find use in Europe, additional products have been developed and implemented in other international regions. Some of these include:

BiblioCommons

BiblioCommons, developed by a Canadian company of the same name, brings many concepts of social networks to the library catalogue. Its interface includes most of the now-standard features, such as single search box, results ordered by relevancy, faceted navigation and visual enhancements and includes a number of advanced search options. BiblioCommons has been implemented by many libraries in Canada, including the public library systems in Edmonton, Ottawa and Vancouver and the Chinook Arch Regional Library; in the United States by the public libraries in Boston, Seattle, Santa Clara County; and by the Christchurch City Libraries in New Zealand.

eXtensible Catalog

The eXtensible Catalog, a research project launched in April 2006 by the River Campus Libraries of the University of Rochester, with funding from the Andrew W. Mellon foundation, has created a number of tools that complement the development of discovery products and services. The main outcomes of the project include a set of connectivity tools, including toolkits for the Open Archives Initiative Protocol for Metadata Harvesting (OAI-PMH) and for NISO Circulation Interchange Protocol, as well as the XC Metadata Services Toolkit. This toolkit offers utilities for the transformation and clean-up of metadata as it is extracted from repositories, such as library management systems, and loaded into discovery services. The eXtensible Catalog project has also created the XC Drupal Toolkit, which provides a discovery interface with customizable faceted navigation based on content from repositories and the library website. Though the toolkits created by the eXtensible Catalog have been used by many projects, no libraries have yet placed the full set into use as their primary discovery interface.

SOPAC

Originally developed at the Ann Arbor District Library in Michigan under the lead of John Blyberg, SOPAC makes use of the open source Drupal content management system as the basis for a new generation library catalogue rich in social features. To date, no major SOPAC installations have taken place in libraries outside the United States.

Library-based developments

In addition to implementation of commercial and open source products, many library organizations have created their own new-generation catalogues or discovery projects.

Beluga

The Beluga project[61] from the State and University Library in Hamburg, Germany, serves as an example of a locally developed discovery interface that aims to provide contemporary features such as relevancy-based results, faceted browsing, and blended content for images and enriched bibliographic information, as well as a social dimension of user-supplied tags, reviews, and other content. The interface presents a single search entry point, uses Apache Solr for indexing and offers visualizations that help users interpret results, such as graphs that summarize the types of materials represented. The Beluga interface interacts with the underlying library management systems to show current availability status and offers users suggestions for similar materials. Though the features and functionality of Beluga are similar to those in other commercially provided or open source discovery products, the project stands out through its emphasis on user-centred design and the usability studies performed to shape its development. Beluga currently spans the content of six academic and school libraries in Hamburg with combined holdings of six million titles. The project was led by Anne Christensen from its inception in November 2007 (see Chapter 1 for more information), with Jan Frederik Maas taking responsibility for the project in January 2011. In December 2012, Beluga was relaunched using VuFind.

Data Wells

In Scandinavia and other parts of Europe, the concept of large consolidated indexes representing broad repositories of content have come to be called 'data wells' and a number of projects have embraced the concept. In the same way that some commercial companies have worked on collaborations and business relationships with publishers, aggregators, and other content providers to gain access to a broad array of resources for the purpose of indexing in a discovery platform, some library organizations have engaged in similar activities, often with a more specific geographic or academic focus. Some of the projects that include a discovery interface extended through a data well include Summa and Ting in Denmark, and Libris in Sweden.

E-LIB Bremen

E-Lib Bremen[62] is the electronic library of the State and University Library in Bremen, Germany. It provides an integrated search across 32 million objects including the library catalogue and digital collections of the library. Of the digital collections an estimated 80% are full-text documents. The search engine has been fully integrated into the library website. The system is built on a search engine product called CIXBase.[63] Further information is available on the project website.[64]

OpenBib

The University of Cologne in Germany has implemented a search environment called Kölner UniversitätsGesamtkatalog, or KUG,[65] based on an open source discovery interface called OpenBib, originally developed by Oliver Flimm. KUG encompasses a broad range of content, including the materials from the catalogues of 190 associated colleges and institutes and external collections, totalling over 11 million titles. The OpenBib interface includes most of the features now expected in new-generation catalogues, such as faceted navigation, recommendations of related materials, tag clouds, and user-supplied tags. Search results can be separated according to target resource or combined. The technology components underlying OpenBib[66] include the Apache Web service, Perl, MySQL and Xapian, an open source search engine.[67]

Summa

Statsbiblioteket, or the State and University Library, based in Aarhus, is one of the national libraries in Denmark. It has been engaged in a project to provide a discovery environment that includes the holdings of libraries throughout the country as well as a large repository of scholarly articles. The initial Summa project included the creation of its own data well. The project took a new turn in mid-2010 when the Statsbiblioteket entered into a development partnership with Serials Solutions, involving licensing Summon to integrate its deep index of articles with the interface created for Summa.[68]

TING.concept

Another effort to create a new discovery environment for Denmark that includes a data well component has been taken on by an organization called the TING.concept, as a collaboration between the public libraries in Aarhus and Copenhagen and DBC, an organization that provides various products and services to libraries in Denmark, including content description and indexing services and library automation infrastructure. The consolidated index, or data well, will be created by DBC. The platform for the TING.concept[69] is based on open source components including Apache Lucene and Solr, Fedora Commons, PostgreSQL, and Drupal. Ting was implemented in the two original library partners in 2010, with new libraries, including Randers Bibliotek, joining in 2011.

UniCat

UniCat,[70] a union catalogue of 14 million records, from nine major academic libraries in Belgium, is based on a proprietary search and retrieval product, called LibHub, developed by Salam Baker and supported by SemperTool, a Danish software development firm. The system is populated through regular transfers of files of MARCXML records from each of the libraries. UniCat provides broad discovery services across the holdings of the participating library and integrates with the national and local interlibrary loan systems. SemperTool has also developed electronic resource management products and has developed custom digital library implementations in Africa and the Middle East.

Based on the consolidated index approach of modern discovery services, UniCat provides traditional union catalogue functionality. Its interface offers some basic faceted navigation, with limiters for holding library, language, resource type and publication year, but not for authors or topical terms as is typical for next-generation discovery services. An availability pop-up shows what library holds a selected title, with a deep link into the local interface to show full bibliographic details, circulation status, and shelf location.

Conclusion

The realm of discovery systems has transformed the ways that libraries interact with their users on the web. These tools have made considerable progress in closing the gap between the way other destinations on the web function and the interfaces libraries offer for access to their collections and services. In this chapter we have described a range of modern alternatives to the clumsy online catalogues created in a previous phase of library technologies. The library discovery products available today routinely offer features such as fast, relevancy-based searching, the presentation of facets for guiding users through results, contemporary interfaces with user-centred design and attractive presentation. More importantly, the scope of these interfaces has broadened beyond the traditional realm of the library management system to increasingly encompass growing amounts of electronic scholarly content at the article level and collections of digital objects. The state of the art of discovery services continues to advance through both improvements in technology and new opportunities to aggregate content. Much of the current movement among discovery projects involves partnerships to index ever-increasing bodies of content and in deeper indexing of the full text of the materials, not just citation metadata. We are also seeing an interesting mix of products and projects, including commercial services produced by some of the giants of the automation industry as well as open source projects with very broad-based communities of developers and implementers, as well as a few initiatives taken on by individual libraries or consortia.

Today, despite the availability of many different options for next-generation catalogues or discovery tools, the majority of libraries continue to rely on traditional online catalogues. We anticipate, however, a tipping point at which legacy catalogues will rapidly become displaced by the modern alternatives, such as those mentioned in this chapter. As we look forward a few years, we can anticipate that traditional library catalogues will be mostly eclipsed; few library management system vendors will continue to develop these modules and they will grow more obsolete year by year. Today, most libraries that have implemented discovery services continue to rely on the legacy online catalogue as an advanced search tool for the library's print collection. As discovery products gain these advanced search and browse capabilities, fewer libraries will feel the need to maintain their legacy catalogues. Open source and proprietary discovery products will continue to prosper: some libraries appreciate the freedom and flexibility inherent in open source software, other libraries will depend on the efforts of commercial organizations to create and maintain massive consolidated indexes of licensed and open access scholarly content. Consistent with general trends in computing technology, increasing proportions of libraries implementing discovery solutions will depend on consortially hosted or cloud-based infrastructure rather than operating their own installations on local hardware platforms.

Discovery services, as the primary experience that libraries present to their users, represent the most critical component of a library's infrastructure. This chapter has described the major products and projects, presenting libraries interested in implementing a new discovery interface with a variety of alternatives.

References

1   http://discover.nls.uk.
2   www.carmarthenshire.gov.uk/english/education/libraries/pages/librarycatalogue.aspx.
3   http://bibliotheekutrecht.aquacatutrecht.nl.
4   http://discover.llgc.org.uk.
5   http://quest.qmu.ac.uk/qmu.
6   http://explore.bl.uk.
7   http://rex.kb.dk.
8   http://solo.bodleian.ox.ac.uk.
9   http://lib.uva.nl/primo_library/libweb/action/search.do.
10   http://encore.bangor.ac.uk.
11   http://bradfinder.brad.ac.uk.
12   http://encore.city.ac.uk.
13   http://encore.exeter.ac.uk.
14   http://encore.wellcome.ac.uk.
15   http://glenelg.spydus.com/cgi-bin/sorcer.exe/MSGTRN/SORCER/HOME.
16   http://bayside.spydus.com/cgi-bin/sorcer.exe/MSGTRN/SORCER/HOME.
17   http://library.hud.ac.uk/summon.
18   http://dundee.summon.serialssolutions.com.
19   http://external.shl.lon.ac.uk/summon/index.php.
20   http://lse.summon.serialssolutions.com.
21   http://library.doncaster.gov.uk/web/arena.
22   http://arena.yourlondonlibrary.net/web/kingston.
23   http://arena.yourlondonlibrary.net/web/lewisham/welcome.
24   www.bibliotheekbreda.nl/iguana/www.main.cls.
25   www.liv.ac.uk/library.
26   www.bournemouth.ac.uk/library/resources/search-resources.html.
27   http://yorksj.worldcat.org.
28   www.swissbib.ch.
29   http://libraries.blackpool.gov.uk/client/default.

30   http://libraries.britishmuseum.org/client/default.

31   http://gren.ent.sirsidynix.net.uk/client/default.

32   http://helibtech.com/Open+Source.

33   https://www.jiscmail.ac.uk/cgi-bin/webadmin?A0=LIS-OSS.

34   http://oss4lib.org.

35   http://code.google.com/p/jisclms.

36   http://code4lib.org.

37   http://vufind.org/wiki/vufind_2.0_conference.

38   http://vufind.org/docs/roadmap2.pdf.

39   www.base-search.net.

40   http://vufind.lib.bbk.ac.uk/vufind.

41   http://finden.nationallizenzen.de.

42   https://ifind.swan.ac.uk.

43   http://catalogue.nli.ie.

44   http://search.books2ebooks.eu.

45   http://books2ebooks.eu/partner.php5.

46   http://vufind.org.

47   http://projectblacklight.org.

48   http://libraryfind.org.

49   http://about.scriblio.net.

50   http://thesocialopac.net.

51   http://vufind.org/wiki/installation_status.

52   http://search.books2ebooks.eu.

53   www.dnb.de/DE/Standardisierung/Formate/MARC21/marc21_node.html.

54   www.nines.org.

55   www.jisc.ac.uk/whatwedo/programmes/inf11/jisclms.aspx.

56   http://code.google.com/p/jisclms/wiki/blathull.

57   http://blacklightathull.wordpress.com.

58   http://credaul.wordpress.com.

59   https://catalyst.library.jhu.edu.

60   http://searchworks.stanford.edu.

61   http://beluga.sub.uni-hamburg.de.

62   www.suub.uni-bremen.de.

63   http://cixbase.dyndns.org/CiXbase/cixdocs.

64   http://elib.suub.uni-bremen.de/projekt_elib_en.html.

65   http://kug.ub.uni-koeln.de.

66   www.openbib.org.

67   http://xapian.org.

68   www.statsbiblioteket.dk/summa.

69   http://ting.dk.

70   www.unicat.be.

4

The mobile library catalogue

Lukas Koster and Driek Heesakkers

Introduction

What is a mobile catalogue? A mobile catalogue is a view of a library's collection, with corresponding services, targeted at customers using mobile devices. This definition summarizes the issues involved and the questions that need to be answered.

What are mobile devices? What are mobile applications? Who are mobile users? What type of library are we talking about? What is the collection? Is the mobile view different from the standard view? Which services are targeted at mobile customers? In this chapter we will find out the answers to these questions.

Beginning with defining exactly what a mobile device is, and what it is not, we will then move on to explore the different kinds of mobile applications it is possible to implement and look at the advantages and disadvantages of each. An overview of a range of mobile platforms is followed by a brief explanation of the mobile phone network technology. As mobile library services need to be developed for the end-users, the user needs of the target audience from a range of different types of library will be explored. Building on this understanding of user needs, the different types of mobile library services are then explored, before looking specifically at what functionalities of a library catalogue can be provided via a mobile device.

With this background knowledge in place, we will then turn our attention to putting it into practice. Using the University of Amsterdam Library's 'UBA Mobile' implementation as a case study, the practical steps that need to be undertaken to 'get a mobile catalogue' will be followed. This part includes practical tips and lessons learned to assist in making the task of implementing a mobile catalogue easier. Next comes a selection of implementation examples spanning various types of library and different software platforms. The chapter concludes with a ten-point checklist outlining the steps to set up a mobile catalogue.

Mobile devices

The first question to be answered is: which mobile devices are we referring to? The main feature that distinguishes mobile computing from previous technologies is the fact that it enables people to have internet access literally any time, anywhere. This limits the type of mobile devices to the ones small enough to carry around in a pocket or handbag such as mobile smart phones and small internet devices like the iPod Touch.

Besides the 'any time anywhere' quality, the other distinguishing feature of mobile devices is location awareness. The physical location of a device can be determined by GPS (Global Positioning System), the telecom provider's network or other means, and subsequently used by programs running on the device.

Both features play an important role in determining the mobile services to offer as an organization. They will be dealt with in the section on mobile library services.

Tablets are usually location aware. Netbooks do not normally connect to mobile networks or GPS, unless explicitly configured for that or connected to a smartphone.

Mobile devices are small, in order to fit in pockets and handbags. Therefore they also have limited display screens and input channels: touch screen, keyboard or both. Mobile services should accommodate these conditions. All essential information should be displayed within the boundaries of the mobile screen, without requiring the user to navigate left–right or up–down, and still be legible. It is important to select carefully what information to show and what to omit. Of course, this should be the practice for all applications and websites, but on larger devices (including tablets and netbooks, which is a reason why they are not focused on in this chapter) there simply is more space to work with.

Navigating, selecting, clicking and entering text on mobile devices is mainly performed by touching specific spots on the touch screen with one's fingers. Even devices with physical keyboards often use finger touch for navigation. Clickable areas such as buttons and links should therefore be substantially bigger than mouse pointer targets, even more so because of the extra-small dimensions of touch screens. As a rule, where 20 pixels diameter is sufficient to easily click a button with a mouse, on a mobile screen this should be 50 to be comfortably touched by a finger.

Simply offering existing applications and websites on mobile devices is not sufficient. Though the device will try to squeeze existing content to fit into its limited screen and input space, the results vary from tolerable to unusable. Users see this as a last resort, and when a mobile-optimized alternative presents itself, they will quickly leave the old site or program behind. Mobile applications should be explicitly designed with these physical limitations in mind. This also applies to mobile content and services in relation to size limitations, as well as location awareness and any time anywhere access, as we will see.

In this chapter, we have chosen not to focus on netbooks and tablets, such as iPads. These devices are closer to regular computers than smartphones. They are too big and heavy to carry around literally 'any time anywhere', and their screens are large enough to accommodate most websites. Of course, they can be used for a number of specific mobile services. In these cases they will be considered.

Mobile applications

What is a mobile application? This seemingly simple question is not as easy as it would appear.

In the current generation of smartphones, the term 'app' is mostly used for so-called 'native applications' (from here on, 'native apps'). These are programs that run on the smartphone, much like programs on traditional computers. Confusingly, however, the term 'app' is also often used for so-called web-applications ('web apps'), which are run from a webserver like any website, but can have much of the look and feel of native apps and can even be stored locally for offline use.

Native applications are generally more polished, but cost significantly more to create than web apps. Which to choose – native, web, or both – depends on an organization's ambition and budget.

Web apps

Five years ago, web application development was marred by browser incompatibilities and slow uptake of new functionality. The new web development standards HTML5[1] and CSS3,[2] actively supported by the Firefox browser, which became a real and important alternative to Internet Explorer, turned that around. Mobile browsers lagged behind and only supported a subset of these standards until the advent of WebKit.[3] This open source software forms the core of the browsers on all iOS[4] and Android[5] devices, as well as the Blackberry browser from version 6 upwards. This common core makes it possible to build feature-rich web applications in one version for all major platforms.[6]

The advantages of web applications are primarily for developers

- One version for all (modern) platforms can be developed.
- Skills required are very similar to those of regular web development, which is likely to be available in-house (and cheaper to contract).
- Updates are made on the server – no need for the user to upgrade.
- Independent of platform vendor and app store.

The disadvantages of web apps lie mostly in the user realm

- Some functionality of the device is not, or is less instantly, available (map and GPS integration, gestures,[7] fast scrolling).
- The lack of a single store makes discovery and installation less simple.
- Most widgets are not device-specific, making the integration into the mobile platform less seamless.

Native apps

The big advantage of native applications is the possibility of creating an enhanced user experience, tailor-made to suit the device or platform. The downside is that for each platform, a separate app needs to be created.

Advantages of native apps over web applications

- **Usability** Native apps are easy to integrate with device-specific user interface guidelines, can use advanced animations to create a smooth user experience, and can use the full screen when needed (although in theory a browser can display a web app in full screen mode, the location bar, buttons and other browser clutter are tricky to hide completely).
- **Functionality** Native apps have better access to low-level device

functionality, such as map and GPS integration, gestures, fast scrolling and smooth animations.

- **Discovery and installation** The various app stores have become the first place to which users turn to look for apps. Easy installation is provided with an icon on the home screen. It is possible to have an icon pointing to a web app on the home screen, but it is less straightforward and many users do not know about this.

Disadvantages of native apps

- **Expensive** Specific programming skills are needed, whether in-house or contracted.
- **Fragmentation** A separate app is needed for each platform, or even device. For each, only part of the development can be reused. In addition, apps need to be suited to the platform; users dislike apps that are obviously 'ported' and use non-standard buttons, gestures and other graphic elements. Cross-platform frameworks that allow easy 'porting' of programs from one platform to the other can be used, but it is difficult to give an app created with such a tool a native feel. Costs can be reduced by limiting support to a selection of platforms. However, this will annoy users of unsupported devices, especially if no web app is provided as an alternative.
- **Deployment** via 'app store' *depends on the vendor* (for example, the Apple App store has gained notoriety due to the opaqueness of the app approval process[8]).
- **No control over updates** – this is up to the user. In practice, older versions of the app will remain in use, and improvements do not reach all users.

The platforms

The Apple iOS platform is simple to oversee. There are two physical forms (iPhone and iPod touch range of devices). Apps can be tailored to screen size, on-screen keyboard and gestures. Apps can only be installed from Apple's App Store (except for the 5–10% of iPhones that are 'jailbroken'[9]).

The Google Android platform is less straightforward. Many physical forms exist, with varying screen sizes and resolution, as well as different input mechanisms. On top of that, there are many versions of Android in use, as often devices are intentionally locked from upgrading (in April 2012, Google reported nearly 94% of android devices were running a version from 2010 or earlier[10]). Vendors also add their own graphical user interface on top (Sense,[11] Motoblur,[12] etc.), creating a user interface that is not consistent across the Android platform. By default, apps can be acquired from the Android Market or downloaded by browser. However, some device vendors or carriers block this, and only allow customers to use their own 'market'. Altogether, this makes it hard to create an Android app that is polished and easily available across the platform.

The RIM platform for Blackberry[13] has traditionally had a large share of the smartphone market. Until recently, Blackberry users typically used their device much less than Android or iPhone users for browsing the web and apps, according to data usage statistics by platform.[14] Blackberries are mainly used for text communication, i.e. e-mail, text messaging and 'ping'.[15] When RIM introduced a new, WebKit-based browser, this pattern seems to have been broken, but this has not stopped the decline in use of the platform.[16]

Windows Phone (the successor to the Windows Mobile platform)[17] is the mobile operating system developed by Microsoft. The first release of Windows Phone 7 has at the time of writing failed to have significant impact on the market. The strength of Microsoft, and its partnership with Nokia, make it unlikely to disappear in the short term, but whether it will become a significant platform remains to be seen. For ageing or niche platforms such as Symbian,[18] Bada[19] and WebOS[20] that is even more doubtful.

Even for a large library, it will be too expensive to create apps for all platforms. Our advice is to focus on iOS and Android, unless it is known that other platforms are widely used in your local community.

Network

A key difference between mobile devices and regular computers is their connection to the internet using the mobile phone network. There are a number of systems in use, some offering faster services than others, but never as fast and reliable as the broadband that users have become accustomed to at work and in their homes.

When available, mobile devices can use Wi-Fi networks to make a fast connection. When designing an application, this should however not be taken for granted, as not only is Wi-Fi not always available (or free), it also quickly drains the batteries. Therefore many users leave it turned off.

Network performance depends on bandwidth and latency. Bandwidth[21] is the capacity of data that can travel the network, latency[22] the reaction time between sending a message and receiving the answer. For a mobile catalogue, large bandwidth is not very important, for browsing and searching requires but a fraction of the bandwidth needed to stream video. Low latency is important, however, as it translates directly into responsiveness. It will reduce the time of waiting for search results to be returned to the mobile application and can create a near-instant experience for the user.

A library has no control over the network. It has some control over the catalogue application on the client and the library management system on the server. Improvements in performance may be achieved by adjusting the way that both systems use the network. On the client side, this can be accomplished by displaying an intermediate page with the first results. The remaining results can be then displayed as they arrive. The AJAX[23] (Asynchronous JavaScript and XML) web development technology can be used for this. Another approach would be to group multiple requests to the server into a single query. On the server side, it may be possible to optimize the network configuration to give priority to requests made to the library management system. This work should be undertaken by experienced system administrators. If such fine-tuning of the network settings is possible in your organization, it will benefit all users of the catalogue, not only the ones using mobile devices.

Types of library and mobile users

Who are the users that libraries want to reach with their mobile services and catalogues? There is no single answer to this question, because there are many different types of libraries with different types of collections and customers. Libraries can be classified using a number of different criteria. The five criteria listed below are directly related to mobile services and user experience:

1 Target audience (local community, staff, students, specific professions, researchers, global community).
2 Number of branches/locations (single location/multiple branches).
3 Collection type (local/remote, physical/digital).
4 Stack type (open/closed).
5 Policy (lending/reference).

Libraries range from small single-location public libraries in a deprived area with an open-stack physical collection to multiple-branch closed-stack university libraries with a large number of online subscriptions, and everything in between.

In the online digital world, access to library web services, including mobile services, is available to everyone. However, access to library services via mobile devices will tend to occur within the actual target audience of a specific library. This is even more the case than for standard web services targeted at non-mobile devices or use. The reason for this is because mobile services are aimed at fulfilling user needs directly related to a particular library. Within a library's target audience, only the owners of mobile devices will use the mobile services. Within this group of mobile device owners, only those who actually have a need for these services will use them.

Mobile services

An academic library offers a range of online services to its users. Two recent projects, the Beluga project, [24] a next-generation catalogue for libraries in the Hamburg area (see Chapter 1 for more information), and the research on mobile technologies from the North Carolina State University (NCSU) libraries[25] recommend the following:

- Aim at saving your user's time.
- Do not simply copy the existing services to a new interface; think of the different user needs in this specific (mobile) context.
- Users have high expectations; they appreciate autocorrect, 'did you mean?' suggestions, thesauri, faceted browsing, etc. On mobile devices this becomes even more important, as tiny or on-screen keyboards mean more spelling mistakes.
- Reuse existing infrastructure.
- For digital resources, access is just as important to the user as discovery, if not more.

Mobile library services can be divided into three groups:

1. Practical information
- address, contact, directions, maps

- opening hours
- information on the current availability of workstations in the learning centre.

Practical information is well suited for mobile presentation. It is limited enough to present on a small screen; it requires relatively little input from the user, which would be cumbersome on a regular workstation; and the location awareness can be used to tailor the information to the user ('what is the nearest open branch?').

2. Discovery

- broad searches
- narrow searches
- finding known items.

When searching widely, a patron typically skims many results from generic subject searches. This is much harder on a small screen. More specific searches and known item searches, however, can still be presented in a useful way.

3. Delivery

- adding the items to bibliographic databases (citeulike,[26] endnote,[27] etc.)
- for physical objects: requesting the item for collection
- skimming (reading the abstract, skimming the full text)
- for digital objects: reading; reading and annotating; reading and writing.

The user can add found items to a reading list, a bibliographic database or another form of social network.

Other uses depend on the object. If it is only available on paper, the user can request it. If an abstract is available, the user can read that. If it is available online – and it can be accessed – the user can read it directly, either to skim it or in depth. Finally, the user can read it while making notes.

With the limitations of the small screen, it seems unlikely that many people will do much reading on their mobile device beyond skimming. This will be different for tablets. The larger the screen, the more skimming may turn into reading.

Mobile catalogue functions

A library catalogue is the gateway to a library's collection. Through the library catalogue users can find items in collections and get access to them. Traditionally, a library has been a physical location for keeping a physical collection of books and other printed or handwritten items. Users had to go to the physical library location and consult the local physical catalogue (in the form of lists or later cards) to find descriptions of items that might be of interest to them, possibly with the assistance of librarians. In the case of a closed-stack item, the user needed the assistance of library staff to actually access the item. If the item in question was available for lending, the customer was allowed to borrow the item.

In the computer age, the digital catalogue made its appearance. Initially, the electronic library catalogue was only available on standalone workstations. Customers still had to come to the library to find and get items. Only after the introduction of the online web catalogue, or OPAC,[28] were customers able to search and find items remotely. However, they still had to come to the library to view or borrow items of interest. Catalogues became digital a long time before collections did.

As library collections are becoming digital, either because items are 'born digital' or because they have been digitized, library users will increasingly be able to not only find items remotely, but also to get access to them online, without having to visit a physical library location. This depends on the type of library and, most importantly, on the nature of its collection. Public libraries will for some time still have largely local physical collections, whereas research libraries tend to have subscriptions to a large number of online digital resources.

The meaning of the concept 'library collection' has changed from 'all items a library owns' to 'everything a library has access to'. This includes both physical and digital items the library owns itself, and physical and digital items owned by other organizations (libraries, publishers, etc.)

For library customers it may well be that finding items (the catalogue function) will become separated from getting access to items (the delivery function). They may find interesting items in Google or other libraries' catalogues, and may even get direct access to freely available content online. However, in order to get access to physical items or restricted access digital material, they need to be affiliated to an organization that can provide that access, for instance a public or university library.

A mobile catalogue will essentially play the same role as the 'standard' online library catalogue does. As catalogues are becoming more and more part of 'discovery tools' which aim to integrate discovery and access, so will their mobile counterparts. The 'any time anywhere' and 'location awareness' features of mobile devices will affect both discovery and delivery. The question is, in what circumstances people will use their mobile devices to search a library catalogue, and what they will subsequently do with the results.

Mobile catalogue functions in practice

Some people will probably use their mobile device to perform a search in a library catalogue only because, for whatever reason, they need to find a library item then and there and have their smartphone at hand.

More interesting is what happens next. What do people do with results from a mobile catalogue search? This is directly related to the user's objective, the nature of the collection and the items found: physical or digital and for borrowing or reference. Library collections generally consist of textual material targeted at reading (books, journals, articles, sheet music, etc.), audio (mainly music), video (films), images (drawings, photographs, paintings, maps, etc.) and games. All of this material can be physical or digital, or both.

Let us look at digital collections and items first. If someone intends to use an item directly on his or her smartphone, they will want to download it immediately. This may be an e-book, a journal article, a film or some music. It will also depend on whether they have permission to access the item and download it. If it is text, people may choose to read it on their tiny smartphone screen, if they do not intend to process it in any other way, such as making notes, writing summaries, analysing data, etc. If people need books or articles for studying or processing in any way, they are likely to just bookmark the results and download or print these later on a laptop, PC, e-reader or other device. This appears to be confirmed by usage statistics. For instance, in their report on *Mobile Device User Research* for the California Digital Library Mobile Strategy,[29] Rachael Hu and Alison Meier quote research from the Library of Texas A&M University, which shows that only 1% of searches in EBSCO Mobile led to a full text download, as opposed to 77% of regular EBSCO searches.

Physical items not only include printed books, journals, images, but also music (in the form of CDs, tapes or vinyl), films (in the form of DVDs, videotapes) and games. Mobile catalogue users can request items to be sent to the nearest branch location. If it concerns items from a reference collection, they can be bookmarked or requested for on-site use. In the case of open stacks, customers could be guided to the location of the item they are interested in by using the location awareness of the mobile device in combination with a map. An even more integrated approach would be to use 'Augmented Reality', in which a live image from a mobile device's camera is overlaid with information relevant to the view.[30] For example, further information about the library's collection, similar to the type of information displayed on signs in a physical library, could be displayed to the user directly on their mobile phone screen.

A useful mobile function for physical items will be enabling users to renew items via their mobile device. After receiving an alert by e-mail or text message, library users can prevent fines this way if they are physically not in the position to return their items. Even paying the fines can be a mobile function.

Paradoxically, the latest digital library developments appear to be closely linked to the physical world.

How to get a mobile catalogue

New library systems, especially the new generation of integrated discovery tools like Summon,[31] Primo,[32] VuFind,[33] etc.,[34] are more likely to offer an out-of-the-box mobile interface than the older library management systems. These are likely to be sometimes rather clunky web apps, and often some customization is needed to create a smooth mobile experience.

If a usable mobile front end is not included in the system used by your library, then there are a number of options to get one with a 'do it yourself' approach:

1 Libraries can build their own native apps using an API to their library system or an export of their catalogue data.
2 Libraries can partner with commercial library app framework vendors like Boopsie or Blackboard.
3 Libraries can build their own web app using an API to their library system or an export of their catalogue data. Optionally an existing web app framework like iWebKit can be used.
4 If their library system allows adding and customizing OPAC front ends, libraries can create extra OPAC front ends optimized for mobile use.

Case study: UBA Mobile

Having explored the mobile applications, platforms and the networks, it is time to put this background knowledge into practice. To do this, we will use the University Library of Amsterdam's 'UBA Mobile' implementation project as a case study.

In the spring of 2010 the library of the University of Amsterdam (UvA)[35] set up a mobile service in a project called 'UBA Mobiel'. This was accomplished with minimal budget and within weeks, using an 'agile' software development approach,[36] making it an interesting case study for libraries on a tight budget.

Several of the library's staff are enthusiastic, early adopters. Early on, they noticed that the library's web presence was rather lacking for mobile devices. It was hard to use, required much scrolling and zooming and looked amateurish. In the spring of 2010 the Technical University in Delft, the Netherlands (TU Delft)[37] was making headlines in both traditional media and high-profile blogs[38] with their iPhone app. Although the app covered the whole university, the library figured prominently. Meanwhile, library staff at the University of Amsterdam noticed a huge increase in mobile device use by library users, especially students, as found in a simple, non-scientific test, namely counting smartphones in the cafeteria. Although in the long term the library system vendor would probably provide a solution, with the users ready and waiting now, we couldn't afford to wait for that to happen. Something had to be done.

Resources were limited. The library had just finished migrating to a new library management system and introduced RFID self-service and was still clearing the backlog. A project was allowed with a limited budget of €1500 and a maximum of 250 hours of staff time. The project structure had to be minimal and the University of Amsterdam library took inspiration from the 'agile' programming style.

A small team was assembled, consisting of staff from the library's user services and IT departments. For the three months of the project, library staff could spend at most four hours a week on the project. To make the most of this limited time, short meetings were held every fortnight to assess and re-assess the priorities. In these meetings, ideas were identified, then prioritized by multiplying two factors: importance and ability to build quickly, both scored on a scale from 3 (most important/easiest to build) to 1 (least important/hardest to build). The outcome was a list of tasks, starting with the highest priority items (the '9s', very important and easy to build), working towards the lower-priority items (less important and harder to build).

Early in the project, the decision was made to focus on creating web apps only. Native apps would cost far too much money and time for a 'quick-win' project.

The spirit of 'eternal beta' was embraced. The prototypes that were built were put out to the public to test. Their feedback was used to reassess the importance of functionality in the priorities list. To complement the spontaneous e-mails, we conducted several short surveys to obtain more detailed feedback.

Simple web app

In a short period of time, the team came up with three products. The first is a simple web app, presenting the library at a dedicated URL, m.uba.uva.nl, as shown in Figure 4.1.

This app gives quick access to the information users find the most important when using a mobile device: opening times, location information, phone numbers and news. The main website has a link to the mobile version, which has a low profile in the regular view, but features more prominently when seen on a mobile browser. The mobile web app includes a link to the 'full' website. Automatic redirection, based on device detection, was considered but rejected as not user-friendly enough. Detection errors cannot be ruled out, especially with new devices, and in such case the user would not have a choice and be forced to use the 'wrong' version.

Staff who were used to creating regular HTML pages learned very quickly how to write mobile HTML,[39] as this is not very different. We did find out that it was important to test the app on real devices, rather than using emulators. Emulating was fine for testing the layout, but the tactile touch navigation cannot be properly understood on a

Figure 4.1 *University of Amsterdam Mobile Library web app home page*

mouse-driven interface. A variety of mobile devices were therefore bought for this purpose.

To encourage users into giving feedback, the bottom of the web app featured Facebook-style 'thumbs-up' and 'thumbs-down' icons. Both linked to a new e-mail message, with either 'like' or 'dislike' in the subject line. This strategy worked, as the team received dozens of replies, most of them positive and, more importantly, with suggestions for improvements and next steps.

Mobile version of the catalogue

The second product delivered was a mobile version of the catalogue, as shown in Figure 4.2.

This would have been impossible to accomplish if it had needed to be built from scratch. Luckily, an active open source community exists for the library management system used, Ex Libris' Aleph.[40] The University of Jönköping in Sweden[41] had already created a mobile 'shell' for the Aleph OPAC and made it available.[42] This uses a simple 'trick'. Aleph uses a template system with a different set of files for each language. The mobile version was added as a new template set, for the language 'Mobile'. This template set was then adapted further.

In line with the advice to 'do less, but better' in the constraints of a mobile internet environment, choices had to be made, for both layout and functionality. The regular OPAC featured a banner and a large menu; both were trimmed. Functionality was brought back to the basics: browsing and searching, requesting and renewing.

Creating a usable advanced search page was especially difficult, as the drop-down menu functionality takes up too much screen space. To complicate things further, web forms display very differently on the iPhone and Android platforms,

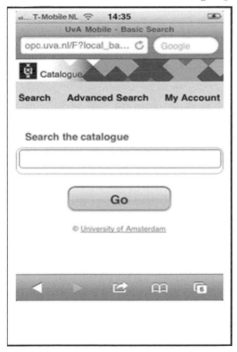

Figure 4.2 *University of Amsterdam Mobile Catalogue simple search page*

which made it very hard to create a layout that worked well across these platforms. The advanced search functionality for the mobile catalogue therefore had to be severely limited compared to the regular catalogue. In the same vein, the default simple search was trimmed down to one field and a large 'go' button.

Although there still is room for improvement in the mobile version of the catalogue that resulted at the end of the project, it is still considerably more usable on a mobile device than the regular web version of the catalogue. Feedback from users showed that although they noticed the shortcomings, they were, on the whole, enthusiastic that the functionality was now available on mobile devices, especially requesting items from the closed stacks.

Recommendations

In addition to the 'simple web app' and the mobile catalogue, the project also delivered a third outcome; recommendations for follow-up. This report was based on the items on the priority list that scored four, or lower, based on the user feedback and the experience of the staff.

The first recommendation was that in future vendor negotiations, for example when considering a new Content Management System (CMS), a mobile interface should be included as a must-have requirement. This mobile interface should work on the various mobile platforms and this should be tested thoroughly on actual devices.

Secondly, it was recommended to continue refining the mobile web catalogue, and to strive to make it function as much as possible like a native application. The regular catalogue should also get QR codes,[43] to make it possible for users to scan an item's QR code with their mobile device and have the location and availability information ready when locating the item in the open stacks.

Finally, the maintenance and further development of both the mobile catalogue and the web app should become part of the core tasks of the appropriate department.

Also, a number of possible 'quick wins' were listed that did not make it in the short duration of the project. Some of these depended on data from third parties. As soon as the relevant data became available, their priority status would be increased to 'high'. The most prominent example was real-time availability numbers for computers in the study centres, which makes it possible to create a 'find the nearest free computer' function. Other possibilities, such as a mobile version of metasearch and full text finder, depended on the suitability and availability of more complex open source software, which needed time to investigate.

It was recommended not to put more effort into location-aware services, such as the automatic detection of the nearest library branch when requesting material, into the OPAC at this time. Technically, creating such a service as a web app is achievable; the NCSU WolfWalk[44] sets a great example. The challenge lies, however, in integrating the app into the existing library system.

Reusing information from the library's Content Management System (CMS) also turned out to be complicated, due to the closed nature of the current CMS: therefore the practical information, such as locations, opening times, holiday schedules, etc. unfortunately would need to be maintained in two places, within the CMS for the main website and in Google Calendar for the mobile app.

Next steps

In August 2010, four months after the launch of the first version of the mobile web app, QR codes were added to the standard OPAC. It was also decided to integrate the opening time and location pages *from* the mobile app *into* the main CMS-driven site instead of vice versa. This provided an alternative way to maintain this data in one place.

In November 2010, after the central university ICT department released real-time workstation availability data, the 'currently available workstations by location' service was added. This turned out to be the most successful mobile library service, as described on the next page under 'Usage'. It proved so popular that VisualSpace, an independent software company, created a free iPhone app, 'Plaats'[45] ('available space' in Dutch) that simply scrapes the page and displays it within a simple native app. This app has seen 394 new downloads (purchases) from the iTunes App Store in the first ten weeks it has been available, which is around 40 a week.

Development of mobile versions of the metasearch and full text finder services was abandoned when the institution decided to acquire Ex Libris' Primo unified discovery tool, which comes with an out-of-the-box mobile interface. Unfortunately, significant work was still needed to make it usable. Primo, including the mobile view, was launched in April 2012.

Usage

After the launch of the mobile web app in early April 2010 collection of usage statistics started in May 2010. Analysis of the usage statistics is made using Google Analytics.[46]

Mobile catalogue

Between 1 May 2010 and 1 April 2012 the mobile catalogue had on average 9 visits per day, with 6 page views per visit. This amounts to 54 page views per day, with 60% of the traffic originating from mobile devices. Of the total number of visits 48% came from returning visitors. For the mobile devices the percentage of returning visitors was 52%. This was less than 1% of the total use of the standard OPAC, which averaged during that same period around 3000 visits per day, with 10 page views per visit, amounting to 30,000 page views per day. The percentage of returning visitors was 66%.

Mobile web app

During the first six months following the launch of the mobile web app, between 1 May and 1 November 2010, the number of unique visits to the mobile web app (excluding the mobile OPAC) averaged 16 per day, with 25% originating from mobile devices. Of the total number of visits 38% came from returning visitors. For the mobile devices the percentage of returning visitors was 60%. The most visited page was the mobile web app home page (80%). The regular library website shows on average around 4100 visits per day on weekdays, with around 45% returning visitors.

Currently available workstations service

After the introduction of the 'currently available workstations' service the number of visits to the mobile web app increased to 150 per day on average (1 November 2010–1 April 2011), with 33% originating from mobile devices. Of the total number of visits, 52% came from returning visitors. For the mobile devices the percentage of returning visitors was 75%. The most visited page was the 'currently available workstations' page (90%, or around 1200 page views per day).

In the period 1 November 2010–1 April 2012 the number of visits to the mobile app was around 100 per day on average, with 45% from mobile devices, 64% returning visitors, and 83% returning visitors for mobile devices. There was a peak in May (214 visits per day) right before the end of term, and a low in July and August (54 visits per day) during the summer break. The most visited page was the 'currently available workstations' page (95%, or around 930 page views per day)

About 75% of visits to the 'currently available workstations' page were direct hits; 17% originated from links from other sites, including the regular library website and only 7% originated from the mobile web app home page.

According to Google analytics, only 6% of the visits originated from mobile devices. As this percentage does not include hits made from the 'Plaats' app, the actual use on mobile devices might be higher. It also indicates that discovery through the app store draws a different audience from the one a regular (mobile) webpage gets. But even if the number of app users is equal to those visiting using mobile device web browsers, seven out of eight visits come from regular computers.

Impact

Both the mobile website and the mobile OPAC appear to attract a steady but limited number of visits per day. Only the 'currently available workstations' service attracts a significant number of visitors, and even then only one in eight comes from a mobile device. This seems to indicate that academic library users prefer regular workstations over mobile devices for their day-to-day work.

Although the number of visits to the mobile catalogue is only a tiny fraction of the usage of the standard OPAC, this does not mean that the service should be discontinued. The high number of returning visitors indicates that those who use it find it handy. The usage statistics of the mobile catalogue do not diverge much from the usage statistics of the other mobile web app services of the library website. However, when a library does not yet have any mobile services, the introduction of a mobile service for practical information should be considered first, before a mobile catalogue.

It is clear that mobile users expect practical services that are useful to them 'here and now.' Libraries should not ignore this. The mobile catalogue offers a number of these 'here and now' services that are really important – for example, search and bookmark for later use, request items for picking up and renewing loans.

The mobile catalogue offers a search window on only a part of the library's content, consisting mainly of the traditional print holdings. As part of the implementation of a new library unified discovery interface the mobile catalogue will be replaced by the mobile interface included in the discovery interface, which will give mobile search access to the catalogue, library repositories, online databases and electronic journals.

Lessons learned

The 'quick-win' approach and 'agile' style worked well. With minimal resources (200 hours of staff time, spread over five staff, and €1100 out-of-pocket costs), the University of Amsterdam Library managed to set up a mobile presence that seems attractive to the users, as the percentage of repeat visitors is average to high.

Secondary results were a boost in staff morale and publicity for the library in various well read magazines and blogs. Also, in-house knowledge of mobile devices and their requirements was gained, especially useful in negotiations with vendors.

Other points:

- Don't be afraid to make mistakes!
- Stimulate the early adopters among your staff and use their ideas.
- It is vital that staff have some freedom to experiment with tools of their own choice. Setting up the mobile website would not have been possible if the webmaster had not had the freedom to use a standard webserver as a playground for experimentation, instead of being limited to the University CMS system, with its technical and political constraints.
- And finally: you cannot work on mobile presence without owning some devices! If smartphones are too expensive, or cannot be purchased due to contractual issues, Wi-Fi-only devices such as Apple's iPod Touch can be an alternative.

Mobile catalogues: implementation examples

To complement the specific case study of the University Library of Amsterdam's 'UBA mobile' project, the following section provides a selection of mobile catalogues that have been implemented in a range of libraries. The examples cover public versus academic libraries, web versus native apps and commercial versus in-house development. They are intended to illustrate the range of possibilities available when considering implementing a mobile catalogue for your library.

Los Angeles Public Library with Boopsie

* Boopsie (www.boopsie.com)
* iOS (http://itunes.apple.com/app/lapl-to-go/id383513855)
* Other platforms (http://lapl.boopsie.com)
* Los Angeles Public Library (www.lapl.org)

Boopsie is a commercial vendor that offers a configurable framework for native apps for libraries. Besides practical library services it also integrates any proprietary ILS. The Los Angeles Public Library chose this approach to create their 'LAPL To GO' app, as shown in Figure 4.3.

In particular, Figure 4.4 shows the 'LAPL To Go' mobile catalogue results page:

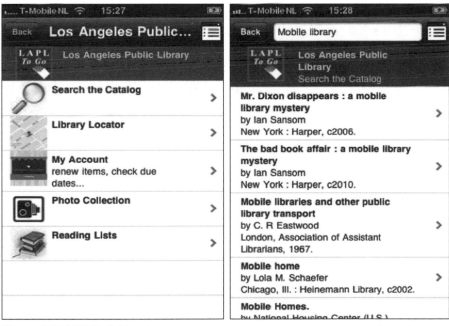

Figure 4.3 *'LAPL To Go', Los Angeles Public Library's iPhone app, home screen*

Figure 4.4 *'LAPL To Go', mobile catalogue results page*

City University London Library with Library Anywhere (by LibraryThing) www.libanywhere.com/m/229

The free social book readers' network LibraryThing offers a commercial framework for web and native (iPhone, Android, Blackberry) apps for libraries. This offers practical library services and integrates with many proprietary library management systems. There is only one app to find and use all libraries that have implemented the framework, but libraries can link to their specific site, as in the example from City University London library shown in Figure 4.5.

University of Minnesota Library (www.lib.umn.edu/mobile)

The University of Minnesota Library developed their own mobile web app in-house using PHP scripts, as shown in Figure 4.6. In addition to practical library services, the mobile web app offers access to a number of catalogue and content services by connecting to the library catalogue Aleph, the discovery interface Primo, the federated search engine MetaLib and the OpenURL link resolver SFX via an Application Programming Interface (API), as shown in Figure 4.7.

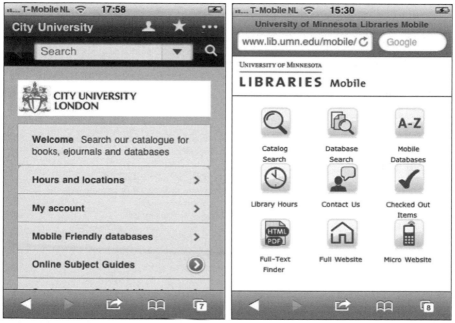

Figure 4.5 *City University London's mobile library interface using libanywhere.com*

Figure 4.6 *University of Minnesota libraries mobile web app home screen*

Figure 4.7 *University of Minnesota libraries mobile catalogue search screen*

North Carolina State University (http://m.lib.ncsu.edu)

'NCSU Libraries Mobile' shows how far a web app can go. The layout remains clear and usable across different devices and is well adjusted to the screen size, as shown in Figure 4.8. In the search and search results screens, only the most important information is shown at first. To keep the search results list compact, the NCSU mobile catalogue only shows title and availability, as shown in Figure 4.9.

Conclusion

There are still many uncertainties surrounding the deployment of

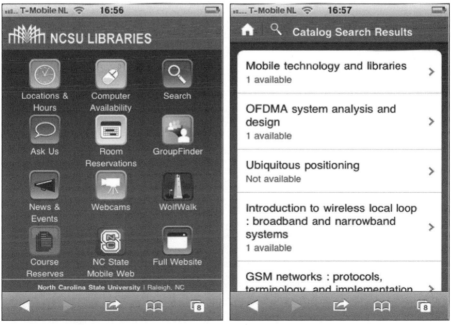

Figure 4.8 *NCSU libraries web app home screen*

Figure 4.9 *NCSU libraries mobile catalogue search results page*

mobile library services, especially when it comes to the catalogue. It appears to be too early to be able to determine what kind of library services will be desired and appreciated on the mobile platform. It is essential that end-user experiences and feedback are monitored closely and that mobile library applications can be adjusted rapidly, based on that feedback.

However, it seems that services of a practical nature are appreciated more than mobile catalogues. Mobile users expect services that are useful to them here and now. This is confirmed by recent studies.[47]

Mobile services providing practical information such as contact information and opening hours are not, of course, specific to libraries. However, requesting physical library material, based on the results of a catalogue search, and renewing loans certainly are valid mobile library services. These services will be used on a mobile platform as long as libraries provide access to physical material.

Providing access to all kinds of information can be considered a core service that libraries offer. However, libraries should start thinking 'outside the box'. In the near future mobile customers will not be satisfied when they only get bibliographic metadata on their smartphones in reply to a search for information.

Offering real 'location-aware' services on the mobile platform will prove to be essential – for example, the automatic provision of the nearest library location when requesting a book. In this case, the physical location is directly related to practical mobile services.

Further in the future, 'location awareness' will be linked more to the need for real information and this will not necessarily be limited to library-related information services. Augmented reality will also play a role, for instance to provide detailed information on a specific building in view. Through an augmented reality application, information will become available in very diverse forms, from a number of different sources. One of these sources might be a library catalogue. However, there will also be museums, archives and local government agencies, providing such information. Based on the users' physical location, one of the mobile services available may be, for example, a reference for a book at the nearest library.

In order to make linking of information from different sources possible, the concept of Linked Data should be embraced by more content providers (for more information, see Chapter 6). The future of mobile internet lies in the combination of location awareness, augmented reality and Linked Data.

Implementing mobile library services: a checklist

1 Identify your target audience or audience groups.
2 Identify the mobile services you want to offer.
3 Identify available and useful internal and external services that can be integrated.
4 Identify level of in-house native app and web app development capacity.
5 Check existing frameworks and suppliers that can be used, both for native and web apps.
6 Determine time frames for implementation.
7 Decide on whether to implement a native or web app.
8 Decide on outsourcing or in-house development.
9 Don't forget PR.
10 Gather and process feedback continuously.

References

1 The HTML5 standard is currently being revised: http://dev.w3.org/html5/spec/Overview.html.
2 www.css3.info.
3 www.webkit.org.
4 iOS, Apple's iPhone Operating System: www.apple.com/ios.
5 www.android.com.
6 Even though most mobile browsers are now based on WebKit, there are still some (relatively minor) differences that need to be considered when developing a mobile web app. See www.quirksmode.org/webkit.html for a detailed overview.
7 Gestures are the finger movements made on a touch-screen mobile device.
8 Approval of iOS apps: http://en.wikipedia.org/wiki/Approval_of_iOS_apps.
9 According to Wikipedia, jailbreaking 'is a process that allows devices running Apple's iOS (also known as iPhone OS prior to iOS 4.0) operating system (such as the iPad, iPhone, iPod Touch, and recently Apple TV) to gain full access (root access) to unlock all features of the said operating system', http://en.wikipedia.org/wiki/IOS_jailbreaking.
10 Statistics taken from the official Google Android Developers Platform Versions page: http://developer.android.com/resources/dashboard/platform-versions.html – retrieved on 14 April 2012, collected during a 14-day period ending on 2 April 2012.

11   http://en.wikipedia.org/wiki/HTC_Sense.

12   http://en.wikipedia.org/wiki/Motoblur.

13   RIM (Research in Motion), the technology behind BlackBerry devices:
www.rim.com.

14   Consumer reports: 'iPhones hog much more data than other smart phones',
http://news.consumerreports.org/electronics/2010/02/iphone-data-usage-smart-
phones-smartphones-blackberry-mb-network-att-carrier-istress.html.

15   Pinging is a BlackBerry-to-BlackBerry messaging system.

16   StatCounter Global Stats report, 1 December 2010, noted the sharp increase in
Blackberry browser usage: http://gs.statcounter.com/press/blackberry-
overtakes-apple-in-mobile-wars. However, from December 2010 onwards the
Blackberry browser share fell from 18% to 6% in March 2012 in the StatCounter
Global Stats: see http://gs.statcounter.com/#mobile_browser-ww-monthly-
201001-201203. This is confirmed by the comScore, see:
www.readwriteweb.com/2012/04/23/microsofts_mobile_comeback_is_
looking_terrible.

17   http://en.wikipedia.org/wiki/Windows_Phone_7.

18   http://en.wikipedia.org/wiki/Symbian.

19   http://en.wikipedia.org/wiki/Bada_(operating_system).

20   http://en.wikipedia.org/wiki/WebOS.

21   http://en.wikipedia.org/wiki/Bandwidth_(computing).

22   http://en.wikipedia.org/wiki/Latency_(engineering).

23   http://en.wikipedia.org/wiki/Ajax_(programming).

24   Beluga is a home-grown next-generation catalogue for all the libraries in the
Hamburg area in Germany, http://beluga.sub.uni-hamburg.de. See also
Christensen, A. (2009) *Next Generation Catalogs: what do users think? Conclusions
from the Beluga project in Hamburg*, IFLA 2009, Satellite Meetings, Florence,
www.slideshare.net/xenzen/next-generation-catalogs-what-do-users-think-
1872446.

25   Sierra, T. (2009) *Mobile Library projects at North Carolina State University*, CNI Fall
2009 Membership meeting, Washington, DC,
www.lib.ncsu.edu/documents/dli/projects/librariesmobile/cni2009f.ppt.

26   www.citeulike.org.

27   www.endnote.com.

28   OPAC: Online Public Access Catalogue

29   Hu, R. and Meier, A (2010) *Mobile Strategy Report, Mobile Device User Research*,
California Digital Library,
https://confluence.ucop.edu/download/attachments/26476757/

CDL+Mobile+Device+User+Research_final.pdf?version=1 (p.27).

30 http://en.wikipedia.org/wiki/Augmented_reality.

31 www.serialssolutions.com/summon.

32 www.exlibrisgroup.com/category/PrimoOverview.

33 http://vufind.org.

34 For more information about new-generation discovery tools, see Chapter 3.

35 Library of the University of Amsterdam (UvA), www.uba.uva.nl/en.

36 Agile software development:
    http://en.wikipedia.org/wiki/Agile_software_development.

37 Technical University (TU) Delft: http://home.tudelft.nl/en.

38 For example, www.mobilegarageblog.com/2010/03/going-mobile-tu-delft-netherlands.html.

39 HTML 4.0 Guidelines for mobile access: www.w3.org/TR/NOTE-html40-mobile.

40 ExLibris' Aleph library management system:
    www.exlibris.co.il/category/Aleph.

41 University of Jönköping, Sweden, http://hj.se/en.html.

42 Aleph Mobile OPAC, created by Daniel Forsman, University of Jönköping, Sweden: www.exlibrisgroup.org/display/AlephCC/Aleph+Mobile+OPAC.

43 http://en.wikipedia.org/wiki/QR_code.

44 North Carolina State University (NCSU) Libraries, WolfWalk project: www.lib.ncsu.edu/dli/projects/wolfwalk.

45 'Plaats' app for iOS: http://itunes.apple.com/app/plaats/id415467214.

46 Google Analytics, www.google.com/analytics.

47 Boopsie: *Non-Catalog Services More Popular With Mobile Library Patrons,* www.prweb.com/releases/2010/11/prweb4787284.htm.

5

FRBRizing your catalogue: the facets of FRBR

Rosemie Callewaert

Introduction

The Functional Requirements for Bibliographic Records, FRBR, is a conceptual model of the bibliographic universe.[1] Although implementations of FRBR are beginning to emerge, it has not yet been implemented widely within the library community. However, one of the successful implementations of FRBR has taken place within the public libraries of Flanders, the Dutch-speaking part of Belgium. Using the Flemish public library web portal, zoeken.bibliotheek.be, as a case study, this chapter will explore how the theory behind FRBR has been applied in practice in Belgium. Attention is paid both to the user experience and how the theoretical concepts of FRBR can be presented in a practical way for the end-user. In addition, the technology, particularly in terms of metadata creation and enrichment, is also described. With a look to the future, the shortcomings of FRBR in this particular case are also explored.

FRBR and its background

FRBR is a conceptual model of the bibliographic universe outlined in a 1998 report from the International Federation of Library Associations and Institutions (IFLA).[2] The report uses entity-relationship analysis to provide a clearly defined framework for structuring bibliographic data to meet the needs of users.

The IFLA Study Group on Functional Requirements for Bibliographic Records worked from 1992 until 1995, drawing up this entity-relationship model as a 'generalized view of the bibliographic universe, intended to be independent of any cataloging code or implementation'.[3]

This chapter is not intended to provide a comprehensive description of the FRBR theory, but to provide a picture of the more general context and a detailed explanation of an example in which the concepts from the IFLA report have been applied.

FRBR visualized
Theoretical
Figure 5.1 shows the theoretical FRBR entity-relationship model:[4]

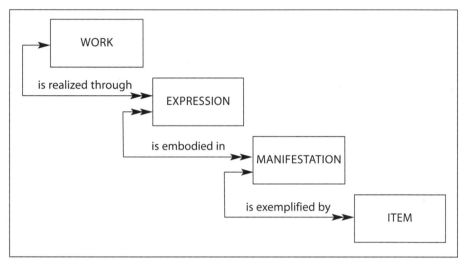

Figure 5.1 *The FRBR entity-relationship model*

Practical
Figure 5.2 shows FRBR visualized with some examples from zoeken. bibliotheek.be.

FRBR: its purpose and its solutions
The most commonly known features of the FRBR report are its four user tasks (Find, Identify, Select and Obtain) and the Group 1 Entities which categorize the products of intellectual and artistic endeavours (Work, Expression, Manifestation and Item).[5] One of the key aims of FRBR is to provide a solution for both browsing large sets of metadata and making the cataloguing process more efficient. Due to a growing diversity in content carriers,[6] library collections are becoming more hybrid, including digital and analogue texts, multimedia productions, etc.

An example: *De ontdekking van de hemel* (The Discovery of Heaven) is a well

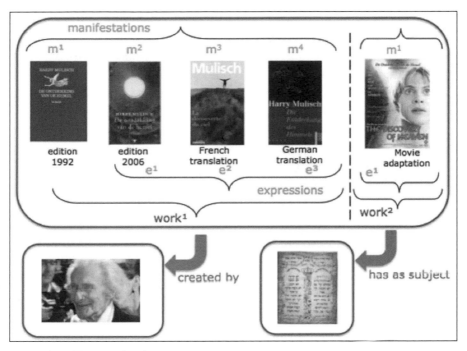

Figure 5.2 *FRBR visualized*

known novel by the Dutch writer Harry Mulisch. This Work has been made into a film, the text has been translated in many languages and the novel is available as an audiobook. It may even be turned into a graphic novel. The e-book versions of this novel can range from ePub[7] to pdf, with many possibilities in between. The intellectual Work – the original text by the author – may even have been made available in different versions or adaptations intended for a specific audience.

In order to make these publications retrievable, libraries traditionally provide a set of metadata (a record) for each content carrier. The FRBR report suggests that linking or re-using the common metadata can organize cataloguing processes more efficiently. Another ambition defined in the report is the development of a metadata navigation model for supporting the four user tasks – Find, Identify, Select, Obtain – in a highly user-friendly way.

These four user tasks are not new to the library world, as the long tradition of cataloguing is intended to help support the user in such tasks. In addition, libraries have a long tradition of grouping similar 'resources' together within the library catalogue, based on the content of author, subject or other control field values. The FRBR report, however, defines cluster concepts that go one step further by grouping collection items at different levels or logical entities as described in the FRBR entity-relationship model.

An example: a user looking for *De ontdekking van de hemel* by Harry Mulisch should at a single glance be directed to all available editions, regardless of the publisher, the year of publication, printed or digital versions, all available translations, film versions, reviews, etc.

The FRBR report of 1998 does not offer practical solutions for these navigation patterns. This may explain the fact that visible implementations of the FRBR concepts have been a long time in coming and even now are not applied on a large scale. The application of FRBR in zoeken.bibliotheek.be in 2006 was one of the first public web environments where FRBR navigation was applied. The implementation in zoeken.bibliotheek.be is not the only possible solution, but can be inspiring for others. The solution applied in zoeken.bibliotheek.be is comparable to the way that WorldCat[8] is FRBRized.

Implementing FRBR in Belgium

The public libraries in the Dutch-speaking part of Belgium have a union bibliographic database called Open Vlacc (VLAamse Centrale Catalogus). This database is made up of records from:

- the physical collections of six major Flemish public libraries: Antwerp, Bruges, Brussels, Ghent, Hasselt and Leuven.
- forthcoming books by Dutch or Flemish publishers (Cataloguing in Publication (CIP) records)
- the music collection of the Centrale Discotheek Rotterdam (CDR)[9]
- a selection of websites categorized by subject.

The bibliographic centre, Vlabin-VBC[10] and the six major public libraries edit and enrich the Onix[11] metadata which the professional organization of the Flemish book trade, Boek.be,[12] provides for bookshops and public libraries in the database Boekenbank.[13] The co-ordination of the union catalogue, Open Vlacc, is undertaken by Bibnet.[14]

Bibnet is a project organization, funded by the Flemish Government, with the aim of raising the profile of the added value that public libraries can provide in the digital age. In this role, Bibnet aims to build innovative public service environments on top of library catalogue data and digital collections. One of the results is zoeken.bibliotheek.be,[15] a public search environment with the AquaBrowser software.[16] Since 2006 the site has continued to innovate, through incremental improvements, starting with the implementation of FRBR. Since 2010 the web interface of zoeken.bibliotheek.be has provided the basis for the Library Portals project (Bibliotheekportalen).[17] This project enables each local public library in Flanders to present its collection on the web in a similar way.

Why FRBR on zoeken.bibliotheek.be?

Open Vlacc, the union catalogue of the Dutch-speaking public libraries, contains records of over a million manifestations. These records represent several million physical items in the public library collections in Flanders. Public library collections are characterized by a large variety of carriers for a wide audience: books, journals, fiction, non-fiction, easy readers, audiobooks, musical sound recordings, films, sheet music, youth collections, collections for the blind people, etc. In order to present these items to the public, clear navigation must be provided.

Another ambition of the public presentation of library collections is the wish to index digital collections in the same search environment as physical collections. So, for each printed edition it is theoretically possible to have one or more digital editions or manifestations. The idea of a clustered presentation is that a printed edition can raise awareness of the digital one, or vice versa.

Creating a next-generation catalogue is more than simply adding Web 2.0 tools. It is also about abandoning the idea of the library catalogue as the only system that can be used for presenting a library's collections to their users. The use of a discovery layer – or a separate indexing platform – clears the way for indexing and presenting different sources in one search environment. (See Chapter 3 for more information.)

An additional benefit of using dedicated indexing software for the web is that data processing capabilities are offered. In zoeken.bibliotheek.be it is the pre-processing of MARC21 records that make the metadata FRBR-ready.

The solutions used for zoeken.bibliotheek.be are described below, starting with what the public 'in front of the screen' gets to see, followed by the technical solutions 'behind the scenes'.

FRBR and zoeken.bibliotheek.be in front of the screen
Dynamic relationships

A possible criticism of FRBR is that, although the hierarchical navigation from Work through Expression and Manifestation to Item may be the desired navigation strategy for some users, it is not the desired navigation path for many other users. A user looking for an exact Manifestation must also be able to find it quickly without being confronted with all possible Expressions or Manifestations of that Work in other languages or in other formats.

One of the challenges of setting up a FRBR interface is in designing the workflow of dynamic navigation strategies. Navigation should not present itself as a straightjacket. A good search leaves it to the user to determine a personal navigation path.

In the search engine design three kinds of indexing and high-level navigation workflows can be identified:

1 **Keyword search:** one or several keywords retrieve a list of search results containing those keyword(s).
2 **Traditional (browse) navigation:** a predefined list of browse terms is provided. Browse navigation can also start with a user entering a keyword, resulting in a list of index terms that contain the keyword. Traditional browse navigation is one-dimensional, as the relationships between the terms are predefined.
3 **Relational (facet) navigation**: relational navigation takes traditional navigation a step further by showing the user the different relationships between the records within the indexed datasets. These relationships can be implicit (for example, field values in a bibliographic record) or explicit (for example, predefined relationships between bibliographic records). Relational navigation combines keyword searching with a browse function. These browse suggestions (also called facets or refinements) are generated dynamically from the indexed datasets based on the search terms entered.

Relational navigation, or faceted browsing, was first seen on commercial sites, such as web shops,[18] to assist the user in finding the full range of products available. The faceted browsing techniques were later adopted in the search engines developed for libraries. The structured metadata in library catalogues is a very good starting point for enabling faceted search. Like other discovery tools (see Chapter 3 for more information), for library collections,

AquaBrowser Library software offers faceted browsing. This functionality was one of the key tools used as a basis for designing the FRBR navigation for zoeken.bibliotheek.be.

The cataloguing workflow in Open Vlacc is, as in many other library catalogues, based on the publication (not the Work) in hand. Every Manifestation is catalogued with its own specific data values about 'publisher', 'publication language', 'year of publication', 'medium', etc., encoded into the appropriate fields within the MARC record. These values can be seen as inherent relations within a publication. In a search interface these relations can be presented as facets or values to refine a search result. As the Work level is not explicitly recorded within the Flemish union catalogue, works cannot be presented as an out-of-the-box facet or option for refining.

Right from the start of the implementation work for zoeken.bibliotheek.be, the aim was to provide a result list at Work, rather than Manifestation level. In a catalogue that is not FRBRized, a keyword search on, for instance, John Boyne leads to a long result list that shows all Manifestations. For the Flemish public libraries union catalogue *The Boy in the Striped Pyjamas* alone would provide more than 20 search results. If we know that most users do not look further than the first page of a search result, it seems wise to present as many different Works as possible on the first page, so that not the quantity, but the diversity of the collection becomes directly visible.

The Work-clustering on zoeken.bibliotheek.be complements the facets in which the other FRBR-groupings are expressed, as shown in Figure 5.3 on the next page. The Work-level clustering is made possible by pre-processing the data. The pre-processing will be explained in detail when discussing 'behind the scenes'.

The FRBR solution within zoeken.bibliotheek.be extends beyond the clustering of Works in the result list. On each of the screens of the search environment, attention is paid to how the different FRBR-relationships and entities are presented to the user.

Result list and facets

1   The Manifestations in the search result are clustered at Work level. The clustering depends on the search query. If a search query has the attributes of an Expression in it, then the result list is grouped on an Expression level. For example in Figure 5.4 (see page 101), the English, Dutch and French and editions are displayed in the 'Expression-level' language facet.

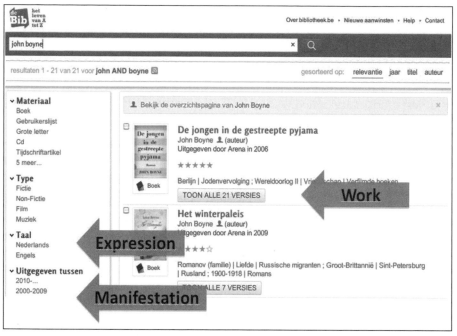

Figure 5.3 *Work clustering with FRBR-based facets in zoeken.bibliotheek.be*

2   For each Work, one Manifestation is shown in the result list. This is the Manifestation that fits in best with the query, based on the relevance ranking. The algorithm defining the relevance ranking was developed to facilitate the implementation of FRBR. For example, in Figure 5.4 a search on an English title gives back an English Manifestation in the result list. The other Manifestations are clustered behind the English Manifestation.

3   In the result list, other Expressions and Manifestations are referred to by a link to a secondary result list. For example, in Figure 5.4 there is a button inviting a user to 'Show all 30 versions' (Toon alle 30 versies).

4   By refining the result list, the Manifestations are regrouped to another of the FRBR entity levels. For example, as shown in Figure 5.4, a user can sort the results list (gesorteerd op), relevance, year, title and author (relevantie, jaar, titel, auteur).

Work list

From the result list, a user can click on a specific Manifestation, or the link to the Work list with all the Manifestations. In this Work list it is possible to

Figure 5.4 *The zoeken.bibliotheek.be results page*

navigate to the Expression or Manifestation level by refining the Work list on one of the facet values. At the top of the Work list, the common metadata values are shown: title and author, subjects, etc.

Detailed presentation screen

On the detailed presentation screen, as shown in Figure 5.5 on the next page, the information about the specific Manifestation is shown. There is also a link that refers to all other Expressions and Manifestations of the Work.

There is also a reference made to publications 'about' the Work shown. If, for instance, there is a review ('recensie') available in another Manifestation, the link to this review is displayed.

The idea behind these interface issues is to make FRBR groupings visible during every step in a search workflow. Groupings can be ignored or used. Each user chooses his or her own path to browse through the library collection.

FRBR and zoeken.bibliotheek.be behind the scenes

The technical infrastructure of zoeken.bibliotheek.be is made up of different components:

Figure 5.5 *The zoeken.bibliotheek.be detailed presentation screen*

- a cataloguing database made and stored in the Aleph 500[19] software from Ex Libris[20]
- conversion and export tools made by Libis [21]
- a storage and data processing platform hosted and developed by Serials Solutions Medialab[22]
- AquaBrowser Library software[23] as the web user interface.

There are three cycles for building the FRBR output: metadata creation and export, metadata processing and enrichment, and metadata indexing and display.

Metadata creation and export

The Open Vlacc metadata is created in the Aleph 500 library management system software from Ex Libris. This means that the input and exchange format is MARC21 in a flat record structure. The cataloguing editor uses MARC21 and the cataloguing rules are AACR2-based. The cataloguing rules for Open Vlacc were revised in 2007 to incorporate FRBR principles and terminology as far as possible. Currently, the question of how the cataloguing rules for Open Vlacc can be attuned to the new content description standard RDA (Resource Description and Access)[24] is being investigated.

The catalogued records in Open Vlacc are descriptions for Manifestations.

Whole-part relationships (for example, the individual tracks on an album) are catalogued in different records, with the use of the MARC21 77X- linking entry fields. All records are exported daily as ISO 2709 mrc files and MARCxml files. These exports are the raw input files to make the records FRBR-ready.

Metadata processing and enrichment

Making metadata FRBR-ready means that a software algorithm infers the Work level from the Manifestation records. The Work level is extracted with a software algorithm that calculates a unique Work identifier. The algorithm goes through the MARC21 fields in search of values that can be used as a textual identifier for the Work. When calculated, the identifier is added as an extra field <FRBRkey>workidentifier</FRBRkey> in the xml that is used for indexing in AquaBrowser. Each bibliographic record is enriched with a FRBR-key. This FRBR-key adds an unambiguous identifier for the Work. The Work identifier is calculated as shown in Figure 5.6.

MARC21 Work extraction algorithm

If there is no100$a or no110$a is, than the frbr-key is the value of 130$a
If there is 100$a or 110$a take this value and combine it with the "best" title value.
To look for best title value:
If there is 240 take these values 240$amnrfgpko (+ 100$a 110$a)
If there is 534 take 534$a
If there is 245 take:
- for fiction : 245$anp (+ 100$a OR 110$a)
- for non-fiction and music : 245$abnp (+ 100$a OR110$a)
The FRBR-key is then stripped of the characters : [, -, !, ;,], comma(,) and interspace ( )

Figure 5.6 *Work identifier calculation*

Next to the FRBR key, the algorithm creates a FRBR-link to establish a relationship between a Work and Works about a Work, e.g. descriptions for book or film reviews that are part of the library collection.

If a Work is found in a subject field (MARC tag 600 or 610) the enrichment indicates a link-to-work-field <frbr_link>workidentifier</frbr_link>. The link-to-work identifier is calculated as shown in Figure 5.7 on the next page.

MARC21 Work-based subject headings

1.   600at (author, title)
2.   610at (author, title)

The FRBR-link is then stripped of the characters : [, -, !, ;,], comma(,) and interspace ( )

Figure 5.7 *Link-to-work identifier calculation*

Metadata indexing and display

All processing for making the MARC-records FRBR-ready is done after the export from the cataloguing system and before the indexing in the discovery platform. The grouping of all Manifestations with the same Work-identifier happens on the fly, at the moment that the search result is built.

Similar data-mining and processing is done on external datasets, for example metadata from a provider of public domain e-books in Dutch (DBNL)[25]. The result of this data-mining is a clustering of printed and e-book versions in the result list and on all other screens mentioning this Work, as shown in Figure 5.8 ('Lees op DBNL').

Figure 5.8 *Link to the Digital Library of Dutch Literature (DBNL) in zoeken.bibliotheek.be*

FRBR and metadata creation

An interesting question is what impact FRBR can have on the cataloguing process. Different answers can be given to this question. The example of zoeken.bibliotheek.be shows that FRBR can be an extension that is applied to metadata that has been created without consciously employing the FRBR-principles. Technically, various approaches are possible for metadata creation: split records with explicit relationships, flat records with implicit relations or a combination of flat and split records.

Bibliographic records with explicit entity-level relationships

A strict interpretation of FRBR can result in building a bibliographic database by creating separate records for each entity level: Work, Expression, Manifestation, Item, Person, Family, Corporate Body, Concept, Object, Event and Place.

These different records must be linked with specific types of relationships (e.g. 'created by', 'about', 'based on', etc.) in an entity-relationship model. A consistent use of this model leads to a maximum reusability of data. Working with split records can result in detailed descriptions of entities, for instance, the year of creation of the original Work or place of birth of the author. This comes close to what we know as Authority Records. Each entity level in this model becomes an authorized record, which can be related to various other records with different relationships. In this context, two additional FRBR-standards, FRAD (Functional Requirements for Authority Data)[26] and FRSAD (Functional Requirements for Subject Authority Data),[27] came into being.

RDA (Resource Description and Access),[28] as the new FRBR-based content standard for cataloguing, formally describes, in the Open Metadata Registry, the different types of relationship for linking the FRBR entity levels to each another in a standardized way.[29]

Bibliographic records with implicit entity-level relationships (flat records)

The solution used for zoeken.bibliotheek.be is almost entirely based on an automated Work-level extraction from the classic MARC21 flat record structure. This means that every Manifestation has its own bibliographic record.

Relationships such as, 'created by', 'about', etc., are an implicit part of the Manifestation record. The entity levels are presented in the search interface by means of carefully chosen refining facets as browse options.

The one-Manifestation-is-one-record world of MARC21-AACR2 can be viewed as a strength for copy cataloguing within the library or book community. On the web, however, this encoding is a weakness, because the data elements are not understood by the outside world.

Mixed database structure: flat records and split records

If we know that the majority of items in a library collection are single-manifestation publications, then a workflow in which a record is made for each entity can be seen as overkill. On the other hand, the model of separate records can enhance cataloguing efficiency for Works with many Expressions and Manifestations, as is for example the case with classical music Works. It is therefore possible to choose a mixed method for building a catalogue. Manifestation records versus Work-based records can be used for some parts of the collection, such as, for example, Works in fields like classical music, that appear in multiple versions or performances over time. In Open Vlacc, the single Manifestation records live in the same database next to Work-based records that are part of another Work.

In addition to finding a cataloguing solution, the visualization of whole-part relationships is a challenge. On zoeken.bibliotheek.be there is, for example, a grouping at music album level and a grouping per Work or track on the album, as shown in Figure 5.9.

Figure 5.9 *Visualizing whole-part relationships with music in zoeken.bibliotheek.be*

Metadata creation and the user interface

A practical application of FRBR does not stop with a solution for modelling metadata. An important part of the solution lies in the design of the interface to present the FRBR concepts with an added value for the end-users.

Developments on the web and in search engine technology have partly caught up with the FRBR concepts. The combination of *search* and *browse* as relational navigation, as applied in zoeken.bibliotheek.be, has become state-of-the-art navigation. Bradley Allen, cited in the FRBR Blog, puts it as follows:

Work + facets = Expressions = Manifestations + tags

By facets he means not the facets that come from a faceted classification system, but the kinds easily divined from MARC records: year of publication, call number range, format (book, music, video, map), language, subject headings, etc.[30]

These results are best-effort solutions with the library data we have as a result of library automation since the early 1970s. The browsing philosophy of the library catalogue in those times was based on the card catalogue. Search strategies today must be based on how search engines handle data to provide service to the end-user on the web. The interface is not the library catalogue alone, but can also be a search engine that can lead us to information about concepts like Works, Subjects, Persons, etc.

The idea of unique internet addresses or URIs (Uniform Resource Identifiers)[31] for concepts can lead to the creation of web pages filled with aggregated content from a variety of sources or users. Initiatives like Open Library,[32] LibraryThing,[33] Goodreads,[34] and Freebase[35] are built as entity-level-based web pages. These landing pages also function beyond the specific search environment that they were originally created for; they are accessible on different levels directly from search engines such as Google. Aggregated data about Authors, Works, Expressions, Manifestations, Subjects, etc. are conceived as full web pages. Depending on the query, you arrive on one of these levels on a rich web page showing references to the other levels and to end-user services such as buying or lending information for physical items or direct access to digital information.

Unlike the faceted browsing mentioned above, these applications require more detailed descriptions of the entity levels. The data requirements for the URI solution correspond to the concepts for the Semantic Web as described by Tim Berners-Lee.[36] Both solutions can, of course, exist side by side. The use of the Semantic Web and Linked Data in libraries is covered in depth in Chapter 6.

FRBR as the beginning of more

In addition to the chosen solutions, the experience with zoeken.bibliotheek.be teaches us that the knowledge of the Work level can lead to features that go beyond the visual clustering of entities.

FRBR and relevance ranking

A kind of record enrichment that has not been mentioned above is the 'FRBR-count'. In the processing and the preparation of FRBR-ready metadata for indexing, the number of Manifestations for each unique Work identifier is counted. A high number gives a boost in the relevance ranking. As a result, popular titles come at the top of the search result.

This is a solution for the cases such as, for example, a search for 'Harry Potter'. Without the 'FRBR-count' solution, secondary sources (e.g. reviews about a Harry Potter book or film) appear at the top of the results lists, while the well known titles appear further down the results list. The FRBR-count solution is similar to the way Google is fine-tuning its ranking algorithms, for the Google books search environment.[37]

FRBR and new interfaces

Following the example of WorldCat Identities,[38] author pages have been created. These pages are created by visualizing the data related to a particular author in the zoeken.bibliotheek.be index. An author page enables users to browse through the work of a writer, a composer, a director, an actor, etc. from the collections of Flemish Public Libraries. The author pages are a result of data-mining all indexed data, including the FRBR data enrichment. The page itself is enriched with content from outside the library catalogue environment, – photos from the Flickr photo community, an abstract from Wikipedia, etc. – as shown in Figure 5.10.

FRBR and collection knowledge

If the Work level is known, it becomes possible to undertake more detailed

Figure 5.10 *Author page for Roald Dahl in zoeken.bibliotheek.be*

analysis of the quantitative content of the collection. For instance, how many unique Works does the library collection hold, how many Works are presented in different Expressions and Manifestations, what are the top ten unique Works, and so on? We learned for example by calculations of this kind that only 17% of the whole non-music collection has more than one Manifestation in our own bibliographic database. When we take a look at the music collection, the figures are totally different: 43% of the Manifestations are grouped with at least one other Manifestation.

FRBR and end-user services

An important challenge in the implementation of FRBR lies in the linking of the user services to the various Entity levels. Currently, in zoeken.bibliotheek.be and related search environments, online services, such as reservations or inter-library loans (ILL) are not provided at Work or Expression level. It is conceivable that someone would want to place a hold on a specific Work, independent of the year of publication, language, publisher, etc. Alternatively, someone else might find language important, but not the publisher or the year of publication. For this kind of differentiated service, the integrated library management system, with its linked circulation database, should support the groupings that are presented in the public end-user interface.

FRBR and metadata enrichment

Internal enrichment

On zoeken.bibliotheek.be content enrichment – not only user-generated content such as tags and reviews by end-users, but also full-text book reviews from literary journals – is added to each of the Manifestations of a Work. This is an experiment that does not always yield the desired results, because for certain sources a good enrichment is more appropriate at the Expression or Work level. In order to know whether a book review or a comment on a musical performance refers to the Work or to a specific Expression of it, the texts should be analysed, or the content creator should be able to indicate the Entity level.

External enrichment

As a result of the knowledge that has been built up in zoeken.bibliotheek.be, a link can be made between an ISBN and a Work, as shown in Figure 5.11. This link is stored and can be accessed by external environments via a web service. In this way, other data sets can be enriched with Work identifiers. Within the network of Flemish Public Libraries this enrichment is applied in the AquaBrowser data platform. Other databases such as WorldCat (xISBN)[39] and LibraryThing (ThingISBN)[40] offer comparable web services.

FRBR and identifiers

The Work identifiers created for zoeken.bibliotheek.be have interesting functions, as becomes clear from the various applications that have been built on them. The Work identifiers also have some weaknesses or restrictions:

- The Work identifier is created after the initial cataloguing process.
- The Work identifier depends on the consistency of the catalogued data.

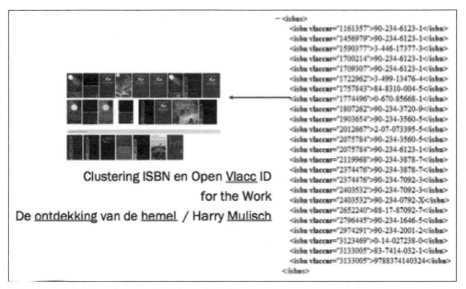

Figure 5.11 *Linking between ISBNs and Works*

- The Work identifier only has significance in the context of the Flemish Public Libraries.

A possible solution to the Work identifier issue is being developed by the publishing community by providing an identifier embedded in the publication itself, just as the ISBN is for a Manifestation. It is the aspiration of the International Standard Text Code (ISTC),[41] a new ISO (International Organization for Standardization) standard (ISO 21047),[42] to assign reliable identifiers to textual Works.

The web as a FRBR user

The FRBR report of 1998 was written with the library catalogue user and the library professional in mind. A lot of library catalogues were already published on the web in 1998, but the web in 1998 differs in many aspects from the web today. In 1998 there was no Web 2.0. In the meantime, Web 3.0, the Semantic Web, the web of things, the web of identities, the web of data have become topics of conversation and real working examples of new services based on these concepts already exist. What these different points of view have in common is that data and metadata can also have a function beyond the one specific web address or the one kind of software, database or interface that it was originally created for. The open and Linked Data community has shown that data can have other functions outside its original context. Therefore, librarians have to be aware of the interdependencies of their data. Not only every user, but also every interface or machine can be a user of library data.

Conclusions: thinking outside the library catalogue box

Few organizations invest more than libraries do in creating information about their collections. The value of library metadata is distinguished by the consistency with which it is created. However, this consistency within the library catalogue does not automatically mean that the individual parts can be used widely outside this isolated box.

Today, it seems that, despite having a long tradition of metadata creation and library-specific data exchange standards the library is, to a certain extent, isolated on the web. Standards used by the library community are slow to evolve and they are not known by the general public, or by the generation of web-developers who are creating innovative applications on top of open datasets.

The ideas behind FRBR are, to a certain extent, timeless. However, FRBR-based implementations that transcend the boundaries of the library domain are somewhat slow in coming. The example of zoeken.bibliotheek.be shows that successful implementations of FRBR within the library domain are possible. However, to make such results available in a broader context, the methodology behind this implementation needs to be rethought. On the web, it is not enough for libraries to only link their data to other library data. There is a lot of other information on the web that is ready for libraries to link to.

It is encouraging that new library standards, such as RDA, are being developed with a broader context and new developments in mind. However, it is a shame that the development of such new standards takes so long because of the consensus-building nature of the library community. In the future, investing in library catalogues will be easier to justify if the products of these investments reach beyond the borders of the library catalogue. The product creation is not the catalogue, but the raw material, data: data that needs to be easily (re)usable in the wider world. The result of an open library data set can be the catalogue of one or several specific libraries. The result can also be every possible application with the same raw material. Libraries are everywhere, as library data should be.

References

1   IFLA Study Group on the Functional Requirements for Bibliographic Records (1998) *Final Report*, www.ifla.org/en/publications/functional-requirements-for-bibliographic-records.

2   IFLA Study Group on the Functional Requirements for Bibliographic Records (1998).

3   Tillett, B. (2003) *What is FRBR?: a conceptual model for the bibliographic universe*, Library of Congress Cataloging Distribution Service, www.loc.gov/cds/downloads/FRBR.PDF.

4   IFLA Study Group on the Functional Requirements for Bibliographic Records (1998). *Final Report*, IFLA Series on Bibliographic Control 19, K. G. Saur Verlag, Munich, www.ifla.org/en/publications/functional-requirements-for-bibliographic-records.

5   Tillett (2003).

6   'Carrier refers to the means and methods by which content is conveyed.' Joint Steering Committee for Revision of AACR (2006) *RDA/ONIX Framework for Resource Categorization*.

7   ePub is a distribution and interchange format standard for digital publications and documents. For further information see http://idpf.org/epub.

8   www.worldcat.org.

9   www.muziekweb.nl.

10 Vlabin-VBC bibliographic centre: www.vlabinvbc.be.

11 ONIX is the international standard representing and communicating book industry product information in electronic form: www.editeur.org/8/ONIX.

12 Professional organization of the Flemish book trade: www.boek.be.

13 www.boekenbank.be.

14 www.bibnet.be.

15 Public search environment of the Flemish public libraries: http://zoeken.bibliotheek.be.

16 See Chapter 3. AquaBrowser: www.serialssolutions.com/aquabrowser.

17 www.bibnet.be/portaal/Bibnet/Publiekstoepassingen/Bibliotheekportalen.

18 An example of a web shop is www.wine.com.

19 Further information on the Aleph library management system is available at www.exlibrisgroup.com/category/Aleph.

20 Ex Libris is a provider of library technology solutions. Further information about Ex Libris can be found at www.exlibrisgroup.com.

21 Libis is a library and information solutions provider. Further information about Libis can be found at www.libis.be.

22   Serial Solutions Medialab, www.medialab.nl.

23   AquaBrowser library software, www.serialssolutions.com/aquabrowser.

24   Resource Description and Access (RDA): www.rdatoolkit.org.

25   DBNL (De Digitale Bibliotheek voor de Nederlandse Letteren) is a digital library of Dutch literature: www.dbnl.org.

26   IFLA Working Group on Functional Requirements and Numbering of Authority Records (FRANAR) (2009) *Functional Requirements for Authority Data (FRAD), Final Report*, www.ifla.org/publications/functional-requirements-for-authority-data.

27   IFLA Working Group on the Functional Requirements for Subject Authority Data (FRSAD) (2010), *Final Report*, www.ifla.org/node/5849.

28   Resource Description and Access (RDA): www.rdatoolkit.org.

29   Open Metadata Registry, RDA relationships for Works, Expressions, Manifestations and Items: http://metadataregistry.org/schemaprop/list/schema_id/13.html.

30   Allen, B. (2007) *Faceted Classification and FRBR*, posted by Willem Denton on The FRBR Blog, www.frbr.org/2007/09/10/allen-faceted-classification-and-frbr.

31   Further information about Uniform Resource Identifiers: www.w3.org/Addressing/URL/URI_Overview.html.

32   http://openlibrary.org. For example, http://openlibrary.org/books/OL7914991M/The_Boy_in_the_Striped_Pajamas and http://openlibrary.org/authors/OL1432532A/John_Boyne.

33   www.librarything.com. For example, www.librarything.com/author/boynejohn and www.librarything.com/work/383608.

34   www.goodreads.com. For example, www.goodreads.com/book/show/39999.The_Boy_in_the_Striped_Pajamas.

35   www.freebase.com.

36   Berners-Lee, T. (1996) *Universal Resource Identifiers – Axioms of Web Architecture*, www.w3.org/DesignIssues/Axioms.html.

37   Madrigal, A. (2010) *Inside the Google Books Algorithm*, www.theatlantic.com/technology/archive/2010/11/inside-the-google-books-algorithm/65422 (1 November).

38   WorldCat Identities provides a summary page for every name in WorldCat: www.oclc.org/research/activities/identities/default.htm.

39   WorldCat's xISBN web service: http://xisbn.worldcat.org/xisbnadmin/index.htm.

40   LibraryThing's ThingISBN is listed on LibraryThing's API page: www.librarything.com/wiki/index.php/LibraryThing_APIs.

41   The International Standard Text Code (ISTC) is a numbering system developed
     to enable the unique identification of textual works:
     www.istc-international.org/html.

42   International Organization for Standardization, ISO 21047, *International
     Standard Text Code (ISTC)*,
     www.iso.org/iso/iso_catalogue/catalogue_tc/catalogue_detail.htm?csnumber=
     41603.

Enabling your catalogue for the Semantic Web

Emmanuelle Bermès

Introduction

The history of cataloguing can be summed up as a struggle to meet users' needs by making catalogues ever easier to access and to use, more interoperable, more flexible and more efficient. Even if the original purpose of catalogues was to be a tool to help manage the library's collection, this vision of the catalogue as a management tool for librarians has never prevailed in the theory of catalogues: the catalogue was considered a bibliographic tool for information retrieval even before the age of information technology and computers.

Today, it's not about the catalogue any more, it's about the data. The efforts undertaken by librarians across the 20th and 21st centuries have converged toward a common goal: free the bibliographic data from the confinement of catalogues. Card catalogues in drawers have been printed in volumes so that they could be disseminated outside the library. Printed catalogues have been digitized so that their content could be processed by machines. This content (the data or at least, a first version of it) has been standardized according to international rules so that it could be easily exchanged and duplicated. Catalogues have been put online, first on the internet and then on the web. Finally, standard protocols such as Z39.50 and OAI-PMH have been developed, so that online catalogues could be accessed at distance by machines in an automated way.

This landscape is where we stand today: online catalogues with standardized, structured data, which can be accessed distantly both by human users and by machine processes. Could there ever be a way for catalogues to be more interoperable than they are today? Can we feel comfortable when we say that library catalogues are on the web?

The impact of library standards, both data formats like MARC and standard protocols like Z39.50, is limited to the library community (a little further, if we consider OAI-PMH, but not beyond the educational, scientific and cultural landscape). Catalogues are part of the 'deep web' and cannot be indexed by search engines: they are deemed to be used only by people who already know they exist. When transferring data from one catalogue to another, duplication is necessary; it is not possible to link the content seamlessly.

Finally, library catalogues are data silos, distinct from one another: they are not part of a global information space; they are not part of the web.

The Semantic Web and, even more, Linked Data are initiatives that could empower the catalogue's interoperability way beyond what it is today. They could make library data really open, available and reusable in a global information space not restricted to libraries and their community. They could make library data really a part of the web. The trend has already begun, even if it is a long and difficult journey for libraries. These technologies are on the edge of changing completely the cataloguing landscape, and the opportunities they offer are promising enough to make it worth trying to understand how they can help libraries achieve their mission. In this chapter, we will provide a short introduction to the Semantic Web and its practical implementation, Linked Data. It will explore the reasons why a library would want to enable its catalogue for the Semantic Web and the different steps that would need to be taken. To help with this process, an introduction to the technology will be provided, even if further reading would be necessary to put these basics into practice. Finally, we will present some ongoing and existing Semantic Web projects in the library domain.

Semantic Web and Linked Data . . . what is it all about?
From the Semantic Web . . .
The Semantic Web is a set of technologies that are being developed by the W3C[1] in order to achieve a vision: the vision of a web of data, a web where structured data that is currently isolated in databases could be expressed in a way that would make it possible for machines to interpret them and process them into new applications and services. In order to do so, the data needs to be shared in a global network and linked with unique, reliable identifiers. This global structure based on relationships between resources is the basis of the RDF (Resource Description Framework) model underlying the Semantic Web. In the article 'The Semantic Web' in *Scientific American* in 2001[2] Tim

Berners-Lee, founder of the web and director of the W3C, and his co-authors James Hendler and Ora Lassila, explain that 'The Semantic Web is not a separate web but an extension of the current one, in which information is given well defined meaning, better enabling computers and people to work in cooperation.'

Hence the Semantic Web is mainly about providing standards that will empower this smarter, more efficient web. These standards include a data model, RDF (Resource Description Framework), tools such as RDFS (RDF Schema), OWL (Web Ontology Language) and RIF (Rule Interchange Format), to describe the semantics and the logic of the data, and also standards to manipulate and process the data, such as SPARQL, the query language and protocol for RDF. We will explore these technologies in more detail shortly.

What is important to note here is that the Semantic Web is deeply rooted in the web. It is not another web: the use of standard web architecture technologies such as the HTTP protocol and URIs (Uniform Resource Identifiers) are as important as the RDF model itself. The Semantic Web is designed to be enabled using the existing web architecture. It is designed to be part of the existing web environment.

. . . to Linked Data

What we call 'Linked Data' today is actually an effort to put these principles into practice. While possibilities opened by Semantic Web technologies include a wide variety of complex applications, such as automatic reasoning, inference deduction or complex ontology modelling, these opportunities have long been the reserve of the research domain. A broader adoption by commercial companies and other entities is needed to shift the Semantic Web from a vision to a reality. The Semantic Web Education and Outreach interest group (SWEO) was created within the W3C in 2006 in order to increase awareness among the web community of the need and benefits of the Semantic Web. In addition, it had an educational role to teach the web community the solutions and technologies of the Semantic Web. The objective of this interest group was to facilitate the adoption of Semantic Web technologies by showing the possibility of short-term realizations and 'quick wins' in the Semantic Web environment.

One of the results of this interest group was the launch of the Linking Open Data initiative. The goal of this initiative was to promote a vision of the web as a global database and to interlink data in the same way that web documents (i.e., HTML pages) are interlinked on the web today. Such a 'Web of Data' (this expression being also widely used to speak about Linked Data) would be understandable not only for humans, as is the web today, but also for machines, which would make it possible to build applications on this interLinked Data.

The Linking Open Data initiative developed guidelines and best-practice principles in order to help build this Web of Data. It also encouraged a variety of organizations to publish copyright-free content as RDF triples and link it on the web with URIs.

The success of this initiative is a result of the pragmatic approach it adopted: it uses straightforward RDF conversions, pragmatic data publishing approaches and step-by-step improvement processes. It can be considered as an easy and simple subset of Semantic Web technologies that could be adopted by anyone. The Web of Data provides a good test bed for prototyping because it brings together a critical mass of data.

For libraries considering the possibility of enabling their catalogues for the Semantic Web, Linked Data is therefore a good option to start with. That is, they will not necessarily challenge their whole data creation process, their software infrastructures and their existing tools. Instead, they will consider the need for publishing their data as part of the Linked Data cloud, so that it is available on the web for reuse by other communities, within that global information space for structured information: the Web of Data.

Organizational, intellectual and legal issues

Starting a Linked Data project in a library actually raises some questions that are not related to the technology but to other kinds of issues, starting with the actual relevance of the project, not in terms of technology, but in terms of service. Semantic Web technologies, just like any other technology, are not a purpose in itself. A Linked Data service should not be built just to provide a Linked Data service, but should have wider benefits for the library service.

Advocating the project

Undertaking a Linked Data project in a library can be a challenge, because the added value to end-users is not obvious. It can often be argued that the same result can be achieved using more traditional technologies. Therefore, the added value of enabling the catalogue for the Semantic Web and Linked

Data has to be clearly demonstrated, beyond sheer interest in innovative technologies.

A Linked Data service can be advocated in two major cases:

- If the library owns datasets that are worth publishing on the web and which will prove relevant for other communities to reuse (rare and unique collections descriptions, authorities, thesauri and vocabularies, user-generated content, etc.).
- If the project improves interoperability, such as merging sources from different databases in heterogeneous formats, or reusing existing datasets from the Web of Data rather than creating new content (DBpedia, Geonames, MusicBrainz, etc.).

In both cases, interoperability is a key feature for the library, either in output (being able to make the library's data more efficient on the web) or input (being able to exploit other data within the library system). If we consider that the web is the main environment for interoperability nowadays, it is obvious that a library project that wants to be innovative, open and extensible to external data, and with a strong web visibility, should embrace Linked Data.

Developing expertise

Another challenge lies in the organizational commitments required to embrace Semantic Web technologies, and first of all, training. In a field where the technology is not yet mature, skills may be lacking, both among librarians and among IT staff. While there is a strong interest currently in the profession, the number of experts is still limited, and expertise is required in order to test and assess the new tools and services.

This is a reason why a Linked Data project can only be undertaken on a step-by-step basis, involving experimentation phases and acknowledging the learning-by-doing aspect. This aspect can also be seen as providing added value, because experts only become experts by challenging their own skills and putting their knowledge into practice. The international library community has been organizing itself in this regard, and many library technology-related events now offer dedicated workshops or events focused on acquiring and experimenting with Linked Data: Code4Lib,[3] ALA,[4] ELAG,[5] IFLA,[6] etc.

Agile methodologies, based on short iterative development cycles, can be a good way to ensure a progressive development of the service and to provide the opportunity to step back if needed. They deliver high-quality services by adapting to users' needs as the project progresses, even if special attention needs to be paid to documentation and quality of the outcome.[7]

It is therefore important to take the time and money needed for staff training into account when setting up the planning and the budget of the project.

Legal issues

The last obstacle, which should preferably be tackled before the actual project starts, is the matter of licensing. The value of publishing data on the Web of Data lies in the opportunity given to others to reuse this data. Unfortunately, the data is often restricted by unclear or unfavourable terms of use.

To provide a comparison: in the early ages of the web, many institutional websites used to require authorization from people who wanted to create deep links to their content; some would even forbid it completely. Today we know that the added value of the web relies in links. A website that is not linked has little interest or value.

It is exactly the same for the Web of Data. Many data providers are the victims of a 'database hugging' phenomenon: they love their data so much that they want to keep it for themselves. Such an attitude is clearly incompatible with the Linked Data approach. In order for data to be useful on the web, it needs to be clear of licensing limitations.

Public domains licences like Creative Commons Zero (CC0), and open licences like the General Public Licence (GPL) or the Open Data Commons licence, are adapted for the publication of datasets in the Web of Data. They allow the data to be reused, thus creating the maximum added value from the Linked Data.

Technical basics: RDF, URIs and Linked Data principles

The first technological building blocks of a Linked Data project are the RDF model and the web standard for identifiers: URIs. Linked Data makes use of these basics, in conjunction with data models, to publish data on the Semantic Web.

A short introduction to RDF

RDF (Resource Description Framework) is a data model where each piece of information is expressed in the form of an assertion composed of three elements: the subject, the predicate, and the object, as shown in Figure 6.1. Such an assertion is also called a triple.

Figure 6.1 *An assertion or triple*

In addition, subjects and predicates are always represented using a standard web identifier: the URI (Uniform Resource Identifier), as shown in Figure 6.2. This requirement ensures that resources are uniquely identified in the context of the Semantic Web. In this way, several assertions can be made about them.

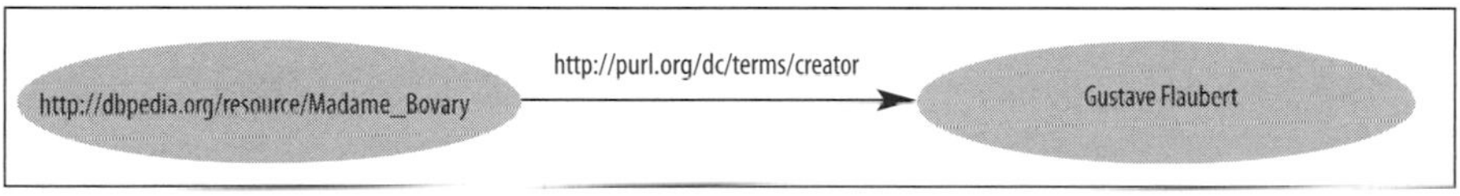

Figure 6.2 *A subject and a predicate represented as URIs*

URIs have a specific syntax. For example, they always begin with a scheme and a colon (e.g. 'http:', 'ftp:', 'urn:', 'info:'). The part after the colon depends on the specification of the scheme. For instance, URLs (Uniform Resource Locators) are a specific type of URIs where the scheme is always 'http:'.[8]

The object of the triple can also be expressed as a URI and can therefore become the subject of another triple, as shown in Figure 6.3. Alternatively, the object can be expressed as text, e.g. 'Gustave Flaubert'. This is known as a literal or a string.

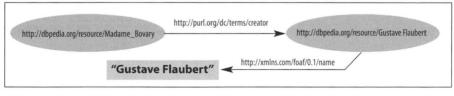

Figure 6.3 *An object represented as a URI*

The combination of several assertions, or triples, composes a directed graph as shown in Figure 6.4. It is a *directed* graph because the predicate, or relation, is orientated or unidirectional. It is only meant to be used one way.

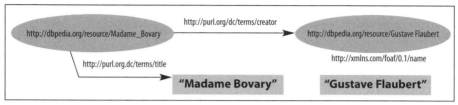

Figure 6.4 *A directed graph*

When a thing has a URI, it is considered to be a resource, as shown in Figure 6.5. This means assertions can be expressed about it. Things include documents, persons, objects, concepts . . . everything that needs to be described. Resources are categorized into classes (types of things).

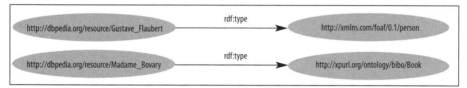

Figure 6.5 *Example resources*

The predicates or relationships between resources are also called properties. Properties can have specific behaviours. For instance, if two resources are linked by a symmetrical property, the property can be reverted, as shown in Figure 6.6. These behaviours allow inferences: new triples can be created by machines, or inferred, from these properties. The inference software interprets what is already known about the data to create new pieces of information.

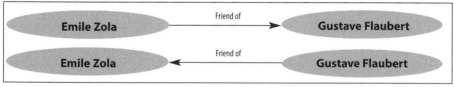

Figure 6.6 *Example properties or relationships between resources*

Classes and properties can have a hierarchy (they can have sub-classes and sub-properties which share the same characteristics). Classes, properties, their behaviours and hierarchy, are declared in vocabularies or ontologies, by using formalisms such as RDFS or OWL.

Linked Data principles

The four major principles of Linked Data, as expressed in the founding poster presented at the European Semantic Web Conference in 2007 (ESWC 2007),[9] are focused on how to design the URIs and what their behaviour should be in the linking environment of the web:

1 Use URIs as names for things.
2 Use HTTP URIs so that people can look up those names.
3 When someone looks up a URI, provide useful RDF information.
4 Include RDF statements that link to other URIs so that they can discover related things.

It is important to note that these principles rely on the basics of web architecture as defined by Tim Berners-Lee in his article *Linked Data*.[10] Berners-Lee refers to these principles as rules. However, they can rather be considered as expectations of behaviour, or guidelines. Not following these principles will not destroy anything; however, it means that opportunities will be missed. This will be a shame, as Linked Data is exactly about that: creating opportunities.

First of all, Linked Data involves providing RDF data on the web.[11] Using URIs to name resources is a must, as it is a requirement of RDF. The use of HTTP URIs is a bit more challenging, as there is a long-held belief that everything starting with 'HTTP' is a URL and is therefore subject to change over time. This has led institutions who want to guarantee the persistent identification of their resources to prefer using other URI schemes such as DOI, URN, etc. However, nowadays it is widely recognized that no identifier system provides persistence.[12] Persistence is an institutional commitment and can be achieved using well managed HTTP URIs.

Once these HTTP URIs have been designed, they must be de-referenceable. This means that it is necessary to provide a mechanism allowing the retrieval of data from the URI. While URIs often correspond to abstract resources (real-world entities, also called non-information resources, in comparison to 'information resources', which are data or documents), the web architecture requires that a web document is provided. This web document can provide information about the resource being referenced. The de-referencing of HTTP URIs, described in the SWEO interest group note 'Cool URIs for the Semantic Web',[13] provides recommendations on how to obtain information about the resource.

The last 'rule' of Linked Data is to provide links from one dataset to other available datasets. Linked Data is built following a bottom-up approach, by aggregating and linking datasets from a variety of sources and owning organizations. It is unrealistic to expect that a worldwide, cross-domain agreement on a global and unique URI that could be used to name a real-world entity can be reached. It is therefore likely that the same real-world entity (for instance, 'Sandro Botticelli' as real-world person) will have a variety of URIs according to the statements that a variety of actors are willing to make about him: Sandro Botticelli as the creator of the *Birth of Venus* in the Uffizi Gallery in Florence, Sandro Botticelli as the subject of a book held by the National Library of France, etc. Linked Data statements can therefore include equivalence statements which enable the existence of URI aliases, i.e. distinct URIs that are de-referenced to different descriptions of the same resource, to be identified. Different views and opinions about the same real-world entity can therefore be expressed.

A data model for the Semantic Web

As we have seen in the previous section, publishing data as RDF requires using existing vocabularies or ontologies. Unlike with XML and other traditional metadata syntaxes, RDF allows a great deal of flexibility in the choice of elements that compose a bibliographic description. This flexibility also implies that there is a need to build rules and define patterns. A data model is the definition of these rules and patterns.

As long as the data is available in RDF, Linked Data does not enforce any modelling requirement regarding how classes and properties should be defined. It is expected that it is built in a bottom-up process, just like the web itself. This means that the various datasets are connected by links, but the form and model of a local dataset does not need to have knowledge of the form and model of another. This is possible because each resource represented by a URI is independent and each triple is self-describing, whatever other statements are made about the same resource, i.e. one resource could be both an object and a subject within the same context or RDF graph. If we compare this with interoperability, as it is usually conceived within libraries, it is just as if you could link a MARC data field inside a record from your catalogue with a Dublin Core element inside a record in another catalogue and then use this link to retrieve and manipulate both records together without the need for any metadata mapping or crosswalk, any record exchange or import or software development. A data model is a set of classes and properties used to express information in a certain context. As we are talking about RDF, all classes and properties need to have URIs. A good practice in the Linked Data is that these URIs are de-referenceable. Another best practice is to reuse existing classes and properties from vocabularies already declared and possibly standardized.

Building a data model therefore means analysing your data and then selecting from existing vocabularies relevant classes and properties fitting your specific needs. The following sections highlight a selection of existing vocabularies that may be of interest.

Dublin Core: simple and powerful

Dublin Core is probably one of the oldest and most famous metadata formats. However, its purpose and principles are often misunderstood, partly because there are a lot of preconceived ideas about this standard and partly because it has evolved significantly since its creation 15 years ago.

The first important thing to know about Dublin Core is that it is meant to be a vocabulary, independent of implementations and applications. It is not limited to the famous 15 historical 'core elements',[14] but has been enriched to compose a comprehensive vocabulary of properties and classes, called the Dublin Core Metadata Initiative (DCMI) Metadata Terms.[15] Each property and class from the list of metadata terms has a URI and information about its hierarchy and use, expressed in RDFS. Dublin Core is therefore enabled for the Semantic Web.

As Dublin Core is intended to be implementation-independent, there are several syntaxes to express it, starting with XML. The XML expression of Dublin Core, with its alternative choice between 'simple Dublin Core' (only the 15 core elements) and 'qualified Dublin Core' (the 15 elements, enriched with refinements taken from the DCMI Metadata Terms), was initially meant to allow the description of resources using only Dublin Core terms.[16]

On the contrary, the RDF expression of Dublin Core follows the logic of the RDF model; each triple is independent. Dublin Core is therefore a simple and powerful standard that plays a major role in the Web of Data, because its main properties can be widely reused. The wide reuse of properties is a key factor for the interoperability of Linked Data. For example, if you are considering publishing your data on the web and if there's something in your data that is a title, it is better to use the Dublin Core 'title' property than to create a specific one that will be less understood by external applications.

In 2007, the DCMI (Dublin Core Metadata Initiative) [17] extensively revised both its Abstract Model[18] and its framework for creating application profiles,[19] in order to acknowledge the RDF model. The revised documents enable application profiles to be created using relevant classes and properties from external vocabularies in addition to those from Dublin Core.

SKOS and FOAF: concepts and persons

FOAF (Friend of a Friend)[20] is an RDF vocabulary adapted for the description of persons, organizations and their relationships.

SKOS (Simple Knowledge Organisation System)[21] is an RDF vocabulary for thesauri, taxonomies, controlled vocabularies and lists of concepts. Its goal is to describe concepts and relationships between concepts such as 'broader', 'narrower' and 'related'. Each concept can have one or more preferred labels and one or several alternative labels. SKOS also provides mechanisms for encoding alignments between similar concepts in different vocabularies (SKOS:closeMatch and SKOS:exactMatch).

Both of these standards have raised an interest in libraries for the description of authority data. Initiatives like the Library of Congress Authorities and Vocabularies service,[22] which has published various authorities such as the Library of Congress Subject Headings (LCSH) as Linked Data and the Virtual International Authority File (VIAF),[23] are using SKOS as a model to represent the structure of the authority file, sometimes enriched by other vocabularies to describe specific resources. For instance, VIAF uses both SKOS and FOAF to describe persons.

Building a data model: the example of EDM

The Europeana Data Model (EDM) was developed by the European project, Europeana v1.0,[24] in order to create an interoperability framework for cultural heritage resources aggregated by Europeana, the European digital library.

The EDM ontology is the result of a long consensus-building process, because the objects to be ingested within Europeana are very diverse and are provided by communities, which have their own – not necessarily compatible – metadata standards: libraries, archives, audiovisual archives and museums.

As described earlier, Europeana follows the best practice to not create new classes and properties, but rather to reuse existing ones from available vocabularies and to combine them into a high-level ontology. This will enable data providers to use a more detailed, often domain-specific metadata format for the mapping to EDM for interoperability.

The basics of EDM are described in the EDM Primer, with the full specification in the EDM Data Model definition document.[25] The ORE[26] vocabulary is used in order to describe complex structures of digital objects, and to track provenance of the descriptions thanks to the proxy mechanism. Then, four main classes (Agent, Event, Place and Concept) are used as nodes to aggregate the bibliographic elements describing the object. Agent and Concept are classes reused from FOAF and SKOS.

The purpose of EDM is to provide an interoperability framework where the semantics of ingested objects will be aligned, and create a global information layer that will allow seamless access to the content.

The European project, Europeana Libraries,[27] investigated how library-domain metadata can be aligned with the EDM. Drawing on the expertise of library-domain metadata experts, a report recommending best practice of aligning library-domain metadata has been produced. By the end of the project the alignments will be implemented and the data provided to Europeana.

Issues with data models

The perspective for data models and vocabularies development is still quite unclear in the library domain. Standardization of these vocabularies is not always a straightforward process, and there are obstacles such as the fact that data and the communities owning them are scattered and very diverse.

As an example, we can take the FRBR (Functional Requirements for Bibliographic Records) model.[28] FRBR is an abstract model, which means that it is not meant for implementation as such. However, being an entity-relationship model, it is very convenient for expressing data in graphs and early interest has risen for the development of a RDF vocabulary for FRBR.

Unfortunately, the lack of commitment and clear ownership for this project has led to a current situation where at least four versions of FRBR in RDF co-exist:

1 The FRBR Core[29] is an unofficial ontology developed by Ian Davis and Richard Newman. Its lightweight interpretation of FRBR and its early release have made it already a reference within Semantic Web and Linked Data early implementations like MusicBrainz and the BBC datasets.

2   The RDA (Resource Description and Access) new cataloguing code intended to replace AACR2 has developed an RDF declaration of its elements within the Open Metadata Registry. As FRBR concepts are key to RDA, it was necessary to declare the main FRBR classes[30] (in particular Work, Expression, Manifestation and Item). As an official ontology was still lacking, the RDA task group decided to declare their own FRBR entities, which they plan to either declare equivalent or deprecate when an official version of FRBR is available.

3   Meanwhile, IFLA's FRBR review group, jointly with a Namespaces Task Group appointed intentionally within IFLA's cataloguing section, has started the work to declare $FRBR_{er}$ entities and relationships as RDF classes and elements within the Open Metadata Registry. This work is still ongoing.

4   Finally, the efforts of convergence between FRBR and CIDOC-CRM (CIDOC Conceptual Reference Model),[31] a major ontology for museums, have led to the definition of an alternative version of FRBR, the $FRBR_{oo}$,[32] which is compatible with CRM-CIDOC and RDF expressions of the latter.

This example shows how difficult it is to standardize these library-specific vocabularies in the still unstable environment of the Semantic Web. Other questions, such as what type of relationships these standards should have with more general standards like Dublin Core, FOAF and SKOS, still remain unclear.

For implementers, another issue will lie in the validation and quality assessment of library data in RDF. Application profiles, such as envisioned in the DCMI Singapore Framework,[33] could be a way to check if the data that is produced is consistent with the guidelines and the data model.

Transformations, alignments
MARC to RDF?

Once the data model has been defined, the next step will be to transform existing library data into this new model. There again, there is no one single appropriate approach to this work. Data conversions are a tedious task that implies a deep knowledge of both the source and the target format. It is also important to be aware that conversion processes, even with a detailed and precise mapping, tend to imply data loss.

One straightforward approach to transforming MARC data into RDF would be to use an intermediate RDF syntax which fits very closely to the initial MARC format. This can be seen as similar to MarcXchange, being a different syntax to express MARC in XML rather than in ISO 2709.

Some work to create a MARC ontology was carried out – for instance, MarcOnt by the DERI (Digital Enterprise Research Institute), Ireland – a few years ago, but the interest in this field seems to have slowed significantly. However, some guidance on how to do that kind of straightforward syntax conversion would be useful, even if the MARC in RDF data created is only intended for back-office data processing and not for dissemination.

In May 2012, the Library of Congress announced a new effort,[34] undertaken together with Zepheira, a Semantic Web-dedicated company in the USA, to undertake a translation of MARC21 to a Linked Data model. This project is part of the Bibliographic Framework transition initiative, which aims at determining a transition path from MARC formats to a new standard, more adapted to the new technology framework at the beginning of the 2010s.

Alignments

Last but not least, a catalogue that is enabled for the Semantic Web should provide links to other resources, as this is a fundamental rule of Linked Data. What kind of links would they be?

In general, we can identify two different ways of linking library data on the open web: alignment of concepts and alignment with real-world entities.

Alignment of concepts would rely on equivalences between authorities and subject headings used by different libraries, at an international level. For instance, the LCSH (Library of Congress Subject Headings) published as SKOS by the Library of Congress have been aligned with the French-language subject headings RAMEAU[35] and the German-language subject headings, SWD,[36] as a result of the MACS (Multilingual Access to Subjects) project.[37] These links can therefore be used to bridge these three vocabularies, allowing, for example, the possibility of multilingual search. VIAF, the Virtual International Authority File, plays the same role for persons, except that the alignments are created prior to the transformation in RDF. VIAF also provides links to DBpedia (the RDF version of Wikipedia)[38].

Alignment of real-world entities is necessary when it comes to create links with datasets outside the library world. These datasets generally describe 'real things'. For example, the Wikipedia entry on Gustave Flaubert is about

Gustave Flaubert as a real-world person, not about an 'authority' in the library sense. Library authorities are about disambiguating names, not about describing real-world entities. This gap needs bridging in the data model.

In both perspectives, providing these alignments is not trivial, especially because the sheer mass of data makes it impossible to do it manually. Algorithms based on comparisons of text strings can be developed in some cases, but alignments will always be more reliable when an identifier is available: for instance, ISBNs for books,[39] ISTCs for textual works, ISNI for persons, etc. Some automated linking services have been developed, such as LD-mapper for music resources, Silk, Knofuss, etc.[40]

Storing and publishing Linked Data

RDF is not a format, it is a model or an abstract syntax. It is necessary to use a formal syntax to encode and store the data. This step is called serialization. There are also software tools available that allow the storage and publication of RDF data.

RDF syntaxes

It is not our goal here to describe in detail the syntaxes that allow the encoding of RDF data. However, it is useful to understand their principles and their objective. We will present only the three most common: Turtle, RDF/XML and RDFa.

Turtle

Turtle (Terse RDF Triple Language) is a simplified syntax to express triples,[41] as shown in Figure 6.7. Turtle is the easiest way to manipulate triples in a human-readable form. In principle, it is only about expressing triples one after the other, using URIs for subjects and predicates, and objects when they are not literals. The syntax also provides a means to shorten the URIs using prefixes and to avoid repetition of the same URI. The Turtle syntax is currently being standardized by W3C.[42]

RDF/XML

RDF/XML is an XML syntax for RDF, standardized by the W3C. Although

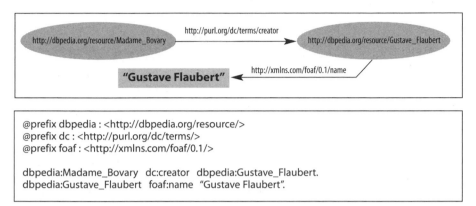

```
@prefix dbpedia : <http://dbpedia.org/resource/>
@prefix dc : <http://purl.org/dc/terms/>
@prefix foaf : <http://xmlns.com/foaf/0.1/>

dbpedia:Madame_Bovary  dc:creator  dbpedia:Gustave_Flaubert.
dbpedia:Gustave_Flaubert  foaf:name  "Gustave Flaubert".
```

Figure 6.7 *A triple expressed in Turtle syntax*

RDF/XML 'looks like' XML, they should not be confused. The main difference is the absence, in RDF/XML, of the notion of validation. A valid XML document is created by making reference to an external grammar, such as a DTD or XML schema, that provides guidelines or constraints about the data elements in an XML document. Validation does not exist in RDF/XML. A RDF/XML document can make reference to several vocabularies or ontologies. Namespaces are used to shorten URIs as in Turtle, only for predicates. Figure 6.8 shows a triple expressed in RDF/XML.

```
<rdf:RDF
 xmlns:rdf="http://www.w3.org/1999/02/22-rdf-syntax-ns#"
 xmlns:dc="http://purl.org/dc/terms/">
 xmlns:foaf="http://purl.org/dc/terms/">
   <rdf:Description rdf:about="http://dbpedia.org/resource/Madame_Bovary">
        <dc:creator rdf:resource="http://dbpedia.org/resource/Gustave_Flaubert"/>
   </rdf:Description>
</rdf:RDF>
```

Figure 6.8 *A triple expressed in RDF/XML*

RDFa

Finally, RDFa is a standardized syntax to express RDF triples within an XHTML page, in order to embed rich metadata within web documents (see Figure 6.9). Within RDFa, triples are expressed within the XHTML mark-up and can be retrieved and processed by software agents. Metadata can be added either as a separate element in the page or by tagging the words in the content. There are other RDF syntaxes that are more development orientated, such as JSON.[43]

```
<p xmlns:dc="http://purl.org/dc/elements/1.1/"
  about=" http://dbpedia.org/resource/Madame_Bovary ">
 In his book
 <cite property="dc:title">Madame Bovary</cite>,
 <span property="dc:creator" resource="http://dbpedia.org/resource/Gustave_Flaubert">
 Gustave Flaubert</span> depicts the french nineteenth century local bourgeoisie.
 </p>
```

Figure 6.9 *A triple expressed in RDFa*

Triple stores

RDF syntaxes are used with the purpose of sharing, exposing or disseminating RDF triples. In order to store the RDF data, it is not necessary to adopt a particular syntax; instead, appropriate tools should be used.

Specific databases have been developed in order to store and manipulate RDF data. They are called triple stores. Virtuoso (by Open Link Software)[44] is an example of a triple store. It has an open-source version and a more scalable fee-based version.

In essence, a triple store is about storing data expressed as 'subject', 'predicate' and 'object'. It is as if you had a database with only these three types of data, which means that you can fit anything in that common model. This is therefore more flexible and extensible than a relational database, where you have to define records and data-fields that are specific to each type of information you want to store. The common model allows storing any kind of content information in a generic structure.

In practice, it is of course, not that simple. In particular, the triple store has to be optimized for queries and other specific functions that may require a more complex implementation. Sometimes, triple stores are associated with a framework for manipulating the data: Sesame,[45] ARC.[46] A triple store/RDF framework is a set of tools that can parse RDF data from various syntaxes, serialize RDF data into various syntaxes, store RDF triples, and query them. It can provide additional functions such as, for instance, inferencing. Work to improve the scalability and performance of triple stores beyond a few billion triples is ongoing.

Using the data
Access and interfaces

The way the data is stored can affect the way it is disseminated. Here we consider three cases: data dumps, queries and exposure.

Data dump

The data dump is the simplest. Once the data set is transformed to RDF, it can simply be made available online for bulk download, for instance as a RDF/XML file. This is the simplest method of making the data available. However, it cannot really be considered as Linked Data because the basic de-referencing requirement cannot be met.

Queries

If the RDF data is stored in a triple store, generally a query mechanism is provided. The W3C standard query language for RDF is called SPARQL.[47] SPARQL is a query language and protocol that allows very precise queries to be run against RDF datasets using a Turtle-like syntax. The results are delivered in a standard output. Queries can be either addressed to the store via a query interface or remotely using the SPARQL protocol. Remote queries make it possible to build new interfaces that use the data, such as mash-ups.

Exposure

Exposure is the classic dissemination requirement of Linked Data. While Linked Data does not enforce any specific architecture, the basics of content negotiation should be respected. Content negotiation means that with the same URI, the application should be able to provide either an RDF view or an HTML view on the same data, depending whether it is requested by an application that can consume RDF data, or by a human user with a regular browser. Exposure can also be achieved by tagging XHTML pages with RDFa as described above.

Applications

The more data is available, the more tools are created to search, browse and use the data. Existing applications are generally similar to the ones that we are familiar with in the Web 2.0 environment and include websites, search engines, browsers, etc. Here we will present a selection of example applications.

Semantic Web browsers such as Tabulator[48] can be used to browse Linked Data. When provided with a URI, they retrieve associated RDF statements from the Linked Data cloud and allow navigating from one URI to another.

The BBC music website[49] is a good example of what can be done by aggregating Linked Data in a way similar to mash-ups. For each artist, a persistent URI is provided and a webpage gathers information and images from Wikipedia via DBpedia discographies from MusicBrainz[50] and radio play data from the BBC database (BBC programmes, also available as Linked Data). The website is both an appealing product for the public and will also help to improve ranking in search engine results.

Semantic Web search engines use de-referenceable URIs to crawl and index the global information space of Linked Data. They provide both human interfaces and machine interfaces where one can present a URI and retrieve all the related statements found on the Web of Data. Sindice[51] from the DERI is an example of a Semantic Web search engine. It monitors, crawls and indexes RDF data available on the web from triple stores, HTML pages including embedded RDFa and RDF files (not only from actual Linked Data datasets). The results are provided as an API so that they can be embedded in a new application. This functionality is an important building block for the Web of Data as it makes it easier to find RDF triples that can then be reused in other applications and websites.

Finally, there are some applications that have the goal of creating the 'read/write Web of Data', or develop the opportunity to create new datasets in a seamless, Web 2.0-like manner. Semantic wikis and social networks such as Semantic Media Wiki[52] and Freebase[53] allow average web users to create RDF data without even being aware of it. This social data will be interlinked with authoritative Linked Datasets such as DBpedia, Geonames, etc. and used to create new triples for the continuing growth of the Linked Data cloud.

Library catalogues as Linked Data

The applications described above foster the real added value of Linked Data by showing how data that is made available in this way can be widely reused. This goes beyond reuse in a selected number of existing data silos, such as when we create a mash-up application using APIs, towards a global shared information space where all available resources are interlinked.

The DBpedia mobile[54] application is a very interesting example of this principle. This project, from the Freie Universität in Berlin, aims at providing Linked Data resources for use on mobile devices, such as a mobile phone. The idea is to use the GPS function of the mobile device to locate the user and then provide him with a map showing all available Linked Data resources nearby.

Geonames and DBpedia are used as hubs to retrieve data linked with a place and other added-value information. This is a great example of the opportunity for a variety of institutions, including libraries, to make their data available as Linked Data. A mobile application dedicated to library information would not be necessarily attractive for users, but if they could find library data, among other things, in such an application, they would probably be encouraged to discover it and use it. The advantage for the library would be twofold: firstly, increased visibility for library data and secondly, no need to invest in costly application development.

Applications such as the RDF book mash-up developed by the Freie Universität Berlin[55] demonstrate the opportunities created by Linked Data for bibliographic information. The BBC websites[56] are probably the most efficient example of how the use of Linked Data can help creating added-value websites out of aggregated information.

Libraries and other related institutions are showing a growing interest in Linked Data. In 2008 LIBRIS, the catalogue of Swedish university and research libraries managed by the National Library of Sweden, undertook a project to rebuild their online public access catalogue, following user-orientated development strategies and agile methodology. One of their main concerns was to make the catalogue machine-readable and the data reusable by other developers. Their decision was not to choose one protocol over the others, but rather to provide a variety of techniques, ranging from the traditional Z39.50 to Linked Data. By being the first to release the whole catalogue as Linked Data, LIBRIS created an important first step for libraries, then followed by many others, including the national libraries of Hungary, Germany, Spain, France, etc.

In 2010 the JISC published the Open Bibliographic Data Guide,[57] a list of use cases demonstrating the possibilities of publishing open bibliographic data. In November 2010 the British Library announced the publication of the British National Bibliography (books published in the UK since 1950), under a CC0 licence.[58] Following up on this announcement, the JISC Open Bibliographic project further worked on the dataset to make it more usable, loading it into a Virtuoso triple store in order to make it available for SPARQL queries. The data contains about 173 million triples to date. The dataset is expressed using existing vocabularies such as Dublin Core and SKOS and provides links to other datasets, including LCSH and Dewey.info, a service provided by OCLC.

Furthermore, the European cultural heritage portal Europeana is beginning to experiment with Linked Open Data and in summer 2011 undertook a pilot project with willing European cultural heritage organizations, including libraries. The ten national libraries of Austria, Czech Republic, Hungary, Ireland, Luxembourg, the Netherlands, Portugal, Serbia, Slovenia and the UK were involved in this pilot.

In 2012 OCLC also announced the release of WorldCat as Linked Data. The data expressed in RDF using the Schema.org vocabulary[59] is embedded in WorldCat's regular HTML pages, using the RDFa syntax. One of the major goals of the initiative is to improve WorldCat's resources ranking in results pages provided by web search engines. Links are also provided to VIAF, Dewey.info, id.loc.gov, etc.

W3C Library Linked Data Incubator Group

In 2010, the W3C created an incubator group[60] in order to assess the state of the art of Linked Data adoption in the library domain and to plan for future developments. The Library Linked Data incubator group (LLD XG) was chartered for one year, with the mission of increasing global interoperability of library data on the web. The group gathered more than 50 use cases and case studies, examples of ongoing work in the cultural domain, or proposed developments and requirements for the future. This gathering of use cases demonstrates the efforts undertaken by libraries across the globe to publish their data on the web and underline issues and challenges that standardization bodies like the W3C and others will have to address in the forthcoming years.

The LLD XG has joined 'The Data Hub' initiative from the Open Knowledge Foundation to describe and reference existing datasets that are part of the Library Linked Data cloud.[61] As of August 2012 58 datasets had been registered with the 'LLD' tag.

The W3C has also worked on identifying the requirements and issues that need to be tackled in order to facilitate the adoption of Linked Data by libraries. Not all issues are technical: management, awareness raising, training, costs and licensing are high on the list. The main challenge is probably to induce change in the library environment, which is characterized by its stability and focus on long-term standards designed specifically for the community. The massive amount of legacy data and libraries' long tradition of collaboration, are both strengths and weaknesses. They create a favourable environment for a shift towards web standards, but a strong co-ordination effort is needed to achieve this transition.

Conclusion

Linked Data offers a very promising framework for publishing library data on the web. The main W3C standards that we have presented in this chapter, starting with RDF, are naturally fit to express complex structured data such as bibliographic data. Well known and well disseminated vocabularies, like Dublin Core, SKOS and FOAF, contribute to providing a favourable environment and help the modelling and conversion of library data to web-compliant forms. A significant number of libraries or library-related projects have placed Linked Data high on their list of priorities. Finally, the technology providing tools for creating, storing and aligning datasets is improving every day. Today, enabling the catalogue for the Semantic Web seems an innovative option. Tomorrow, Linked Data technologies may be the ones that will undermine the design of new library systems and provide the main interoperability framework, not only for the library community, but beyond, reaching out to museums, archives, publishers and others.

References

1   World Wide Web Consortium (W3C), a major standardization body for web technologies.
2   www.scientificamerican.com/article.cfm?id=the-semantic-web.
3   In 2009, Linked Data Tutorial at Code4Lib:
    http://wiki.code4lib.org/index.php/LinkedData.
4   In 2010, pre-conference at the ALA meeting titled 'Linked Data: Making Library Data Converse with the World':
    www.ala.org/ala/alcts/events/pastala/annual/10/linked.
5   Workshops and presentations about Linked Data at ELAG 2010:
    http://indico.cern.ch/conferenceProgram.py?confId=75915;
    http://elag2011.techlib.cz/en/787-programme.
6   IFLA session on Libraries and the Semantic Web at WLIC 2010, Göteborg:
    http://conference.ifla.org/conference/past/ifla76. A Semantic Web Special Interest Group has been created within IFLA during the 2011 Congress in Puerto Rico.
7   For an example of use of agile methodology in a library project, see Lindström, H. and Malmsten, M. (2008) User-Centred Design and Agile Development: rebuilding the Swedish National Union Catalogue, *Code4lib journal*, **5**, http://journal.code4lib.org/articles/561.
8   About URI syntax, see RFC 3986: http://tools.ietf.org/html/rfc3986. The

difference between URI and URL is explained in the W3C note *URIs, URLs, and URNs: clarifications and recommendations 1.0*, www.w3.org/TR/uri-clarification.

9   http://linkeddata.org/docs/eswc2007-poster-linking-open-data.pdf.

10   July 2006, www.w3.org/DesignIssues/LinkedData.html.

11   Bizer, C., Cyganiak, R. and Heath, T. (2007) *How to publish Linked Data on the Web*, http://wifo5-03.informatik.uni-mannheim.de/bizer/pub/ LinkedDataTutorial.

12   See the NISO report on identifiers in 2006 : NISO Identifier Roundtable. 13–14 March 2006, http://niso.kavi.com/news/events/niso/past/ID-06-wkshp/ ID-workshop-Report2006725.pdf.

13   www.w3.org/TR/cooluris.

14   Title, Subject, Description, Source, Format, Type, Creator, Contributor, Publisher, Rights, Relation, Coverage, Language, Date and Identifier.

15   http://dublincore.org/documents/dcmi-terms.

16   See Guidelines for encoding DC in XML.

17   http://dublincore.org.

18   http://dublincore.org/documents/abstract-model.

19   http://dublincore.org/documents/profile-guidelines.

20   www.foaf-project.org.

21   www.w3.org/TR/skos-reference.

22   http://id.loc.gov.

23   http://viaf.org.

24   http://pro.europeana.eu/web/europeana-v1.0.

25   The EDM Primer and the EDM Data Model Definition are available in the EDM Documentation section of the Europeana Professional website: http://pro.europeana.eu/web/guest/edm-documentation.

26   ORE (Object Reuse and Exchange) is a vocabulary developed by the OAI (Open Archive Initiative) community for describing complex object aggregations. It enables the representation of the relationships between the entities which constitute the objects, express their structure and associate metadata at the appropriate level.

27   www.europeana-libraries.eu.

28   www.ifla.org/publications/functional-requirements-for-bibliographic-records.

29   http://vocab.org/frbr/core.html.

30   http://rdvocab.info.

31   www.cidoc-crm.org.

32   www.cidoc-crm.org/frbr_inro.html.

33   http://dublincore.org/documents/singapore-framework.

34   The announcement and more information regarding the Bibliographic
     Framework transition initiative can be retrieved from: www.loc.gov/bibframe.

35   http://rameau.bnf.fr.

36   SWD (Schlagwortnormdatei):
     www.dnb.de/DE/Standardisierung/Normdaten/GND/gnd_node.html

37   The MACS (Multilingual Access to Subjects) project aims at offering a cross-
     language search to library databases using controlled subject terms. The project
     has up to now concentrated its efforts in linking terms from the Library of
     Congress Subject Headings (LCSH), RAMEAU and SWD. Currently, there are
     60,000 trilingual links covering subject headings most often used in the
     collections of the French National Library (BnF), the British Library (BL), the
     German National Library (DNB) and the Swiss National Library (SNL).

38   http://dbpedia.org/About.

39   For more information about ISBN, see: www.isbn-international.org; ISTC, see:
     www.istc-international.org; and ISNI, see: www.isni.org.

40   These tools have been explored by the Melinda project (Meta Linking Data) in
     2009: http://melinda.inrialpes.fr.

41   Turtle is a subset of a more complex syntax called N3. There is also a subset of
     Turtle, which is even simpler, called N-Triple.

42   www.w3.org/TR/turtle.

43   www.w3.org/2011/rdf-wg/wiki/TF-JSON.

44   http://virtuoso.openlinksw.com.

45   www.w3.org/2001/sw/wiki/Sesame.

46   www.w3.org/2001/sw/wiki/ARC.

47   www.w3.org/TR/rdf-sparql-query.

48   www.w3.org/2005/ajar/tab. Tabulator was the first Linked Data browser,
     developed by the W3C.

49   www.bbc.co.uk/music.

50   http://musicbrainz.org.

51   http://sindice.com.

52   http://semantic-mediawiki.org/wiki/Semantic_MediaWiki.

53   www.freebase.com. In 2010 the company responsible for Freebase, Metaweb,
     was bought by Google.

54   http://wiki.dbpedia.org/DBpediaMobile.

55   http://wifo5-03.informatik.uni-mannheim.de/bizer/bookmashup.

56   BBC Music: www.bbc.co.uk/music; and BBC wildlife finder:
     www.bbc.co.uk/nature/wildlife.

57   http://obd.jisc.ac.uk.

58   www.bl.uk/bibliographic/datasamples.html.

59   http://schema.org is a vocabulary jointly created by Google, Bing and Yahoo! in order to help search engines improve the ranking of web resources.

60   www.w3.org/2005/Incubator/lld. The final report of the group, released in November 2011, can be retrieved from www.w3.org/2005/Incubator/lld/XGR-lld-20111025.

61   http://thedatahub.org/dataset?tags=lld&q=lld.

7

Supporting digital scholarship: bibliographic control, library co-operatives and open access repositories

Karen Calhoun

Introduction

Research libraries have entered an era of discontinuous change – a time when the cumulated assets of the past do not guarantee future success. Bibliographic control, co-operative cataloguing systems and library catalogues have been key assets in the research library service framework for supporting scholarship. This chapter examines these assets in the context of changing library collections, new metadata sources and methods, open access repositories, digital scholarship and the purposes of research libraries. Advocating a fundamental rethinking of the research library service framework, this chapter concludes with a call for research libraries to consider collectively new approaches that could strengthen their roles as essential contributors to emergent, network-level scholarly research infrastructures.

Changing collections, the 'control zone' and resource discovery

Scholarly collections have changed. Now dominated by licensed online content, academic library collections are becoming more universally available and less institutionally focused. Other types of collections – digital libraries and open access repositories – are gaining in visibility and importance. With the transformation of the scholarly information landscape wrought by the web, it is no longer possible for one individual library to own, license or point to all the information objects of value to the academy. The roles and value of locally housed, largely paper-based collections are being reconsidered (for some recent examples see Lewis, 2013; Malpas, 2011; Henry et al., 2011; University Leadership Council, 2011; Payne, 2007).

The state of the scholarly research collection

The demand for online content has seemed insatiable. In response, starting in the mid-1990s, research libraries began expending at first modest and now large shares of their budgets on commercial online content controlled by publishers. Many foresaw the large impact that the shift to online access would have on library collections and collection-centred services such as reference and cataloguing. Ross Atkinson, an exceptional librarian who helped to define modern research library collection development, wrote a seminal paper on the roles of library collections up to the mid-1990s (Atkinson, 1996). As he observed more and more scholarly publications moving from paper to online, Atkinson sought to define research library collections in terms of their fundamental purpose 'to reduce the time needed by individual client-users to gain access to that information they need to accomplish their personal or institutional work objectives.'

In the paper environment, research libraries 'privileged' certain information objects by acquiring and transferring them to be physically available to the library's user community – a function 'disintermediated' by the displacement of paper by high-priced commercial online content. Atkinson was an early advocate for research libraries' reclaiming their roles supporting essential components of scholarly research *infrastructure* (the content, technology, tools, services, systems, organizations and facilities on which the continuance and progress of scholarship depend). Since Atkinson published his article, the research library community has vigorously sought ways to carry forward its roles supporting scholarship, through advocacy, open access publishing and the establishment of open access repositories.

While Atkinson's 1996 proposal was more radical than what has since unfolded, his intent was widely shared in the research library community. He proposed reclaiming libraries' central role in scholarly communications through the establishment of a *control zone* (a global digital library, in fact) that would carry forward the purpose of privileging, drawing attention to and adding value to scholarly content. He regarded the selection and preservation of the scholarly subset of the universe of information as a social and ethical imperative of librarianship. It is in this context that he argued:

> It is time – past time – for the academic library community to begin work on the creation and management of a single, virtual, distributed, international digital library, a library that has (conceptual, virtual) boundaries, that defines its services operationally on the basis of the opposition between what is inside and outside those boundaries, and that bases that service on the traditional social ethic that has motivated all library operations in modern times. The academic community must consider, in other words, the creation of a control zone.
>
> (Atkinson, 1996, 254)

He recognized the practical limits of realizing a single, universal control zone and proposed regional and other instances, linked interoperably to a larger whole.

Ten years later, Atkinson (2006) convened an important conference of collection development leaders to consider the future of research library collections. By that time, while the disintermediation of library services that Atkinson foresaw in 1996 was coming to pass, pieces of the control zone had begun to emerge in unanticipated ways.

Pieces of the control zone on the web

Research libraries have not developed the control zone that Atkinson envisioned, but pieces of it (that is, of a new scholarly research infrastructure) have nevertheless begun to emerge as a result of the development of the web and the tumultuous, technology-driven changes in the practices and tools of scholarship over the past 20 years. Efforts to rethink scholarly communications and advance toward 'the system that scholars deserve' (Van de Sompel et al., 2004) are having an impact. Three lines of development – some scholars' establishment of subject-based repositories; research libraries' persistent efforts to establish institutional repositories; and parallel developments resulting from the transformative impact of search engines – have combined to produce a nascent, 'network-based system that . . . provides interoperability across participating [scholarly communications] nodes.' (Van de Sompel et al., 2004).

These developments occurred against a backdrop of changing user behaviours with respect to collections. By the middle of the first decade of the new millennium, students had expressed clear preferences for starting their research with search engines (see De Rosa, 2005) and faculty perceived themselves as less dependent on the library (Schonfeld and Guthrie, 2007).

By the beginning of the second decade of the millennium these trends had become even stronger (De Rosa et al., 2011; Schonfeld and Housewright, 2010). For example, across disciplines, faculty members now prefer to begin research with network-level services (common search engines or discipline-specific online resources) instead of using the library catalogue or visiting the library. Faculty and researchers expect that scholarly content will be online, and it is: the Cox and Cox (2008) study reported that over 95% of science, technology and medicine and 85% of arts, humanities and social science journal titles are now online.

In other developments, search engines have improved their abilities to index the deep web (Zillman, 2012), and scholarly content providers are increasingly willing to allow search engines to crawl their metadata or content so that it is easily discoverable there. Also part of the fabric of this transformation is rethinking the role of little-used print collections (for usage statistics see Anderson, 2011). In addition to developing storage facilities, research libraries are making their print collections work harder through successful innovations like Borrow Direct, a user-initiated book borrowing programme that essentially makes multiple libraries' print collections available to a larger audience (Nitecki, Jones, and Barnett, 2009). The Hathi Trust (www.hathitrust.org/about) gathers together partner research libraries' collections in digital form for preservation and effective access.

Scholarly journals and articles

In practice, Google and Google Scholar are identifying a network-level, scholarly control zone of licensed and open access scholarly articles. Google Scholar has been in place since 2004. The CIBER study (2009) and other research findings (Hampton-Reeves et al., 2009) indicate that both faculty and students now discover online scholarly content more often through Google, Google Scholar and Google Books. Now that the content of scholarly aggregations (like ScienceDirect and the content of open access repositories) is crawled and indexed by Google, a huge amount of traffic to online scholarly content comes from Google. Google Scholar includes open access versions of articles in search results when possible. Norris, Oppenheim and Rowland (2008) evaluated four search tools' utility for locating open access articles and found that Google and Google Scholar did the best job of locating them.

Metadata for commercial e-journals generally is originally sourced from publishers and passed along in a supply chain to a number of stakeholders, including national libraries and registration agencies, subscription agents and vendors. The work of CONSER, the Cooperative Online Serials Program (www.loc.gov/acq/conser/index.html) remains relevant in the metadata supply chain for online journals; however most libraries are more consumers than creators of the descriptive metadata for e-journals.

Metadata for journal articles has more sources. It is generally provided by publishers, abstracting and indexing services, aggregators of online articles, authors and those acting on behalf of authors (such as e-print repository managers or staff). Producing metadata for journal *articles* has never or rarely been the domain of the library cataloguing community. Following the launch of Google Scholar in 2004, more and more article content providers agreed to expose their metadata for harvesting by search engines and for inclusion in the central indexes of library discovery services.

New library discovery services

By tradition, discovery of articles has been the domain of abstracting and indexing agencies and bibliographers, not cataloguers. Article-level metadata has typically been absent from the catalogue. With the massive changes that led to the direct online delivery of articles, and the high user demand for this content, it became critical for the catalogue to somehow integrate and surface article level content. Starting around 2005, new discovery services began to replace traditional library online public access catalogues (OPACs), because the traditional catalogue could not scale to this purpose (for example, at the date of writing the author's ARL library's discovery service indexes over 71 million journal articles).

The new discovery services (Summon, EBSCO Discovery Services, WorldCat Local, Primo, Encore, etc.) provide a common interface to a centralized index of pre-harvested, pre-indexed metadata or content from heterogeneous sources, thus enabling a library to present a much larger view of scholarly content to its users. In additional to indexing e-content (journals, books and articles) to which the library has access, typically the discovery service also indexes the library catalogue, institutional repository and digital collections. See Chapter 3 for more information.

Open access repositories

Open access repositories grew out of the desire to transform scholarly communications and reduce dependence on commercial publishing. They exemplify what Atkinson had in mind when he envisioned 'reclaiming' the control zone from publishers. On balance, they have been successful: a directory of open access repositories, OpenDOAR (http://opendoar.org), lists nearly 2200 repositories, a figure that has been steadily rising each year.

Repositories, both subject- and institutionally based, are gaining in visibility and impact. Several of the subject-based repositories have succeeded in transforming scholarly communications and fostering worldwide collaboration in the disciplines they support. Institutional repositories have been challenged with low deposit rates, but they are gradually becoming more successful at attracting submissions. Deposit mandates (governmental or institutional requirements that researchers make their papers available in open access repositories) have begun to stimulate growth in the number of open access papers available (see for example http://publicaccess.nih.gov). The result is that the number of articles published in open access journals or available from open access repositories (both subject-based and institutional) or authors' web pages represents an increasing proportion of annual scholarly output. Björk and colleagues conducted a number of analyses (Björk, Roos and Lauri, 2009; Björk et al., 2010; Laakso et al., 2011) and estimated that a little over 20% of all the articles published in 2008 were openly available a year later. The results of the study that the team published in 2011 suggested that the number of open access journals has grown at an annual rate of 18% since 2000, and the number of open access articles has grown 30% a year.

Open access repositories have become increasingly important for improving the discoverability and accessibility of not only articles, but also reports, theses and dissertations, conference and working papers, teaching materials and presentations. Universities have had some incentive to invest in repositories as ways of better organizing and disclosing the scholarly output they support.

To provide a sense of the scope and scale of attention received by selected repositories compared to other sites of interest to scholarly information seekers, Figure 7.1 compares US traffic in October 2011 across a number of sites including:

- a highly ranked institutional repository (dspace.mit.edu)
- three of the top subject-based repositories
- several library-related sites (Yale, the catalogue of the Library of Congress, the University of Michigan, New York Public Library and

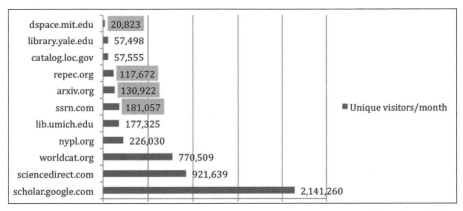

Figure 7.1 *US Traffic to selected repositories, library sites, ScienceDirect and Google Scholar (October 2011). Source of data: siteanalytics.compete.com*

OCLC's public interface to WorldCat)
- a leading commercial site for science, technology and medicine (STM) research (ScienceDirect)
- Google Scholar.

Numbers of unique monthly visitors to the repositories are shaded in grey.

The metadata for repositories generally comes from authors or repository managers on behalf of authors. Sometimes metadata librarians or cataloguers participate in this process. Authors and subject experts have proved to be good sources of metadata (see for example Wilson, 2007), especially when the author or contributor interface provides helpful guidance. A variety of investigations (for example see Duranceau and Rodgers, 2010) are looking into how metadata might be more easily generated and transferred to multiple repositories at the point the content is deposited.

Digital libraries

An analysis of digital libraries and digital library aggregations suggests the categories of digital objects shown in Figure 7.2. There are indications that larger digital library collections are attracting a good deal of attention. Figure 7.3 is a chart using 2012 data from Alexa.com showing the percentage of visitors who go to different parts of a site. The chart shows the top three visitor destinations for the national libraries of France, New Zealand and Australia. Gallica, PapersPast and Trove are digital libraries.

Figure 7.2 *Types of digital objects*

*Pandora is Australia's web archive

Figure 7.3 *Percentage of visitors to digital library subdomains on national library sites, 2012. Source of data: alexa.com*

The metadata for digital library collections comes from many sources and different metadata communities, which deploy a variety of content rules, frameworks, schemes, reference models, element sets and encoding rules. NISO's Understanding Metadata (Guenther and Radebaugh, 2004) provides helpful guidance for anticipating the scope, complexity, and interoperability requirements for representing large-scale digital libraries of cultural heritage materials. While many digital library sites are crawled by Google and are thus discoverable through search engines, their easy discovery alongside other types of content of interest to scholars and students remains problematic. The new library discovery services (Summon, Primo and the like) can sometimes index the metadata from digital library collections so that these collections are discoverable from a common library interface.

Books

The transformation of discovery and access to the scholarly journal literature has progressed fairly rapidly from the mid-1990s until now. The transformation of discovery and access to books is progressing more slowly, but developments over the last decade have continued to alter the landscape of book collecting and metadata for many types of books, for example:

- The development commencing in 1999 of the ONIX (Online Information Exchange) standard for representing and communicating book industry product information in electronic form. The importance of ONIX has grown among publishers, booksellers and other participants in the book industry supply chain. Luther's white paper (2009) explores the possibilities for moving to an environment where metadata is exchanged more easily throughout the supply chain. In the process of her investigation she prepared an excellent Book Metadata Exchange Map which is well worth the reader's time to study. The map illustrates how publishers, metadata aggregators, wholesalers, booksellers (e.g. Amazon), Google, buyers and readers, and national/local libraries participate in the books metadata supply chain. Libraries are one of many participating types of organizations.
- The success of Amazon, founded in 1994, which has raised reader expectations for books metadata creation and management well above what libraries can accomplish with library-based methods (for a comparison of library and Amazon metadata see Calhoun, 2011, slide 23).
- The availability of machine-to-machine web services (e.g. from Amazon, Google Books, Ingram, etc.) that enable web developers to easily capture metadata for books for reuse in their own sites.
- The latest figures suggest that a total of 22 million books may have been

digitized in various projects, the majority by the Google Books project (estimated September 2012 from figures at http://sustainablecollections.com). Hathi Trust provides APIs and other methods that web developers can use to retrieve metadata for a subset of these titles (www.hathitrust.org/data).

- The gradual acceptance of commercially produced e-books. With the rising popularity of e-book readers and tablets, the pace of e-book acceptance has quickened in the last two years. In 2012 Amazon e-book sales exceeded sales of both paperback and hardcover books (Malik, 2012). The metadata for these e-books is often produced outside the library cataloguing community and adapted by vendors for use by libraries.

Library cataloguing's role has shifted from a central position to one of many methods supporting resource discovery and delivery on the network. It is important to point out some exceptions to the trends in how mainstream published books and e-books are selected, packaged, and delivered to libraries: metadata creation and dissemination for non-English text, music, video, maps, special collections, images, archives and new formats will likely continue to be resistant to these trends.

Special collections and archives

As more scholarly content moves online and academic libraries license the same or similar e-content packages, individual libraries' online collections become less distinctive. There is also considerable overlap in many legacy print collections. Special collections and archives are what remain most distinctive about library collections. These types of collections are far from being part of the nascent research infrastructure that is emerging on the web. The results presented in a previous section of this chapter suggest that, if special collections of cultural heritage materials were more discoverable online, they would be heavily used.

Unfortunately, improving discoverability and access to special collections and archives is difficult, because many of them are hidden (either not catalogued at all or not represented in online catalogues). A UK study of hidden collections (Loughborough University, Library and Information Statistics Unit and Research Information Network, 2007) found that half of UK research library collections were not represented in online catalogues at the time of the study. Given today's information-seeking preferences, this means these materials may as well not exist. The study's conclusions urged a UK-wide strategy and programme to uncover these hidden collections.

Based on the number of hidden collections documented by a 1998 survey by the Association of Research Libraries (ARL), an ARL task force worked from 2001 to 2006 to advance a seven-point action plan to promote and surface hidden special collections in US libraries (Association of Research Libraries, 2008). Subsequently, in 2008 the US Council on Library and Information Resources (CLIR) began to administer a national effort with the support of the Mellon Foundation, awarding grants to support efficient description and processing of large volumes of hidden special collections material of high value to scholars (www.clir.org/hiddencollections). OCLC Research conducted a study in 2009 to evaluate progress since the 1998 ARL survey (Dooley and Luce, 2010). They found some progress, but not enough. Many still lack any online representation.

Metadata, cataloguing, bibliographic control
Change
Metadata has changed as collections have changed. It remains important, but it comes in many forms and from many sources. The centrality of bibliographic control has been disrupted. It has become just one piece of a large puzzle that must be assembled to provide for discovery and access to changing collections. Discovery and access for online and print books and journals and scholarly articles are supported through metadata supply chains in which libraries are one of many participants. Metadata for providing aggregation, discovery, access and management of e-content and the contents of open access repositories and digital library collections increasingly come from outside traditional library cataloguing environments and co-operative cataloguing systems. As previously noted, there are some exceptions to these trends: (1) currently received non-English texts, music, video, special collections, images, archives and new formats; and (2) hidden collections.

Metadata management
The traditional manual methods of bibliographic control employed in libraries have not easily scaled as scholarly content has moved online and user demand for electronic resources has grown. A transition to a metadata

management approach began in the 1990s, featuring metadata reuse, automated methods and distributed participation in metadata creation and enrichment, including authors and end-users. The new library discovery services are another indication of the transition from bibliographic control to metadata management: they create a common interface through a central index to heterogeneous sources. The most recent example of a metadata management approach is PDA (patron-driven acquisitions), a vendor-assisted workflow that obviates the need for local cataloguing services for these books. Metadata management approaches are variously supported in current co-operative cataloguing systems.

Table 7.1 compares bibliographic control and metadata management practices. In large research libraries, the shift to metadata management (in line with the changes in the right column of the table) has generally occurred in parallel with, rather than as a replacement for, the traditional workflows of bibliographic control. In her extensive literature review of the cataloguing literature of 2009 and 2010, Gardner (2012, 68) poses the question 'To what extent has the cataloging community embraced non-MARC metadata creation and interoperability?' and answers 'not much.'

Table 7.1 *Toward distributed systems for metadata management*

Bibliographic control	Distributed metadata management
• For finding and managing library collections (mostly print)	• For finding and managing many types of materials, for many user communities
• Catalogue records (well understood rules and encoding conventions)	• Many types of records, many sources, disparate treatment
• Shared co-operative cataloguing systems	• Loosely coupled metadata management, reuse and exchange services among multiple repositories
• Usually handcrafted, one record at a time	• Multiple batch creation and metadata extraction, conversion, mapping, ingest and transfer services
• Record creation and editing generally a solitary activity undertaken by library-trained professionals	• Distributed metadata creation and manipulation; dynamic records; digital library metadata – a fundamentally collaborative activity involving various specialists

Wolven (2009), pondering the waning role of traditional cataloguing as the library moves to the web, nevertheless expresses optimism that the library community will 'reach a new consensus on best practices, less grounded in 20th-century publishing patterns.' As the cataloguing community's debate about bibliographic control rages on, downward pressure on library budgets, shrinking cataloguing departments, the search for efficiencies and opportunities for new ways of doing things have continued to propel the shift from traditional cataloguing toward metadata management.

Responses to disruption

Since the new millennium, the disruptive new conditions brought by the internet and web have eroded prior certainties and produced an entire body of reports and articles around the future of catalogues and cataloguing. On behalf of the Library of Congress (LC), this author produced one of these reports (Calhoun, 2006). A number of extensive investigations have produced recommendations (US and UK examples include Library of Congress, Working Group on the Future of Bibliographic Control, 2008; Reynolds et al., 2009; Chad, 2009). Practising cataloguers, technical services managers, and other library professionals have expressed a range of views around implementing the recommendations of these studies, from strong support and calls for action (for example Hruska, 2009; Hruska, 2011) to fervent opposition (for example Bade, 2009). The community discussion so far has not created consensus.

The long development and implementation path of a new cataloguing code, Resource Description and Access (RDA), has not clarified the way forward. At least in the USA, RDA has been a topic of debate. The recommendations of the US RDA Test Coordinating Committee stated 'the test revealed there is little discernible immediate benefit in implementing RDA alone. The adoption of RDA will not result in significant cost savings in metadata creation. There will be inevitable and significant costs in training.' The committee reported the results of a survey of US cataloguers that indicated mixed support for implementation of RDA (Cole et al., 2011, 4–5). For a variety of reasons, the committee did nevertheless recommend that the three US national libraries move ahead with RDA implementation, provided some key issues could be addressed and that implementation begin no sooner than early 2013.

One of the Test Committee's pre-RDA implementation requirements was 'demonstrate credible progress towards a replacement for MARC.' The committee urged the development of a more flexible cataloguing standard that would address the needs of a changing digital environment. In 2011 LC announced it would work with Library and Archives Canada and the British Library on an initiative whose focus would be 'to determine a transition path for the MARC 21 exchange format in order to reap the benefits of newer technology while preserving a robust data exchange that has supported resource sharing and cataloguing cost savings in recent decades' (Library of Congress, 2012a).

LC later announced a Bibliographic Framework Initiative to 'translate the MARC 21 format to a Linked Data (LD) model' (Library of Congress, 2012b). The LC initiative follows an initiative by the British Library to release the British National Bibliography as Linked Data (Wallis, 2011), with the intent to provide opportunities for experimentation among those wanting to interact with bibliographic data in ways that are aligned with web-based practices. While the intentions of these new initiatives are laudable and hold promise for improving the utility and reusability of legacy collections metadata, their focus appears to be limited to how bibliographic and authority data will be modelled, structured and encoded for distribution and consumption on the web. More change is needed than replacing MARC with a Linked Data model. The Framework Initiative as well as the work of the W3C Library Linked Data Incubator Group (www.w3.org/2005/Incubator/lld – see Chapter 6 for more information) appear to be centred primarily on standards, metadata, technical issues and advocacy for a Linked Data approach, while the burning discovery and access issues for research libraries are social (how do scholars and students find the information they need? what roles do and should libraries and library systems play in how they accomplish their work?); economic (what are the costs, what are the benefits of various choices going forward? who pays?); and organizational (how should research libraries be structured to provide for discovery and delivery of content? what partners do and should they have?).

Co-operative cataloguing
Foundations
The co-operative model of bibliographic control has been tremendously successful at supporting the development of local library collections and access to these collections.

Early automated co-operative cataloguing systems carried forward 1960s and 1970s requirements for collection building and access. This was a time when collections were on site and catalogues were (necessarily) separate from but physically available in the same space as the collections. There was no doubt about what the 'collection' was because it was in the building (or buildings), and there was little doubt about what the local catalogue needed to describe.

Co-operative cataloguing today

Co-operative cataloguing databases reflect what library collections once were, not what they have become. For example, the content of the bibliographic database that supports OCLC co-operative cataloguing services represents mainly print-based collections. Most (80 to 85%) of the records in OCLC's bibliographic database describe books (see Figure 7.4 on the next page), and while the proportion of e-book records has grown in recent years, over 90% of the books records still represent printed books (OCLC, 2011, 14). Schuitema (2010), in her review of the history of co-operative cataloguing, concludes that the shared catalogues that libraries have been producing 'while still scalable in terms of providing access to print materials if significant changes were made, will no longer meet the discovery needs of our clientele seeking information in today's expanding digital environment.' A helpful discussion of the OCLC bibliographic database's representation of digital content is available (Lavoie, Connaway, and O'Neill, 2007); however the number of records describing digital content has until recently grown more slowly than searchers' appetites for digital content.

Stores of MARC records

Co-operative cataloguing systems serve principally as sources of MARC records that are copied and reused in local library systems and institution-level catalogues. Several writers (for example Chad, 2009; Eden, 2011; Sellberg, 2010) have questioned the necessity of continuing with this model, which exists to facilitate the duplication of cataloguing data. As scholarship moves to the network level and research library collections change, and as metadata becomes available from numerous sources, the central position of local catalogues produced using traditional cataloguing practices is diminished. Many of the new metadata management approaches described earlier, while making local processing more efficient and less costly, merely perpetuate the current model, which is based on duplicating MARC records in local catalogues.

When MARC and co-operative cataloguing databases of MARC records first emerged, it was necessary to copy the machine-readable records onto

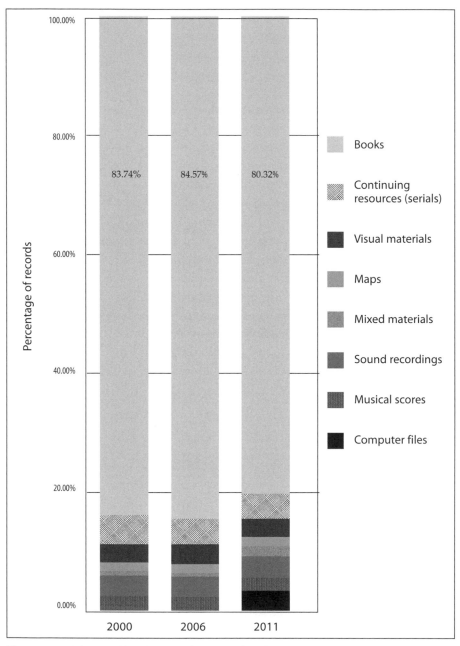

Figure 7.4 *OCLC WorldCat by type of material described, 2000, 2006, 2011. Source: OCLC annual reports (www.oclc.org/en-UK/publications/annual-reports.html)*

some type of physical media – usually cards – because at that time libraries had no online systems in which to store them. Multiple local catalogues representing multiple local collections made sense in the print environment, and the duplicative costs of building and maintaining them were justifiable.

In the mid-1980s, when libraries began to move away from card catalogues toward local online systems, the same practices were carried forward: upon acquiring a new item for the collection, search for a cataloguing record, then copy it for the local system (rather than order a set of catalogue cards). Once a cataloguing record had been obtained, the rest of the work to support discovery, access, and collection management has tended to be done at the institutional level. This set an important precedent and operational model which persisted even as collections moved online in the 1990s; in keeping with the local catalogue model, libraries generally provide for e-content discovery and management locally and redundantly rather than at the network level.

A recent survey of North American MARC record providers, commissioned by LC, provides a fairly complete picture of who produces and distributes MARC cataloguing records in the US and Canada (Fischer and Lugg, 2009) for reuse in local systems. By far the largest North American suppliers are OCLC and LC. The results of Fischer and Lugg's survey also reveals the extent to which vendors have entered the MARC record supply business, notably as sources of MARC records for books but also new types of library materials (e.g. e-books). Ken Chad's study (2009) reveals the flow of bibliographic records and the role of vendors and shared cataloguing aggregators in the UK.

Redundant catalogues

Ken Chad examines the distinction between redundant *cataloguing* (re-editing records to suit local practices) and redundant *catalogues*. Pointing out the duplication of effort required to produce and maintain multiple individual library catalogues, he enumerates the benefits of moving from the UK higher education sector's 160 standalone catalogues to a single shared catalogue at the network level for all of these libraries. Eden (2011) has urged the cataloguing community to turn decisively from its past focus on local operations toward working at the network level.

An option is to move from multiple standalone catalogues to larger shared, co-operative frameworks at the network level that would register many libraries' holdings and be able to feed this information to multiple locations on the web. Such frameworks might operate at a global level or as participating nodes at local, regional or national levels. Roxanne Sellberg (2010), in an article on the future of co-operative cataloguing, writes:

The identity of individual libraries has traditionally been based on locally defined, but highly duplicative, collections. The need to build equally duplicative catalogs has provided incentive for co-operative cataloging. In the future, the collections of libraries will be not so much duplicated as shared, and separate libraries may not have separate public catalogs. Is there a place for co-operative cataloging in such a future?

Sellberg observes that collections are now more web-based and advocates that the library community work together to build a worldwide shared catalogue on the network. This worldwide catalogue would be fundamentally different from today's co-operative cataloguing databases. Her recommendations for creatively reshaping co-operative cataloguing systems include:

- reorganizing such systems around metadata that individual libraries can point to (or from) instead of copy
- providing better functionality to enable the contribution of metadata for rare and unique library holdings
- offering additional support for contributing metadata for born-digital information resources not well covered by other players in the scholarly information space.

Rethinking
Bibliographic control

Scholarship has moved online, and the universe of information objects of potential interest to scholars and students can never again be captured as part of a single research library's collection. In this fundamentally changed world of scholarship, the role of bibliographic control has been diminished and marginalized. There is less need and place for traditional bibliographic control as a set of methods for providing for discovery, access and management of the content of mainstream books and serials. For other types of digital objects, there are other sources of metadata (or other techniques based on crawling and/or indexing) that are better suited for and less costly to use in a web environment.

Even if other sources of metadata and techniques were not available, the manual and semi-automated methods of bibliographic control have not and will not scale to the size of the new universe of scholarly information objects. It is unreasonable to think that even enhanced methods of bibliographic control could support the discovery, delivery and management of this wider array of objects. As for legacy bibliographic data, experimentation with repackaging and distributing it as Linked Data for consumption by web services is of interest and worth pursuing; however, such experimentation is unlikely to address the fundamental issue that, going forward, the techniques of bibliographic control have diminished utility in a transformed world of research and learning.

The library community already takes advantage of other metadata supply chains for journal articles and other types of scholarly information objects. This chapter suggests that the library community consider the feasibility of turning away from the traditional methods of bibliographic control for mainstream books and journals in favour of methods used in the book industry and scholarly publishing.

Bibliographic control would continue to have a role: creating metadata for unique content that is unlikely to be described any other way. As noted earlier, some types of content are resistant to the trends around metadata for mainstream published books and journals (electronic and print): for example non-English text, music, video, maps, special collections, images and archives. In addition, many hidden collections containing unique content remain to be described using more traditional methods of bibliographic or archival control. It would be tremendously useful if effort now tied up in building and maintaining redundant local catalogues could be freed up and systematically applied to improve the discoverability and management of these types of unique non-digital content.

Registries of library holdings

Arguably, what is most important about the data stored in local catalogues is the holdings information – not the bibliographic data. In information systems consisting of brief metadata disconnected from content (such as bibliographic descriptions), what the information seeker usually wants to know is the location of the content and how to get it. This chapter proposes that the library community consider the feasibility of a set of network-level registries of library holdings information that would serve the functions now provided by local catalogues. This set of registries could allow the library community to free itself from the necessity of redundant catalogues (and redundant discovery layers that rely on the existence of copies of bibliographic records in redundant integrated library systems).

Registries are already widely used on the web. Google Scholar is already close to functioning, in practice, as a 'registry' of library holdings for scholarly articles. Further, OCLC and Google already have an agreement to provide a 'Find in a library' service from Google Books. This service needs further enhancement to make it more functional, usable and visible, but in effect it is a registry of many libraries' holdings of books. E-journal 'A to Z' lists are produced from a data set or knowledge base that functions as a registry of the e-journals to which a particular library has access. Through collaborative action and partnerships, research libraries could feasibly move to registry-based systems. While there is some risk that Google's interest in Google Scholar and Google Books will not persist, it would be a pity if library-supported registries were not integrated with what Google Scholar and Google Books already do. These registries would point from cloud-based discovery services to what libraries hold (or license, or want to point to), as suggested by Sellberg. Web services-enabled registry services could be the basis of a range of cloud-based library services that would obviate the need for copy cataloguing as well as the local catalogue in its current form. Instead of downloading a copy of a record (or obtaining copies of records for loading into a local system) as libraries do now, they would register their holdings of new titles (or sets of titles) that they want to make accessible to the communities they serve.

Standards

Collections of value to scholarship (and their metadata) are diverse and widely distributed in multiple digital and non-digital stores. Libraries have generally approached the challenge of providing coherent access to diverse, distributed content by agreeing on and implementing library-specific standards and using metadata to achieve integration and enable data exchange. These measures have worked well to the degree that everyone complies with the standards; implements them in the same way; and not only uses metadata, but also uses types of metadata that can be crosswalked or converted. These methods have not been widely adopted outside the library community. They have been perceived as more complex than the generally simpler, lighter-weight approaches used by many web developers (and increasingly by open access repository developers, as will be discussed shortly).

Building for the web

It is possible that the time has come for new approaches that are built on and for the web. The new global research infrastructure that is emerging to support digital scholarship operates on the network; it deploys standards, protocols and methods native to the internet and web. Any new research library service frameworks would need to be built the same way. Such frameworks need to be web services-enabled, support collaboration and user community engagement, and provide for easy and open data reuse and sharing. Semantic Web approaches may provide part of needed solutions and tools, but all hopes should not be pinned on them, as they are relatively untested. A number of avenues, methods and means should be explored.

Enlarged roles for open access repositories

Open access repositories have become increasingly important for responding to changes in scholarly communications and improving the discoverability and accessibility of scholarly information. In keeping with US and other national policy changes related to publications from grant-funded research, they are expected to become increasingly important components of research infrastructure (Borgman, 2007, 243). They have potential for becoming key building blocks in frameworks supporting e-research data (for further discussion of e-research and repositories see for example Michener et al., 2011; for research library roles in e-research and data management see for example Soehner, Steeves and Ward, 2010).

Emerging, next-generation open access repositories are built on and for the web. They manage, reuse, repurpose and share/disseminate heterogeneous content and metadata. Interesting starting points for further discussion might be generated from work being done in the Hydra Project (Green and Awre, 2009) and to advance ORE (Object Reuse and Exchange; Lagoze et al., 2008; Witt 2010) and SWORD (Simple Web-service Offering Repository Deposit; Lewis, de Castro and Jones, 2012). Both the Hydra Project and ORE feature Semantic Web methods (data models and encoding). The Australian Research Data Commons (described at http://ands.org.au) is another potential source of ideas: the Commons enables flows for depositing and disclosing content and metadata for reuse and integration in a variety of locations: institutional and domain-specific portals, national services and search engines (Burton and Treloar, 2009).

The contents of repositories are usually crawled by search engines and so are highly visible on the web. Google Scholar indexes and provides links to both licensed and open access versions of articles in search results when possible. The potential and feasibility of replacing the current redundant framework of multiple local catalogues with a network of better integrated open access repositories, tied to a larger co-operative infrastructure of 'participating nodes' (as defined by Van de Sompel et al.) should be explored. The research library community and its partners have the opportunity to consider substantially different, collectively supported, network-level services that enhance the positive impact and visibility of scholarly content, using a set of loosely connected participating nodes – open access repositories – as a starting point. A later section and Figure 7.5 on page 167 explore one possibility for how such a framework of services might be tied together.

A library co-operative commons

The notion of displacing multiple library catalogues with a more centralized system or radically different frameworks has been suggested before (for example Coffman, 1999; Bell, 2003; El-Sherbini and Wilson, 2007). Coffman's proposal for 'earth's largest library' in particular set off a storm of controversy (see for example Napier and Smith, 2000). Yet it seems important to consider at this point that local and union library catalogues are not ends in themselves; they are means. When collections change significantly, and information seekers' preferences change, it is necessary to evaluate the means for managing collections and providing discovery, access and preservation. As for research libraries, it seems important to articulate a new, shared strategy for their roles supporting scholarship and learning, a role that otherwise seems well on the way to disintermediation.

Perhaps conditions have now changed enough for research libraries to begin a new conversation. The global scholarly research infrastructure is emerging; however, progress toward aligning research library service frameworks with new scholarship has been largely incremental and reactive. Nevertheless, pieces of a new research library service framework already exist, and it may prove feasible to further develop this framework using registries and other web-based techniques. The purpose would be to enable the drawing of virtual boundaries on the network that define 'holdings' (digital and non-digital, licensed and open access) of interest to scholars and students. These are not wholly new ideas. In particular, Dempsey anticipated by years the immense impact of network-level discovery environments on local and shared library catalogues. Among many other thoughts about how to develop library systems in a network environment, he expressed early interest in system-wide registries as ways of re-connecting network-level discovery to library fulfilment without placing additional burden on local library development (Dempsey, 2006, under 'Routing').

Much attention has recently been focused on the possibilities for cloud-based library systems that will allow libraries to replace their local library systems with web-based applications that are accessed via common web browsers and whose infrastructure is supported in the cloud (see Chapter 3 and Breeding, 2012 for more information). Since these offerings are so new, it is difficult to predict how libraries will respond, but it seems clear that there will be a role for cloud-based platforms in renewed frameworks for library operations and library co-operative cataloguing. One question is whether the cloud-based library systems now in development, testing or early adoption phase have been or are being designed with the changing requirements of digital scholarship in mind. It would be a missed opportunity if they merely carry forward current library system functionality (acquisitions, inventory control, collection management, holdings maintenance, etc.) for mainly online and print book and journals plus licensed aggregator packages of licensed articles.

A recombinant, cloud-based service framework

Lavoie, Henry and Dempsey (2006) wrote of the need for a 'service framework' or shared view of how library services should be organized in a radically changed information landscape. They called for 'reusable, recombinant, and interoperable library services.' Subsequent sections of this chapter lay out some possibilities for two components of a new service framework for consideration. The first component is a set of recombined, interoperable open access repositories managed by research libraries; these would operate as 'participating nodes' in the framework. The second component is a cloud-based set of services and registries – one or more library co-operative commons platforms? – that provide interoperability across participating nodes at local, regional, national and global levels. The intent of both is to create a new, network-level research library service framework that aligns and integrates well with network-level scholarly infrastructure and better supports research library roles in 21st century research, teaching and learning.

Why a new role for open access repositories? Open access repositories already operate on the network and their contents and metadata are crawled and indexed by search engines. Next-generation open access repositories are beginning to emerge. Fundamentally, their purpose is to support scholarship as it is now practised, disseminated and discovered on the web. They are designed to support researchers and to engage the scholarly communities they serve, so they have both user and machine interfaces to support deposit (including deposit in multiple stores of content and metadata). Research libraries might also use them (some already do) to enter the content and/or metadata for digitized, digital or non-digital special collections – instead of putting the metadata in local catalogues or other systems that can't be crawled, harvested and integrated in other discovery services. Metadata for unique hidden collections could also be ingested or entered manually in repositories for disclosure and registration.

As envisioned, in addition to open access repositories, new library co-operative commons services would be essential components of a cloud-based, virtual research library service framework. The commons services would help to tie the repositories loosely together, ingesting unique metadata or content, registering library holdings or other information, and dispersing and/or exchanging data with other nodes or services in the framework.

Considered as a whole, the service framework's purposes would include promoting the sharing of knowledge; enabling researcher and student engagement, participation, content exchange and collaboration; and reducing the time required for scholars and students to identify and gain access to needed information. The objectives of such a framework would include helping research libraries to progress open access to scholarly outputs; extend their institutional roles supporting the infrastructure of digital scholarship; promote the visibility and use of unique collections; and free up local resources for investment in new priorities.

One possibility among many

Figure 7.5 attempts to provide a functional view of one possibility for a new research library service framework from the perspective of one 'participating node' (repository). The figure attempts to depict a hypothetical framework that loosely connects and recombines locally created content and metadata deposited in next-generation, institutionally based open access repositories with other aggregations and/or repositories at various levels (domain-specific,

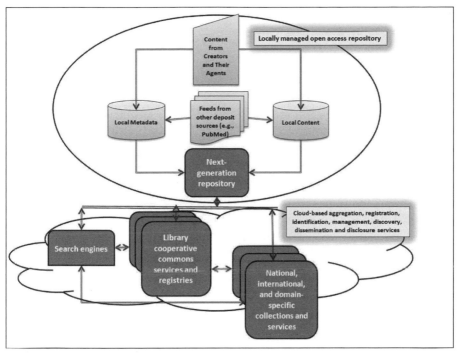

Figure 7.5 *A hypothetical service framework for research libraries*

regional, national, international); search engines; and one or more library co-operative commons. These local next-generation repositories would take the place of local catalogues and expand the catalogue's functions. Within this hypothetical framework, unique (new) content and/or metadata can come from content creators or their agents (one type of agent could be a cataloguer or metadata specialist) or from a variety of feeds from other repositories or aggregations. A current example of this kind of workflow is described by Duranceau and Rodgers (2010), who report on an experiment to enable automated deposit of their university's faculty papers into the university's institutional repository when these papers are first deposited elsewhere. The locally managed repository would also support the registration of library holdings in a variety of network-level services, including one or more library co-operative commons.

In this hypothetical framework, the role of a library co-operative commons is to provide cloud-based services supporting:

- local library collection-centred activities (acquisitions; inventory control;

licensing; registration of holdings, e.g. for non-unique content; circulation; preservation; digitization)
- services that promote the visibility and reuse of digital scholarship (including, for example, e-research data)
- services and registries that tie the infrastructure together, provide interoperability, and integrate work done across participating nodes (e.g. other locally managed repositories).

Registries and identifier services would play a key role in this hypothetical framework, as they would be the means for (1) registering library holdings, thus enabling libraries to move toward *sharing* metadata instead of *copying* it locally, (2) tracking hidden collections and promoting their processing and (3) providing more efficient means for linking and pointing to content. There could be other types of registries or knowledge bases in addition to registries of library holdings, as discussed by Dempsey (2012).

The idea for this figure came from an illustration describing the infrastructure supporting Research Data Australia, a network-based service that connects data, projects and researchers across organizations and promotes the visibility of Australian e-research data nationally and in search engines (Australian National Data Service, 2012). Figure 7.5 is not an architectural view and makes no attempt to comment on how content and metadata are actually stored or how the infrastructure works from a technical perspective. It merely sketches one hypothetical possibility from an institution-level processing or workflow point of view.

Conclusions

Atkinson's control zone has not and will not emerge as he anticipated it could. Nevertheless pieces of the control zone have come to exist in the form of:

- Google Scholar and Google Books
- an informal network of subject-based and institutional open access repositories; plus
- a number of national and international-level digital libraries of cultural heritage materials.

It is not too late for research libraries to lay claim to the scholarly control zone – or at least to participate more strategically and intentionally in the pieces of the network-level scholarly research infrastructure that have already emerged. Should research libraries and their partners choose to engage collectively in these emergent research infrastructures, they could reclaim now fully or partially disintermediated roles supporting research, teaching and learning, for example:

- promoting the visibility and recognition of valuable collections and scholarship on the web
- engaging more actively with scholars and students
- reducing the time required to identify and gain access to needed information.

This chapter advocates a fundamental rethinking of the apparatus (service framework) that research libraries now deploy to support scholarship. Today's local library systems and catalogues, regional and union catalogues and co-operative cataloguing systems collectively constitute key components of a service framework that was useful when print collections stood at the centre of scholarship and traditional library methods for providing discovery and access were sufficient. To continue to focus solely on improving this long-successful service framework (and on bibliographic control alone) implies a choice to limit the role of research libraries to supporting a subset of the information environment, leading eventually to a diminished role in higher education, scholarly communication and cultural heritage.

Open access repositories, while they have their own challenges, look to the future and have great potential for directly engaging scholars and students and for supporting scholarship as it has become. This chapter calls for an exploration of the possibilities for a new, network-level research library service framework – one that features a substantially larger role for open access repositories. This chapter proposes that 'catalogue 2.0' is not a catalogue at all, but a participating node (a repository) in a new library service framework for supporting scholarship and learning.

The challenges that the research library community now face have some similarities to what the computer and information science communities regarded as opportunities in the early and mid-1990s. Atkinson was writing about the control zone in an identifiable context (before the launch of Google in 1998), at a time when digital library pioneers were pursuing a vision of 'tens of thousands of repositories of digital information that are autonomously managed yet integrated into what users view as a coherent digital library system' (Lynch and Garcia-Molina, 1995, under Executive Summary section III).

Atkinson concluded his 2006 conference paper with the thought that 'none of these challenges can be met by research libraries working independently. They can only be confronted collectively.' There is reason for optimism if the research library community collectively re-examines the early vision of thousands of interconnected repositories and identifies what elements of that vision are relevant today. Thanks to 20 years' work on digital libraries and repositories, many more tools, knowledge and expertise are available now to assemble a more coherent scholarly research infrastructure to which research libraries can substantively contribute. What is lacking is, on the one hand, the collective will to begin, and on the other, a commitment to face unequivocally forward, fully embracing an approach that builds on and for the web.

Questions

The previous sections lay out one possibility among many for consideration. Whether or not the ideas sketched in the previous sections prove worthy of further thought, a collective forum or series of forums that bring stakeholders together could explore a range of new ideas for collaboration and collective action. Nine questions that might be considered in such a forum or forums follow. Some of them have been asked before or in different forms; others are new. They are offered to stimulate further research library community discussions about the future of bibliographic control, cataloguing and catalogues, co-operative cataloguing systems, and how all of these relate to digital scholarship and research libraries' missions.

Nine questions to consider

1 Web-based discovery and access methods generally use fully automated processing and low-barrier standards. In comparison, library cataloguing tends to be more complex. Do the benefits of library cataloguing, as it is currently practised, still justify its additional costs? Are there other methods, better integrated with web practices and metadata supply chains, that are already being used or that could be further developed to meet the needs of researchers, instructors and students?
2 The traditions of book cataloguing have stood apart from the practices of publishers and booksellers. Should these traditions and practices

continue to exist and evolve separately? Might national libraries with responsibility for legal deposit programmes directly use metadata from other participants in the metadata supply chain for books?

3 Co-operative cataloguing systems are large stores of MARC records from which cataloguers download copies for separate local catalogues. Are there other means to achieve the same ends? What would it take to move to sharing records/holdings information at the network level as opposed to copying records for local use?

4 How might current or future co-operative cataloguing systems provide for e-content discovery and management at the network level so that investments in redundant local infrastructures and costs (e.g. for local instances of e-resource management systems and knowledge bases, duplicative purchases of MARC record sets for e-content, etc.) might be recouped?

5 In what ways might current or future co-operative cataloguing systems provide additional incentives or more support for efficiently creating and enriching resource descriptions of unique or hidden materials?

6 In what ways might current or future co-operative systems raise awareness and stimulate more use of library print collections?

7 What roles might network-level, web services-enabled registries and/or knowledge bases (e.g. for holdings, work sets, persistent identifiers, researcher names, etc.) play in current or future co-operative library systems?

8 In what ways might today's co-operative cataloguing systems be altered to help research libraries advance their roles supporting scholarship?

9 How might a new library service framework blend with the information-seeking practices and preferences of scholars and students, attracting their attention and helping them to get their work done? What are the best ways to reach out to, engage with and include scholars and students in future research library conversations about local services, domain-specific services, regional or national services, and/or new library co-operative commons services?

Acknowledgements

This paper is a personal commentary, and all opinions and any errors are the responsibility of the author. It includes rewritten and substantially expanded portions of an earlier short paper, which grew out of a strategic analysis undertaken in 2009 with OCLC colleagues John Chapman, Ted Fons, Glenn Patton, Renee Register, Bob Van Volkenburg and David Whitehair. That early paper was translated into Japanese by Hisako Kotaka and published two years ago in a Japanese information science journal (Calhoun, 2010). The author is grateful for these colleagues' contributions to the early paper and for the opportunity that Sally Chambers provided to update and rewrite it for this book.

References

Anderson, R. (2011) Print on the Margins: circulation trends in major research libraries, *Library Journal*,
http://web.archive.org/web/20110607210432/http://www.libraryjournal.com/lj/home/890835-264/print-on-the-margins-circulation.html.csp.

Association of Research Libraries (2008) *Special Collections Task Force Final Status Report, 2006*,
http://web/archive.org/web/20130126120219/http://www.arl.org/rtl/speccoll/spcolltf/status0706.shtml.

Atkinson, R. (1996) Library Functions, Scholarly Communication, and the Foundation of the Digital Library: laying claim to the control zone, *Library Quarterly*, 239–65.

Atkinson, R. (2006) Six Key Challenges for the Future of Collection Development, *Library Resources & Technical Services*, **50** (4), 244–51.

Australian National Data Service (ANDS) (2012), *Australian National Data Service Brochure*, http://ands.org.au/ands-brochure-12-web.pdf.

Bade, D. (2009) *Irresponsible Librarianship: a critique of the report of the Library of Congress Working Group on the Future of Bibliographic Control and thoughts on how to proceed*, http://eprints.rclis.org/bitstream/10760/12804/1/MOUG_2009.pdf.

Bell, M. E. (2003) *Human Interaction at Earth's Largest Library: the current state of a global information infrastructure design*, unpublished manuscript,
http://syndeticsystems.com/Bell%20-%20Human%20Interaction%20At%20Earth's%20Largest%20Library.pdf.

Björk, B-C., Roos, A. and Lauri, M. (2009) Scientific Journal Publishing–Yearly Volume and Open Access Availability, *Information Research*, **14** (1), 391.

Björk, B-C., Welling, P., Laakso M., Majlender, P., Hedlund, T. and Guðnason, G. (2010) Open Access to the Scientific Journal Literature: situation 2009, *PLoS ONE*, **5** (6), (June), doi:10.1371/journal.pone.0011273,
www.plosone.org/article/info%3Adoi%2F10.1371%2Fjournal.pone.0011273.

Borgman, C. L. (2007) *Scholarship in the Digital Age*, MIT Press.

Breeding, M. (2012) Automation Marketplace 2012: agents of change, blog entry in *The Digital Shift*, 29 March, www.thedigitalshift.com/2012/03/ils/automation-marketplace-2012-agents-of-change.

Burton, A. and Treloar A. (2009) Publish My Data: a composition of services from ANDS and ARCS. In *Fifth IEEE International Conference on e-Science*, 164–70, http://ieeexplore.ieee.org/xpls/abs_all.jsp?arnumber=5380872.

Calhoun, K. (2006) *The Changing Nature of the Catalog and Its Integration with Other Discovery Tools*, Washington DC, Library of Congress, www.loc.gov/catdir/calhoun-report-final.pdf.

Calhoun, K. (2010) Rethinking Bibliographic Control in the Web Environment, (trans. Hisako Kotaka), *Joho no kagaku to gijutsu (Journal of Information Science and Technology Association)*, **60** (9), 378–83.

Calhoun, K. (2011) *Library Process Redesign: renewing services, changing workflows*, presented in February at Cambridge University Library, www.slideshare.net/amarintha/library-process-redesign-renewing-services-changing-workflows.

Chad, K. (2009) *Creating Catalogues: bibliographic records in a networked world. A Research Information Network Report*, Research Information Network, http://rinarchive.jisc-collections.ac.uk/our-work/using-and-accessing-information-resources/creating-catalogues-bibliographic-records-network.

CIBER (2009) *E-Journals: their use, value and impact. A Research Information Network Report*, Research Information Network, www.rin.ac.uk/our-work/communicating-and-disseminating-research/e-journals-their-use-value-and-impact.

Coffman, S. (1999) Building Earth's Largest Library: driving into the future, *Searcher*, **7** (3), 34–47, www.fileformat.info/other/library/coffman_mar99.pdf.

Cole, C., Marrill, J., Boehr, D., McCutcheon, D. and Wiggins, B. (2011) *Report and Recommendations of the U.S. RDA Test Coordinating Committee*, www.loc.gov/bibliographic-future/rda/source/rdatesting-finalreport-20june2011.pdf.

Cox, J. and Cox, L. (2008) *Scholarly Publishing Practice: academic journal publishers' policies and practices in online publishing*, Brighton, UK, Association of Learned and Professional Society Publishers.

Dempsey, L. (2006) The Library Catalogue in the New Discovery Environment: some thoughts, *Ariadne* **48** (4), www.ariadne.ac.uk/issue48/dempsey.

Dempsey, L. (2012) *Linking not Typing . . . Knowledge Organization at the Network Level*, blog entry in Lorcan Dempsey's Weblog, 1 January, http://orweblog.oclc.org/archives/002195.html.

De Rosa, C. (2005) *Perceptions of Libraries and Information Resources: a report to the OCLC membership*, Dublin, OH, OCLC Online Computer Library Center, www.oclc.org/reports/2005perceptions.en.html.

De Rosa, C., Cantrell, J., Carlson, M. and Gallagher, P. (2011) *Perceptions of Libraries, 2010: context and community. Report to the OCLC Membership.* Dublin, OH, OCLC Online Computer Library Center, www.oclc.org/reports/2010perceptions.en.html.

Dooley, J. M. and Luce, K. (2010) *Taking Our Pulse: the OCLC Research survey of special collections and archives*, Dublin, OH, OCLC Research, www.oclc.org/content/dam/research/publications/library/2010/2010-11.pdf.

Duranceau, E. F. and Rodgers, R. (2010) Automated IR Deposit via the SWORD Protocol: an MIT/BioMed Central experiment, *Serials: The Journal for the Serials Community*, **23** (3), 212–14, http://uksg.metapress.com/content/l437x1631052407r/fulltext.pdf.

Eden, B. (2011) *The Status Quo Has Got To Go*, presented at the Charleston Conference, 8 November, www.slideshare.net/CharlestonConference/the-status-quo-has-got-to-go-by-brad-eden-dean-of-library-services-valparaiso-university-sat-930-am.

El-Sherbini, M. and Wilson, A. J. (2007) New Strategies for Delivering Library Resources to Users: rethinking the mechanisms in which libraries are processing and delivering bibliographic records, *Journal of Academic Librarianship*, **33** (2), 228–42.

Fischer, R. and Lugg, R. (2009) *Study of the North American MARC Records Marketplace*, R2 Consulting, www.loc.gov/bibliographic-future/news/MARC_Record_Marketplace_2009-10.pdf.

Gardner, S. A. (2012) Cresting Toward the Sea Change, *Library Resources & Technical Services*, **56** (2), 64.

Green, R. and Awre, C. (2009) Towards a Repository-enabled Scholar's Workbench, *D-Lib Magazine*, **15** (5/6), (May), doi:10.1045/may2009-green, http://dlib.org/dlib/may09/green/05green.html.

Guenther, R. and Radebaugh, J. (2004) *Understanding Metadata*, Bethesda, MD, NISO Press, www.niso.org/publications/press/UnderstandingMetadata.pdf.

Hampton-Reeves, S., Mashiter, C. , Westaway, J. , Lumsden, P., Day, H. and Hewertson, H. (2009) *Students' Use of Research Content in Teaching and Learning: a Report for the Joint Information Systems Council (JISC)*, University of Central Lancashire, Centre for Research-Informed Teaching, http://ie-repository.jisc.ac.uk/407/1/Students_Use_of_Research_Content.pdf.

Henry, C., Spiro, L., Henry, G., Courant, P., Nielsen, M., Smith, K. and Schonfeld, R.

C. (2011) *The Idea of Order: transforming research collections for 21st century scholarship*, Washington, DC, Council on Library and Information Resources, www.clir.org/pubs/reports/pub147/reports/pub147/pub147.pdf.

Hruska, M. (2009) Where Are We With the Staffing Transition from Cataloging to Metadata Management?, *Technicalities*, **29** (2) (1 April), 1.

Hruska, M. (2011) Is It the Next Generation Yet?, *Technicalities*, **31** (4) (1 July), 1.

Laakso, M., Welling, P., Bukvova, H., Nyman, L., Björk, B.-C. and Hedlund, T. (2011) The Development of Open Access Journal Publishing from 1993 to 2009, *PLoS ONE*, **6** (6), doi:10.1371/journal.pone.0020961, www.plosone.org/article/info:doi/10.1371/journal.pone.0020961.

Lagoze, C., Van de Sompel, H., Nelson, M. L., Warner, S., Sanderson, R. and Johnston, P. (2008) Object Re-Use and Exchange: a resource-centric approach, *arXiv*: 0804.2273 (14 April), http://arxiv.org/abs/0804.2273.

Lavoie, B., Connaway, L. S. and O'Neill, E. T. (2007) Mapping WorldCat's Digital Landscape, *Library Resources & Technical Services*, **51** (2), 106–15.

Lavoie, B., Henry, G. and Dempsey, L. (2006) A Service Framework for Libraries, *D-Lib Magazine*, **12** (7/8) (July), doi:10.1045/july2006-lavoie, www.dlib.org/dlib/july06/lavoie/07lavoie.html.

Lewis, D. W. (2013) From Stacks to the Web: the transformation of academic library collecting, *College & Research Libraries* (forthcoming).

Lewis, S., de Castro, P. and Jones, R. (2012) SWORD: facilitating deposit scenarios, *D-Lib* Magazine, **18** (1/2) (January), doi:10.1045/january2012-lewis, www.dlib.org/dlib/january12/lewis/01lewis.html.

Library of Congress (2012a) *Bibliographic Framework Transition Initiative*, www.loc.gov/bibframe.

Library of Congress (2012b) *The Library of Congress Announces Modeling Initiative (May 22, 2012): Bibliographic Framework Transition Initiative (Library of Congress)*, www.loc.gov/bibframe/news/bibframe-052212.html.

Library of Congress, Working Group on the Future of Bibliographic Control (2008) *On the Record: report of the Library of Congress Working Group on the Future of Bibliographic Control*, Washington, DC, Library of Congress, www.loc.gov/bibliographic-future/news/lcwg-ontherecord-jan08-final.pdf.

Loughborough University, Library and Information Statistics Unit, and Research Information Network (2007) *Uncovering Hidden Resources: progress in extending the coverage of online catalogues: report of a study undertaken for the Research Information Network*, London, Research Information Network, http://rinarchive.jisc-collections.ac.uk/our-work/using-and-accessing-information-resources/uncovering-hidden-resources-extending-coverage-on.

Luther, M. J., National Information Standards Organization (US) and OCLC (2009) *Streamlining Book Metadata Workflow*, Baltimore, MD and Dublin, OH, NISO and OCLC, Inc., www.niso.org/publications/white_papers/ StreamlineBookMetadataWorkflowWhitePaper.pdf.

Lynch, C. and Garcia-Molina, H. (1995) *Interoperability, Scaling, and the Digital Libraries Research Agenda: a Report on the May 18-19, 1995, IITA Digital Libraries Workshop*, www.sis.pitt.edu/~repwkshop/papers/DL1995.pdf.

Malik, S. (2012) Kindle Ebook Sales Have Overtaken Amazon Print Sales, Says Book Seller, *The Guardian*, 5 August, www.guardian.co.uk/books/2012/aug/06/ amazon-kindle-ebook-sales-overtake-print.

Malpas, C. (2011) *Cloud-sourcing Research Collections: managing print in the mass-digitized library environment*, Dublin, OH, OCLC, Inc., http://dcommon.bu.edu/xmlui/handle/2144/1391.

Michener, W., Vieglais, D., Vision, T., Kunze, J., Cruse, P. and Janée, G. (2011) DataONE: Data Observation Network for Earth – preserving data and enabling innovation in the biological and environmental sciences, *D-Lib Magazine*, **17** (1/2) (January), doi:10.1045/january2011-michener, www.dlib.org/dlib/january11/michener/01michener.html.

Napier, M. E. and Smith, K. A. (2000) *Earth's Largest Library – Panacea or Anathema? A socio-technical analysis*, Bloomington, IN, Center for Social Informatics, Indiana University, https://scholarworks.iu.edu/dspace/handle/2022/165.

Nitecki, D., Jones, C. and Barnett, J. (2009) Borrow Direct: a decade of a sustained quality book-lending service, *Interlending & Document Supply*, **37** (4) (13 November), 192–8, doi:10.1108/02641610911006283; www.emeraldinsight.com/journalshtm?articleid=1827186.

Norris, M., Oppenheim, C. and Rowland, F. (2008) Finding Open Access Articles Using Google, Google Scholar, OAIster and OpenDOAR, *Online Information Review*, **32** (6), 709–15.

OCLC Online Computer Library Center (2011) *OCLC Annual Report 2010/2011*, OCLC, www.oclc.org/content/dam/oclc/publications/AnnualReports/2010/2011.pdf.

Payne, L. (2007) *Library Storage Facilities and the Future of Print Collections in North America*, Dublin, OH, OCLC Programs and Research, www.oclc.org/content/dam/research/publications/library/2007/2007.pdf.

Reynolds, R. R., Knarr, B., Library of Congress, On the Record Report Implementation Working Group, and Library of Congress, Library Services (2009) *On the Record: report Recommendations the Library of Congress should pursue over the next four years report to the associate librarian for library services*, www.loc.gov/bibliographic-future/news/OTR_rep_response_final_091509.pdf.

Schonfeld, R. C. and Guthrie, K. M. (2007) The Changing Information Services Needs of Faculty, *EDUCAUSE Review*, **42** (4), 8.

Schonfeld, R. C. and Housewright, R. (2010) *Faculty Survey 2009: key strategic insights for libraries, publishers, and societies*, Ithaka, www.sr.ithaka.org/research-publications/us-faculty-survey-2009.

Schuitema, J. E. (2010) The Future of Cooperative Cataloging: curve, fork, or impasse?, *Cataloging & Classification Quarterly*, **48** (2–3) (10 February), 258–70, doi:10.1080/01639370903536088, www.tandfonline.com/doi/abs/10.1080/01639370903536088.

Sellberg, R. (2010) Cooperative Cataloging in a Post-OPAC World, *Cataloging & Classification Quarterly*, **48** (2–3), 237–46.

Soehner, C., Steeves, C. and Ward, J. (2010) *E-Science and Data Support Services: a study of ARL member institutions*, Washington, DC, Association of Research Libraries.

University Leadership Council (2011) *Redefining the Academic Library: managing the migration to digital information services*, Washington, DC, Education Advisory Board, www.eab.com/Research-and-Insights/Academic-Affairs-Forum/Studies/2011/Redefining-the-academic-library.

Van de Sompel, H., Payette, S., Erickson, J., Lagoze, C. and Warner, S. (2004) Rethinking Scholarly Communication, *D-Lib Magazine*, **10** (9) (September), doi:10.1045/september2004-vandesompel, www.dlib.org/dlib/september04/vandesompel/09vandesompel.html.

Wallis, R. (2011) Significant Bibliographic Data Release from the British Library, *Data Liberate blog*, 14 July 2011, http://dataliberate.com/2011/07/significant-bibliographic-linked-data-release-from-the-british-library/.

Wilson, A. J. (2007) Toward Releasing the Metadata Bottleneck, *Library Resources & Technical Services*, **51** (1), 16–28.

Witt, M. (2010) Chapter 4: implementations of ORE, *Library Technology Reports*, **46** (4), 26–34.

Wolven, R. (2009) Cataloging Without Silos, or, Where Do We Go From Here?, *Technicalities*, **29** (5) (September/October), 1, 6–9.

Zillman, M. P. (2012) *Deep Web Research 2012*, www.deepwebresearch.info.

8

Thirteen ways of looking at libraries, discovery and the catalogue: scale, workflow, attention

Lorcan Dempsey

Introduction

There is a renaissance of interest in the catalogue. This volume is evidence of that. Yet it comes at a time when the catalogue itself is being reconfigured in ways which may result in its disappearance as an individually identifiable component of library service.[1]

This is because the context of information use and creation has changed, as it transitions from a world of physical distribution to one of digital distribution. In parallel, our focus shifts from the local (the library or the bookshop or . . .) to the network as a whole. We turn to Google, or to Amazon, or to Expedia, or to the BBC. Think of two trends in a network environment, which I term here the **attention switch** and the **workflow switch**. Each has implications for the catalogue, as it pushes the potential catalogue user in other directions. Each also potentially recasts the role of the catalogue in the overall information value chain.

The catalogue as an identifiable service

The catalogue emerged at a time when information resources were scarce and attention was abundant. Scarce because there were relatively few sources for particular documents or research materials: they were distributed in print, collected in libraries and were locally available. If you wanted to consult books or journals or research reports or maps or government documents you went to the library. However, the situation is now reversed: information resources are abundant and attention is scarce. The network user has many information resources available to him or her on the network. Research and learning materials may be available through many services, and there is no need for physical proximity. Furthermore, users often turn first to the major network level hubs which scale to provide access to what is visible across the whole network (think for example of Google, Wikipedia, Amazon, PubMed . . .). This is natural as interest gravitates to the more complete resource rather than a local selection, which seems increasingly partial. Studies show the high value placed on convenience and the importance of satisficing: users do not want to spend a long time prospecting for information resources.[2]

The second trend is related. In an environment of scarce information resources and physical access, users would build their workflow around the library. This centrality was visible in the corresponding centrality of library buildings on campus or in communities. However, on the network, we increasingly expect services to be built around our workflows. And this has led to resources being designed to be present to us in multiple ways. Think of the variety of ways in which the BBC, Netflix or Amazon tries to reach its users, and the variety of experiences – or workflow integrations – they offer. Think of the Whispersynch feature of the Kindle for example, which allows a continuous reading experience across multiple network entry points (phones, tablets, PCs, e-reader, etc). Or think of the multiple ways in which the BBC or Netflix makes programming available (website, iPlayer, Apps . . .).

The catalogue has been an institutional resource. How does it operate in this network environment? Some trends have been to make the data work harder (facets, FRBR, etc.), syndicating data to other environments (learning management, Google Book Search . . .), developing apps, widgets and toolbars to move the catalogue closer to the workflow.

At the same time the catalogue itself may give way to other environments which may deploy catalogue data. An important case is discovery across the whole library collection, not just the 'catalogued' material. Another is the desire to see catalogue resources represented in higher level 'group' services (e.g. OhioLink, German Verbundkataloge, Copac) and in web-scale services (WorldCat, Google . . .). Another is to reuse catalogue data in personal and institutional curation environments (resource guides, reading lists, citation managers, social reading sites . . .).

There have also been developments with the data itself. Catalogue data is closely associated with print and other physical collections. As more of these materials become digital, as they are related to each other in various ways, and as they are delivered in packages rather than one by one, this raises issues for the management of metadata about them. At the same time, there is an interest in more closely aligning data structures with the broader web environment. And knowledge organization systems may also be reconfigured by network approaches.

Ironically, then, as a set of issues around the catalogue is more clearly coming into relief, it may be that the classic catalogue itself may be receding from view. Its functionality and methods may not disappear, but they may be unbundled from the catalogue itself and rebundled in changing network environments.

In this piece, I copy Stevens's conceit in his poem *Thirteen Ways of Looking at a Blackbird*. Even though this results in some repetition it seemed appropriate to a topic about which we don't yet have a single story. Much of the discussion is relatively neutral, covering recent developments. I bracket these 13 sections with this introduction and with a conclusion which looks beyond current developments to speculate about likely direction.

Environmental . . . the library in the network
i: Moving to the network level: web scale

In a physical world, materials were distributed to multiple locations where they were organized for access by a local user population. In this way, the institution was the natural focus for discovery: a catalogue described what was locally available. It provided breadth of access across a large part of what a user was interested in: that which they could gain access to in the library. It was at the right scale in a world of institutional access: it was at institution scale. Similarly a record shop was the natural focus for discovery and purchase of music, or a travel agent for discovery and purchase of flight or rail tickets. They aggregated materials, services and expertise close to their users.

However, access and discovery have now scaled to the level of the network: they are web scale. If I want to know if a particular book exists I may look in Google Book Search or in Amazon, or in a social reading site, in a library aggregation like WorldCat, and so on. My options have multiplied and the breadth of interest of the library catalogue is diminished: it provides access only to a part of what I am potentially interested in.

In this context, it is interesting to note the longitudinal study of faculty use of the library carried out by Ithaka S+R.[3] They have observed a declining role for the 'gateway' function of the library. This is partly because it is at the wrong level or scale. Google and other network level services have become important gateways.

What are the implications for an institution-level service like the catalogue in a world where much of our access has moved to the network level? We can see several responses being worked through, although it is not clear which will be most effective in the longer term. These include network level consolidation strategies (think of Hathi Trust, WorldCat, Europeana, Melvyl, Libraries Australia . . .), syndication and leveraging strategies (where library resources are directly connected to network level resources, as where Google Scholar or Mendeley recognize your institution's resolver, for example), and open approaches, whether at the API or the data level (where others can reuse catalogue data or services). This phenomenon highlights the important locator or inventory role of the catalogue or local discovery environment. While discovery and exploration may move elsewhere, such external discovery environments may link to the library environment for location and fulfilment.

ii: Not a single destination: multiple presences on the web

We sometimes still think of the website as the focus of institutional presence on the network. And, often, mobile or other presences are seen as derivative. Clearly the importance of mobile – especially now with tablets and smartphones – has changed that view and changed the way we think about design and expectations.[4]

The boundary between mobile and fixed has dissolved into multiple connection points, each with its own grade of experience and functional expectations (the mobile phone, the tablet, the desktop, the iPad app, the xBox or Wii, the Kindle or Nook, the media centre, the widget or gadget, the social networking site). At the same time, more functions are being externalized to network-level providers of communications and other services (e.g. social networking services, YouTube, Flickr . . .). Providing service in this environment is very different than in one where the model assumes a personal desktop or laptop as the place where resources are accessed and used and the institutional website as the unified place where they are delivered. As our entry points have become more varied, what might have been on the website is being variably distributed across these entry points. So, selected information may be on a Facebook page, selected functionality may be available through apps and widgets, selected communications may be available on Twitter, and so on.

Libraries have worked with their discovery services in this context. We have seen the catalogue 'put' in multiple places, in Facebook, in Libx style toolbars, in widgets, apps and gadgets, and in mobile apps. Interesting as some of these developments have been, they have highlighted three issues. First, there is the divorce between discovery and delivery. The mobile experience shares with the app a preference for simplicity: it is important to do one thing well. It is also important to get to relevance quickly. The catalogue may not be best suited here, as the connection to delivery is often not immediate, and accordingly may not be directly applicable in such environments. Second, and related, we are seeing a reconfiguration of functions in app/mobile environments, as functionality is disembedded from the fuller website experience and re-embedded in smaller, more discrete experiences. Computer or meeting room availability and scheduling in the library is an example. In this context, it is interesting to think about what types of catalogue functionality lend themselves to this treatment: a simple search may not be the best choice. Finally, while the catalogue is interesting, attention is shifting to the full collection – across print, licensed and digital – and to the discovery layers which make them available. Should the mobile app be at this level or at the level of the catalogue?

iii: Community is the new content: social and analytics

The interaction of community and resources – in terms of discussion, recommendation, reviews, ratings, and so on – is evident in some form in most of the major network services we use (Amazon, iTunes, Netflix, Flickr . . .). Indeed, this is now so much a part of our experience that sites without this experience can seem bleached somehow, like black and white television in a colour world.

Think of two aspects of our interaction with resources: social objects and analytics.

People connect and share themselves through 'social objects' (music, photos, video, links, or other shared interests) and it has been argued that successful social networks are those which form around such social objects.[5] This encourages reviewing, tagging, commenting. We rate and review, or create collections, lists and playlists, which disclose our interests and can be compared to make recommendations or connect us to other users based on shared interests (think of Last.fm or Goodreads, for example). We are becoming used to selective disclosure and selective socialization through affinity groups within different social networks. Together, these experiences have created an interesting expectation: many network resources are 'signed' in the sense that they are attached to online personas that we may or may not know in 'real life', but whose judgement and network presence we may come to know. Think of social bookmarking sites or Amazon reviews, for example, or social reading sites. And although a minority of people may participate in this way, their contribution is important in the overall experience of the site. People are resources on the network, and have become connectors for others.

Second, as we traverse the network we leave an invisible data trail in our wake; we leave traces everywhere. We click, navigate, and we spend both money and time. Services collect and analyse this subterranean data and use it to transform our experience. They do this by providing context and by configuring resources by patterns of relations created by shared user interests and choices. Google revolutionized searching on the web by recognizing that not all websites are equal, and by mobilizing linking behaviours; Amazon made 'people who bought this, also bought this' types of association popular. iTunes will let me know about related music choices.

An important part of each of these trends is that it is an emergent response to the issue of abundance. Where resources are abundant and attention is scarce, the filtering that social approaches and the use of analytics provide becomes more valuable. The data that users leave, intentionally in the form of tags, reviews and so on, or unintentionally, in the form of usage data, refines how they, and others, interact with resources. They allow services to more effectively rank, relate and recommend.

What about the catalogue in this context? Some catalogues have experimented with collecting tags and reviews but it does not seem that the catalogue has the centrality, scale, or personal connection to crystallize social activity on its own. There is some activity at the aggregate level (e.g. WorldCat, BiblioCommons) and there is some syndication of social data from commercial social collecting/reading sites (e.g. LibraryThing). Similarly, catalogues have not generally mobilized usage data to rank, relate or recommend, and again this seems like something that might best be done at the aggregate level, and syndicated locally (as with the Bx service from Ex Libris, for example).

There are some places where catalogue data gets used – reading lists and resource guides, for example – which seem to be especially appropriate for such attention. The choices involved in this additional layer of curation could be aggregated to provide useful intelligence. What items occur frequently on reading lists, for example? Would it be useful to provide an environment where students rate, review or comment on assigned readings? Is there enough commonality across institutions to make it useful to aggregate this data?

Our web experiences are now actively shaped by ranking, relating and recommending approaches based on social and usage data. For library services this is a major organizational challenge, as supra-institutional approaches may be required to generate appropriate scale.

iv: The simple single search box and the rich texture of suggestion

We are used to hearing people talk about the 'simple search box' as a goal. But a simple search box has only been one part of the Google formula. PageRank has been very important in providing a good user experience, and Google has progressively added functionality as it included more resources in the search results. It also pulls targeted results to the top of the page (sports results, weather or movie times, for example), and it interjects specific categories of results in the general stream (news, images, …). Recently Google has begun pulling data from its 'Knowledge Graph' – a resource created from Freebase, mined user traffic, and other sources – and presenting that alongside results. Amazon also has a simple search box, but search results open out onto a rich texture of suggestion as it mobilizes social and usage data to surround results with recommendations, related works and so on. In fact, the Amazon experience has become very rich, with the opportunity to rate reviews themselves, to preview text or music, to look at author/artist pages, to check Amazon-enabled Wikipedia pages, and so on.

We can see this emerge as a pattern: a simple entry point opens into a richer navigation and suggestion space. In this way, the user is not asked to make choices up front by closely specifying a query. Rather they refine a result by limiting by facets (e.g. format, language, subject, date of publication, etc.), or they branch out in other directions by following suggestions. This is also emerging in our library catalogues which are moving to think about how to better exploit the structure of the data to create navigable relations (faceted browsing, work clusters . . .). We are making our data work harder to support interesting and useful experiences.

A next step is actually to recombine the record-based data into resources about entities of interest. The work on FRBR is an example here, to show a work as it is represented in versions and editions. Author or creator pages is another example. See WorldCat Identities for an example of this approach.

Finally, one might note here an interesting difference in approach between a single stream of results across formats (with the ability to filter out using facets), and a multiple pane approach ('bento box'),[6] where results for a particular format or resource stream in an individual pane. There may be usability arguments for this approach, but a principal issue is synthesizing ranking approaches across quite different resources. The 'bento box' style mitigates this issue by presenting multiple streams of results. This approach is used to good effect in Trove, the discovery system developed by the National Library of Australia. Several institutions use Blacklight to support more well-seamed integration between results from, say, a discovery layer product, a catalogue, other local data, and so on, where local control is desired. Again, the 'bento box' approach is common here.

Institutional . . . the library
v: An integrated experience

The library website aims to project a unified library experience, not a set of unrelated opportunities. This is harder than it might at first seem because typically the website provides a layer over a variety of heterogeneous resources. There is the administrative information about organization, strategy, facilities and so on. There is information about library services and specialist expertise. And there are various information systems – catalogue, discovery layer, repository, resource guides, and so on.

If we look at the information systems aspect of the website, we can see that the library has been managing a thin integration layer over two sets of resources, which has brought challenges in creating an integrated experience. One is the set of legacy and emerging management systems, developed independently rather than as part of an overall library experience, with different fulfilment options, different metadata models, and so on. These include the integrated library system, resolver, knowledge base, and repositories. The second is the set of legacy database and repository boundaries that map more to historically evolved publisher configurations and business decisions than to user needs or behaviours (for example, A&I databases, e-journals, e-books, and other types of content, which may be difficult to slice and dice in useful ways). From a user perspective these distinctions are variably important. A student may want access to a unified index across many resources. A researcher may still be interested in a particular disciplinary database, independently of its merger into a larger resource. The desire for better integration has been supported by the emergence of discovery layer products.

This push for a unified experience has also influenced the construction of websites, and has promoted the alignment of user experience across the services presented in the website. So, for example, libraries are using approaches like Libguides or Library à la Carte to assemble subject or resource guides. It may also now be more common to use a content management system to support the library website, or it may use a wider institutional one. This enhances the sense of the pages as a professionally curated resource, and seems to support better overall user interface consistency. What about the catalogue in this context? It is a little shocking still to experience a complete transition in navigation and design when going from some general websites to a page with a catalogue on it. Modernizing these catalogues – making them more 'webby' – was an important part of the interest a while ago in 'next-generation catalogues' and now in the discovery layer products. It is also apparent in the use of Drupal, VuFind, or Blacklight to provide a more integrated approach across such tools.

vi: Four sources of metadata about things

We are very focused on bibliographic data, and have evolved a sophisticated national and international apparatus around the creation and sharing of catalogue data. National libraries, union catalogues, and commercial sources of record supply all play a part. That apparatus is likely to change in coming years, as the nature of physical collections changes and as more data is assembled in packages associated with e-book collections or other significant sets (Hathi Trust or Google Books, for example). A further pressure for change is the need to free time or attention for digital materials, archives, or other materials which the library needs to record but which are typically outside the current collectively managed bibliographic apparatus. The nature of the metadata of interest may also change. I have found it useful to think of four sources of metadata about library materials.

1 **Professional.** Produced by staff in support of particular business aims. Think of cataloguing, or data produced within the book industry, or A&I data. This is the type of metadata that has dominated library discussion. While the approach has worked reasonably well in the physical publishing environment, where the work, or the cost of the work, could be shared across groups of libraries, we are seeing that it may not scale for digital materials and poses issues for special and archival materials.

2 **Crowdsourced.** Produced by users of systems. Think of tags, reviews and ratings on consumer sites. This type of metadata has been less widely used on library sites for reasons discussed above. Although libraries are social organizations, the library website or catalogue is probably at the wrong level to crystallize activity. One area with some promise is asking for user input on rare or special materials, where the library will not have local or specialist knowledge about contents. Think of digitized community photographs, for example.

3 **Programmatically promoted.** Think of automatic extraction of metadata from digital files, automatic classification, entity identification, and so on. This will become more common, but will require tools and practices to become more widespread. We can see how this would be useful as we look at describing digital documents, web resources, images and so on. As digital resources become more common, so will these methods. Of course, they may go hand in hand with 'professional' approaches, as, for example, names extracted from text are matched against authority files.

4 **Intentional or transactional.** Data about choices and transactions which support analytics or business intelligence services. Think about ranking, relating, recommending, in consumer sites (e.g. people who like this also like this) based on collected transaction data. I have also discussed this type of data above, and again for it to be very useful it is likely that it needs to be aggregated above the institutional level and made available back to the library. We are beginning to see some examples of this.

What I call here crowdsourced, programmatically promoted and intentional data are all again ways of managing abundance. Our model to date has been a 'professional' one, where metadata is manually created by trained staff. This model may not scale very well with large volumes of digital material or as it becomes more common to license e-books in packages. Nor does it necessarily anticipate the variety of ways in which resources might be related. The other sources of metadata discussed here will become increasingly important. For libraries and the industry supporting them, this means thinking about sustainable ways of generating this type of data for use throughout the library domain.

vii: In the flow . . .

Libraries are working hard to place bibliographic data or services more directly in the workflow, as workflows are variously reconfigured in a network environment. Practices here are evolving but here are some examples, pulled together in three overlapping categories: institutional and personal curation, syndication and leverage. Increasingly libraries understand that their users may encounter bibliographic references in places other than the library's own web presence. The challenge then may be twofold: first, in some cases, to support the deployment of bibliographic data in these places (e.g. reading lists, learning management systems, citation managers) and second, to provide a path into library resources for users for whom discovery happens elsewhere in this way.

Think of this range: lists, reading lists, resource guides, personal bibliography, researcher/expertise pages, citation managers, reading management sites, campus publication lists. They all involve the management of bibliographic data to serve some end, and may draw on data across the catalogue, A&I resources, and elsewhere. In some ways they are like bibliographic playlists, selections curated to meet particular personal, pedagogical or research goals. In this way they provide useful contextual framing for the items included. Products have emerged to support particular requirements. Think of Libguides, for example, which provides a framework for managing resource guides, or the range of reading management sites (Anobii, Shelfari, Goodreads, LibraryThing . . .). There is quite a lot of activity around researcher/expertise page management, with or without the assistance of third-party tools or services. Think here of Vivo, Bepress, Community of Science. There is growing interest in managing institutional bibliographies, especially where some form of research assessment is in place and CRIS systems have a bibliographic dimension. And, of course, faculty and students want to manage their references, again using a variety of approaches (Easybib, Zotero, Mendeley, Refworks . . .). I put these together because typically they involve collection of metadata from several resources, and ideally they link back through to library resources where it makes sense. However, the connective tissue to achieve this conveniently is not really in place. Think of reading lists, for example. Often, they involve a lot of mechanical labour on the part of faculty to assemble, and they may not easily link through to the most relevant library resources. The ability to create these playlist-style services, drawing on library resources where relevant, and to link them to relevant fulfilment options, is an area where attention would be useful.

The second category I mention is syndication. By this I mean the direct work the library does to place access to the catalogue in other environments.

One might syndicate services or data. Think of providing access to catalogue resources in the learning management system or student portal; think of RSS feeds, widgets, toolbars, and so on, which can be surfaced in blogs and other websites; think of Facebook or mobile apps. On the data side, think of how libraries and the organizations working with them are interested in better exposing data to search engines or other aggregators. Of particular interest here is visibility with Google Book Search and Google Scholar. In the former case, Google works with union catalogue organizations around the world, including OCLC and WorldCat, to place a 'find in a library' link on book search results. In the latter, Google has worked with libraries to link back to library materials through their resolvers. More generally, libraries have become more interested in general Search Engine Optimization principles across the range of their resources. They recognize that findability or discoverability in the search engines is an important goal.[7]

Finally, leverage is a clumsy expression used here to refer to the use of a discovery environment that is outside the library's control to bring people back into the catalogue environment. Think of the Libx toolbar, for example, which can recognize an ISBN in a web page and use that to search the home library catalogue. Or think of adding links in Wikipedia to special collections on relevant entries. Leverage might overlap with a syndication approach, as with the relationship between Google Scholar and an institutional resolver.

The use and mobilization of bibliographic data and services outside the library catalogue is an increasingly important part of library activity.[8]

viii: Outside-in and inside-out: discovery and discoverability

Throughout much of their recent existence, libraries have managed an 'outside-in range' of resources: they have acquired books, journals, databases and other materials from external sources and provided discovery systems for their local constituency over what they own or license. As I have discussed, this discovery apparatus has evolved, and now comprises catalogue, A-to-Z lists, resource guides, maybe a discovery layer product, and other services. There is better integration. However, more recently, the institution, and the library, has acquired a new discovery challenge. The institution is also a producer of a range of information resources: digitized images or special collections, learning and research materials, research data, administrative records (website, prospectuses, etc.), and so on. And how effectively to disclose this material is of growing interest across libraries or across the institutions of which the library is a part. This presents an 'inside-out' challenge, as here the library wants the material to be discovered by their own constituency but often also by a general web population.[9] The discovery dynamic varies across these types of resources. The contribution of the University of Minnesota report mentioned earlier is to try to explain that dynamic and develop response strategies.

In the outside-in case, the goal is to help researchers and students at the home institution to find resources of interest to them across the broad output of available research and learning materials. In the inside-out case, the goal is to help researchers and students at any institution to find resources of interest to them across the output of the institution itself. In other words, the goal in the inside-out case is to promote discoverability of institutional resources, or to have them discovered. This creates an interest in search engine optimization, syndication of metadata through OAI-PMH or RSS, collection-specific promotion and interpretation through blogs, and general marketing activity.

Organizational . . . working across libraries
ix: The emergence of the discovery layer: the full capacity of the library

The catalogue has provided access to only a part of the collection. However, increasingly, the library would like the user to discover a fuller range, not only the full collection but also expertise and other capacities.

Think of collections first. Historically the catalogue provided access to materials that are bought and processed within the cataloguing/integrated library system workflow. Materials that are licensed pass through a different workflow and historically have had different processing and discovery systems associated with them (knowledge base, metasearch, resolver . . .). Similarly, institutionally digitized or born-digital materials have yet other workflows and systems associated with them (repository, scanning, preservation . . .).

As noted above, a major recent trend has been to provide an integrated discovery environment over all of these materials, and a new systems category – the discovery layer – has emerged to enable this. This embraces catalogue data as one of its parts – and whether or not the catalogue remains individually accessible is an open question.

Such systems depend on aggregating data from many sources, providing an integrated index, and typically access to a centralized or 'cloud-based' resource. While many libraries see these systems as a necessary integrating step it will be interesting to see how the model develops. Now, the model is still one in which each library has its own view on the data, which is linked to local environments through the resolver/knowledge base and local catalogue apparatus. However, maybe over time, the model will shift and libraries will register their holdings with one or more central services and manage the authentication/authorization framework to determine what parts of such central services their users have access to.

The discovery layer raises some interesting questions for practice. How should the results be presented? As a single stream? Or sectioned by format as is nicely done in results from Trove[10] at the National Library of Australia for example (note the ranking discussion above)? There are some longer-term metadata issues. Where this service is offered, the catalogue data is mixed with data for articles, for digital collections, and so on. What this means is that differently structured data is mixed. Catalogue data will have subject data (LCSH or Dewey, for example), names controlled with authority files, and so on. Other data is created in different regimes and will not have this structure.

What does this mean for library metadata? A certain amount of mapping and normalization is possible and is done at various levels (library, service provider . . .). Should national libraries extend the scope of their authority files beyond catalogued materials, to include, for example, authors of journal articles? There may be greater integration at the network level, between initiatives like VIAF, which brings together authority files, and emerging author identifier approaches in related domains (ISNI and Orcid). This type of merged environment should also encourage the emergence of Linked Data approaches, where shared linkable resources emerge for common entities. Rather than repeating data in multiple places, with different structures, it makes sense to link to common reference points. VIAF or Orcid provide examples here.

The determination of similarity and difference as data is clustered across multiple streams becomes more difficult, and it makes it desirable to have firmer agreements about those aspects of the metadata which help to determine identity and relationship. Examples include relating open access material to published versions, clustering digital copies and the original, combining metadata for e-books in multiple packages, and so on.

The focus of these systems has been on search of collections. One can see some other possible directions. Here are three:

1 I discussed institutional and personal curation environments earlier: resource guides, reading lists, social reading sites, citation managers, faculty profiles, and so on. These add a particular context to bibliographic data, where this is a research or learning task, a personal or professional interest, or something else. They can frame the data, which is an important aspect of discovery. Library resources sit to one side of these at the moment, although it would be beneficial to be able to easily provide data to them and to be linked to by them.

2 Library users are interested in other things than collections: library services or expertise for example. One aspect of the resource guides just mentioned is the inclusion of a library liaison person to contact. In an interesting further step, the University of Michigan has worked to include relevant liaison librarians in results. Library websites can be very anonymous. If libraries wish to be seen as expert, then their expertise should be visible. And discovery environments are one place where that might happen.

3 Some libraries are investing in additional local integration layers, which may allow customization to particular institutional interests. Look at the community of Blacklight users, for example. Here, a local unifying layer may pull in results from a discovery layer product, a catalogue, local databases, the library website, or other resources. In this way, the library can more readily control a local experience, add additional resources, and so on. The University of Michigan, for example, currently uses Drupal for this purpose.[11]

x: The collective collection: network level access

In the network environment described above, there is a natural tendency to scale access to the highest supra-institutional level that is convenient, so as to make more resources potentially available to a library user. And we do indeed see a growing interest in consortial or national systems which aggregate supply across a group of libraries. This typically is within a 'jurisdictional' context, which provides the agreement between libraries: the University of California system, a consortium such as the Orbis Cascade alliance, a public regional or national system such as BIBSYS, the German regional union catalogues, Abes in France, and so on. The level of integration within such systems is growing, so that it is becoming easier to discover, request and have delivered an item of interest. At another level, one role WorldCat plays is as a union of union catalogues, and it allows libraries to 'plug into' a wider network of provision. This aggregation of supply makes sense in a network environment and is likely to continue. Libraries then have to make choices about what levels of access to present: local through the catalogue, 'group' through a union catalogue of some sort (e.g. OhioLink across Ohio libraries), and potentially WorldCat or some other resource at a global level.

xi: The collective collection: managing down print

The catalogue is intimately bound up with the 'purchased' collection, historically a largely 'print' collection (together with maps, CDs, DVDs, etc). As the importance of the digital has increased, we have begun to see an institutional interest in managing down the low-use print collection. There are various drivers here: the demands on space, the emergence of a digital corpus of books and the cost of managing a resource that releases progressively less value in research and learning. Libraries are increasingly interested in configuring their spaces around the user experience rather than around print collections. Print runs of journals have been an early focus, but interest is extending to books also. In summary, we might say that the opportunity costs of managing large print collections locally are becoming more apparent.

At the same time, we are seeing that system-wide co-ordination of print materials is desirable as libraries begin to retire collections – to offsite storage or removing them altogether. I believe we are moving to a situation where network-level management of the collective collection becomes the norm, but it will take some years for service, policy and infrastructure frameworks to be worked out and evolution will be uneven. The network may be at the level of a consortium, a state or region or a country. At the moment, this trend is manifesting itself in a variety of local or group mass storage initiatives, as well as in several regional and national initiatives. Think of WEST (the Western Regional Storage Trust) in the USA, for example, or the UK Research Reserve in the UK.

Each of these discussions notes the importance of data: to make sensible decisions you need to have good intelligence about the collective collection of which individual libraries are part. Holdings and circulation data, especially, come to mind. It will become important to know how many copies of an item are in the system, or how heavily used a copy is. It will be important to be able to tie together different versions of an item, different editions, for example, or digital copies and originals. It may also become necessary to record additional data, retention commitments, for example. Libraries have traditionally not shared information at the copy level; however, this becomes more important in this context.

As can be seen, the move to shared responsibility for print raises interesting service and policy issues, as well as very practical management issues. One aspect of this is thinking about our bibliographic data at the aggregate level more, and developing it in the direction which will support the above requirements across the system as a whole. It is likely that union catalogues will have an important role here.

xii: Moving knowledge organization to the network level (and Linked Data)

'Knowledge organization' seems a slightly quaint term now, but we don't have a better in general use. The catalogue has been a knowledge organization tool. When an item is added, the goal is that it is related to the network of knowledge that is represented in the catalogue. This is achieved through collocation and cross-reference, notably with reference to authors, subjects and works. In practice this has worked variably well.

In parallel with bibliographic data, the library community, notably national libraries, have developed 'authorities' for authors and subjects to facilitate this structure. From our current vantage point, I think we can see three stages in the development of these tools. In the first, subject and name authorities provide lists from which values for relevant fields can be chosen. Examples are LCSH, Dewey, and the Library of Congress Name Authority File. These provide some structuring devices for local catalogues, but those systems do not exploit the full structure of the authority systems from which they are taken. Think of what is done, or not done, with classification, for example. The classification system may not be used to provide interesting navigation options in the local system, and more than likely is not connected back to the fuller structure of the source scheme.

The second stage is that these authority systems are being considered as resources in themselves, and not just as sources of controlled values for biblio-graphic description. So, we are seeing the Library of Congress, for example, making LCSH and the Name Authority File available as Linked Data. OCLC is working with a group of national libraries to harmonize name authority files and make them available as an integrated resource in the VIAF service.

In a third stage, as these network resources become more richly linkable, knowledge organization moves to the network level as local systems link to network authorities, exploiting the navigation opportunities they allow. Of course, alongside this, they may also link to, or draw data from, other navigational, contextual or structuring resources such as DBpedia or Geonames. Important reference points will emerge on the network.

Much of the library Linked Data discussion has been about making local data available in different ways. Perhaps as interesting as this is the discussion about what key resources libraries will want to link to, and how they might be sustained. An important question for national libraries and others who have systems developed in the first phase above is how to move into the web-scale phase three.[12] The relationship between the Deutsche Nationalbibliothek and Wikipedia in Germany is an interesting example here.[13]

xiii: Sourcing and scaling

One of the major issues facing libraries as the network reconfigures processes is how appropriately to source and scale activities. An activity might be entirely local, where a locally developed application is offered to a local community. However, this is now rare. It is increasingly common to externalize activity to other providers. In this context, sourcing and scaling provide interesting dimensions to consider options.

Scaling refers to the level at which something is done. Consider three levels:

1 **Institution-scale**. Activity is managed within an institution with a local target audience. For our purposes here think of the local catalogue.
2 **Group-scale**. Activity is managed within a supra-institutional domain, whether this is a region, a consortium, or a state or a country. The audience is correspondingly grouped. In educational terms think of the activities of JISC in the UK or SurfNet in the Netherlands. In library terms think of the Hathi trust, or of Georgia Pines, or of OhioLink. For our purposes here think of union and group catalogues: the German regional systems (Verbundkatalogen), COPAC in the UK, Libris in Sweden, Rero in Switzerland, OhioLink, Trove in Australia, and so on.
3 **Web-scale**. Activity is managed at the network level, where we are now used to services like Amazon, Flickr, Google and YouTube providing e-commerce, collection, discovery and other functions. Here, the audience is potentially all web users. For our purposes here think of Amazon, Goodreads, Google Book Search, or, in library terms, WorldCat.

As I discussed above, we have seen more activity move to higher places in the network. There is both a trend towards more group approaches, and towards using the web-scale services. Again, think of knowledge-base data in Google Scholar, for example, or links to special collections materials added to Wikipedia.

The other dimension is a sourcing one. Again, consider three possible ways in which a product or service might be sourced outside the institution:

1 **Collaborative**. Activity is developed in concert with partners (e.g. purchasing consortium, shared offsite storage, open source software).
2 **Public**. This is common in those jurisdictions where library infrastructure is provided as part of educational or cultural public infrastructure. Think for example of union catalogue activity in various countries.
3 **Third-party**. Activity is secured from a third-party provider. A third party might be a commercial or not-for-profit supplier.

As shown in Figure 8.1, there is a lot of overlap between these cells, of course. A publicly supported service like OhioLink, for example, has a strong collaborative component. As the network reduces transaction costs, it is now simpler to externalize in this way. The reduced cost and effort of collaboration or of transacting with third parties for services has made these approaches

Sourcing		**Scaling**		
		Institution	Group	Web
Collaborative		VuFind	Tripod: (Tri-college library catalog)	RePEc
Public		Bibliographic Standards (LC Classification, MESH, LCSH)	German regional union catalogues (Verbundkataloge)	PubMed
Third-party		Hosted ILS/Discovery layer	JISC Collections	worldcat.org

Figure 8.1 *Sourcing versus scaling*

more attractive and feasible. There are also scale advantages. One aspect of moving services to the cloud is the opportunity to reconfigure them. For example, within agreed policy contexts, there will be greater opportunities for sharing and aggregation of transaction or crowdsourced data in group or web-scale solutions.

Libraries face interesting choices about sourcing – local, commercial, collaborative, public – as they look at how to achieve goals, and as shared approaches become more crucial as resources are stretched. At the same time, decisions about scale or level of operation – personal, local, consortial, national, global – have become as important as particular discussions of functionality or sourcing.

Library approaches to scaling and sourcing will be interesting for several years to come as questions about focus and value are central. In general it is likely that infrastructure (in the form of collections or systems) will increasingly be sourced collaboratively or with third parties, while libraries focus on deeper engagement with the needs of their users.

Coda . . . libraries and discovery: futures?

I have reviewed a variety of trends. I conclude briefly with some broad-brush suggestions about how matters will evolve in the next few years, acknowledging that such speculation is invariably ill-advised.

Discovery has scaled to the network level

Although the players may change, this trend seems clear. Constraining the discovery process by institutional subscription or database boundary does not fit well with how people use the network. General discovery happens in Google or Wikipedia. And there are a variety of niches. Amazon, Google Books, Hathi Trust or Goodreads for example. arXiv, repec, or SSRN. PubMed Central. And so on. These services benefit in various ways from scale, and mobilize the data left by users – consciously in the form of recommendations, reviews and ratings or unconsciously in the form of transaction data – to drive their services. Within the library arena, several providers are creating 'discovery layers', centralized indexes of scholarly material to which libraries are subscribing, and to which they are adding their own local resources. In some cases, libraries are providing additional local customization of this material. While this landscape will invariably change, and providers evolve or disappear, this shift seems set to continue.

Personal and institutional curation services

These are now also central to reading and research behaviours, and will also evolve. These include citation management sites, sometimes as part of more general research workflow tools (e.g. Mendeley, Refworks), social reading/cataloguing/clipping sites (e.g. Goodreads, Small Demons, Findings), and resource guides (e.g. Libguides) or reading lists. This is in addition to a range of other support services for reading or research. Think, for example, of how book clubs or reading groups are supported in various ad hoc ways (this seems like an area where network based services or support will emerge). These services create personal value (they get a job done) as well as often creating network value (they mobilize shared experiences). They put the management of bibliographic data into personal workflows, and the resulting pedagogical, research or personal framing provides important contextual data which can be mobilized to improve the service (think of Mendeley's 'scrobbling' for example).

This means that library services may focus differently. Here are several ways in which that will happen.

1   **Location and fulfilment**. If 'discovery happens elsewhere' it is important for the library to be able to provide its users with location and fulfilment services which somehow connect to that discovery experience. Typically this will involve some form of 'switch' between a discovery experience and the location/fulfilment service. Think of configuring Mendeley or Google Scholar with resolver information, or how Google Books uses WorldCat and other union catalogues to provide a 'find in a library' link. Some other approaches were discussed above, and it is likely that they will become more routine over time as these 'switch' services mature.

2   **Disclosure**. Libraries are recognizing that the presence of institutional resources – digitized materials, research and learning materials, and so on – needs to be promoted. Unless it is particularly significant or central, an institutional resource is unlikely to have strong gravitational attraction. For this reason search engine optimization, syndication of metadata to relevant hub sites, selective adding of links to Wikipedia, and other approaches are becoming of more interest.[14]

3   **Consortial or group approaches become more common**. As activity in general moves 'up' in the network, and repetitive work gets moved into shared services, many libraries seek collaboration around discovery

activity at a broader level. The emergence of consortial or group discovery environments is a growing trend.

4 **Particularization**. Some libraries will want to invest in how a variety of local discovery experiences are presented, particularizing general resources to local conditions or aligning them with specific local approaches. The University of Michigan provides an example,[15] as do those libraries experimenting with Blacklight.[16] It will be interesting to see if the software layer supporting this desire becomes more sophisticated.

5 **Research advice and reputation management**. Researchers and universities are increasingly interested in having their research results and expertise discovered by others. There is a growing interest in research analytics supported by tools from Thompson Reuters and Elsevier, as well as by emerging alternative measures. This means that in addition to supporting disclosure of research outputs, and expertise,[17] there is an opportunity for the library to provide advice and support to the university as it seeks to maximize impact and visibility in a network environment.

Knowledge organization will move to the network level

The collective investment that libraries have made in structured data about people, places and things is now not mobilized effectively in the web environment. The cataloguing model makes it now geared around the local catalogue. What is likely to emerge is that authorities, subject schemes and other data will become network-level resources to which data creators link. These in turn can link to Wikipedia or other resources, or be linked to by those other resources. This of course raises questions about sustainability and construction. A purely national model no longer makes sense. The Virtual International Authority File may provide a model here.

Conclusion

This chapter, as with the others in this volume, have outlined how the catalogue is changing. It is becoming a part of a larger discovery environment. National libraries and others are reviewing how catalogue data is created and how it might participate in a broader web of data. They are also exploring how the cumulative expertise and knowledge which is invested in authority files might be mobilized in new ways. There is growing interest in using catalogue and usage data to help drive decisions about collections. There is a growing interest in placing catalogue data and services in other environments, where it can act as a switch back to library resources. I have suggested above that this renewed interest in the catalogue and in catalogue data is emerging at the same time as the catalogue itself is becoming less central as an individual destination. Together, all of this means that libraries are facing some interesting questions about investment and direction. And it is always good to be asked questions.

References

1   An earlier article also discusses the catalogue: Dempsey, L. (2006) The Library Catalogue in the New Discovery Environment: some thoughts, *Ariadne*, **48**, 30 July, www.ariadne.ac.uk/issue48/dempsey. It is interesting how much has changed in the interim. The piece makes extensive use of blog entries from Lorcan Dempsey's Weblog, http://orweblog.oclc.org.

2   Connaway, L. S., Dickey, T. J. and Radford, M. L. (2011) 'If It Is Too Inconvenient, I'm Not Going After It': convenience as a critical factor in information-seeking behaviors, *Library and Information Science Research*, **33**, 179–90. Pre-print available online at www.oclc.org/content/dam/research-publications/library/2011/connaway-lisr.pdf.

3   Schonfeld, R. C. and Housewright, R. (2010) *Faculty Survey 2009: key strategic insights for libraries, publishers, and societies*, New York, NY, Ithaka S + R, www.sr.ithaka.org/research-publications/us-faculty-survey-2009.

4   Dempsey, L. (2009) Always On: libraries in a world of permanent connectivity, *First Monday*, **14** (1), 5 January, www.firstmonday.org/htbin/cgiwrap/bin/ojs/index.php/fm/article/viewArticle/2291/2070.

5   Dempsey, L. (2008) Some Thoughts About Egos, Objects, and Social Networks . . . , *Lorcan Dempsey's Weblog*, 6 April, http://orweblog.oclc.org/archives/001601.html.

6   This is a phrase introduced by Tito Sierra.

7   www.educause.edu/ero/article/thirteen-ways-looking-libraries-discovery-and-catalog-scale-workflow-attention.

8   See Hanson, C. et al. (2011) *Discoverability Phase 2 Final Report*, from the University of Minnesota, for examples: http://purl.umn.edu/99734.

9   Dempsey, L. (2010) Outside-in and Inside-out, *Lorcan Dempsey's Weblog*,

11 January, http://orweblog.oclc.org/archives/002047.html.

10   http://trove.nla.gov.au.

11   Varnum, K. (2012) *Don't Go There! Providing services locally, not at a vendor's site,* presentation posted on Slideshare, May, www.slideshare.net/KenVarnum/ dont-go-there-providing-discovery-services-locally-not-at-a-vendors-site.

12   See Dempsey, L. (2012) Making Things of Interest Discoverable, Referencable, Relatable . . . , *Lorcan Dempsey's Weblog,* 10 June, http://orweblog.oclc.org/archives/002199.html.

13   Hengel, C. and Pfeifer, B. (2005) Kooperation der Personennamendatei (PND) mit Wikipedia, *Dialog mit Bibliotheken,* **17** (3), ISSN 0936-1138, 18–24.

14   See Hanson, C. et al. (2011), cited above, for a discussion of approaches.

15   See, for example, Ken Varnum's discussion of design choices at the University of Michigan: *Keeping Discovery in the Library,* presentation, November 2011, www.slideshare.net/KenVarnum/keeping-discovery-in-the-library-10008918.

16   For libraries using Blacklight see: https://github.com/projectblacklight/blacklight/wiki/Examples.

17   I have not discussed the growing interest in disclosing and discovering expertise through profile pages, research networks, and so on.

Index